The Power of Presence

The Power of Presence

*Be a Voice in Your Child's
Ear Even When You're Not with Them*

Joy Thomas Moore

Foreword by Wes Moore

GRAND CENTRAL
Life & Style
NEW YORK · BOSTON

Grand Central Life & Style
Hachette Book Group
1290 Avenue of the Americas, New York, NY 10104
grandcentrallifeandstyle.com
twitter.com/grandcentralpub

First Edition: September 2018

Grand Central Life & Style is an imprint of Grand Central Publishing. The Grand Central Life & Style name and logo are trademarks of Hachette Book Group, Inc.

The publisher is not responsible for websites (or their content) that are not owned by the publisher.

The Hachette Speakers Bureau provides a wide range of authors for speaking events. To find out more, go to www.hachettespeakersbureau.com or call (866) 376-6591.

Library of Congress Cataloging-in-Publication Data

Names: Moore, Joy Thomas, 1950- author.
Title: The power of presence : be a voice in your child's ear even when you're not with them / Joy Thomas Moore ; foreword by Wes Moore.
Description: First Edition. | New York : Grand Central Life & Style, [2018] | Includes bibliographical references.
Identifiers: LCCN 2018003719| ISBN 9781538743805 (hardcover) | ISBN 9781478921363 (audio download) | ISBN 9781538743812 (ebook)
Subjects: LCSH: Parenting. | Self-presentation. | Influence (Psychology)
Classification: LCC HQ755.8 .M6336 2018 | DDC 649/.1—dc23
LC record available at https://lccn.loc.gov/2018003719

ISBNs: 978-1-5387-4380-5 (hardcover), 978-1-5387-4381-2 (ebook)

Printed in the United States of America

LSC-C

10 9 8 7 6 5 4 3 2 1

To Mom, my original lioness, who taught me the journey to true presence is achievable with or without a partner

To Michael, Holley, Noelle, Earl, Bryce, Alexander, Marcus, Tenai, and Elijah, whose bright futures are dazzling

And to Nikki, Shani, Jamaar, Wes, Dawn, Mia, and Jaime, who prove every day that the power of presence is its ability to ultimately provide a lifetime of joy

Contents

Foreword

"I really wish your mom would write a book."

Ever since *The Other Wes Moore* was published in 2010, I have had the privilege to travel all over the country and the world, sharing the stories of these two boys, their journeys into manhood, and what I hoped the world would take away from my book. At many of the talks or gatherings I led, I would have question-and-answer sessions. At these sessions, questions about my mom were omnipresent: how she felt about her journey, what she learned, what advice she would give. Those questions were constants. And the truth is that when those questions came to me, unable to speak for her, I left the answers bare. It was not just that I didn't feel comfortable answering for her. I didn't know the answers.

The love I have for my mother cannot be explained simply by words, cannot be contained in a foreword. I believe my little sister said it best when she once said, "Our mother wore sweaters so we could wear coats." This is a woman who sacrificed everything she had and everything she was for her kids because she knew she was all we had. She watched her soul mate die in front of her, and the thing that kept her together after that was her faith in God and her faith in her children. We, my sisters and I, are the direct products of her love, commitment, and undying faithfulness to God and to us.

I watched her struggle and sacrifice. I watched her need, but never want. I watched her strive for perfection—and even the times when she fell short, it was never from a lack of effort. I also watched her cringe as the conversation around single parents continued to evolve and devolve in this country.

So as my mom writes this book, my pride in who she is and what she stands for only grows. This book is not just a response to the questions I received from countless people about my mom. It's a call to action about a larger dynamic in our society. The truth is, my mother is not alone: Half of all children are growing up in single-parent households. If you happen to be a child of color, the number is even higher. And we have noticed a correlation and a causal relationship between single parents—single moms and single dads—and poverty. The point of this book is not to question the stats, it's to question the context and the takeaways from these dynamics.

The parents who for whatever reason are raising their children on their own have been demonized. They have been told their choices are the reasons for societal ills and manifestations of a lack of responsibility or concern. We have been taught to point fingers at them instead of lifting our hands to support them. We have been served the "welfare queen" line as a prevailing narrative, instead of calling that offering what is it, a hateful misrepresentation.

This book is a celebration of resilience, an homage to the fact that single mothers are not our nation's burden, but our nation's backbone. Instead of preaching to them, we need to be learning from them. And hearing their voices as our national consciousness, in many cases, lies in their words. And in their prayers for their children.

In Mom's words, and in the lives she shares in this book, I see hope. I see unexpected victory. I see the best of us, dressed in struggle. Worn. Tired. Victorious.

The greatest human gift God gave me was one I did not earn, nor one I asked for. The greatest gift was that He asked Joy Thomas Moore to give birth to me. My uneven and complicated journey was steadied by those beautiful Jamaican hands and the woman who was willing to give it all for her children. That reality I will never forget nor understate. But I know she did not do it alone. She could not have. The people who surrounded her, and surrounded us, when we needed it most, helped us through. The goal of this book is to ensure that our story, which in essence is laced with luck, doesn't have to feel exceptional. Nor should the celebration of this book's author feel exclusionary; my hope is that it is trendsetting.

Maya Angelou once said, "To describe my mother would be to write about a hurricane in its perfect power. Or the climbing, falling colors of a rainbow." Our parents are our force field, and our external immune systems: the ones who keep outside forces and illnesses from permanently derailing us and keep small challenges from becoming ending ones. They are our lions and lionesses, the ones who tend to their pride diligently, with a sole focus on protection. They are our air traffic controllers, whose counsel gives us an ability to understand when potential complications are ahead and how to navigate through the turbulence. They are our daily reminders of God's love.

Thank you, Mom, for all you have given Nikki, Shani, and me. And thank you, through your example and through this book, for making me a better parent to your grandkids.

Wes Moore
February 2018

Introduction

Out of Sight, Ever Present

Draped with an old-fashioned checkered plastic tablecloth and mismatched plates and utensils, our kitchen table in the parsonage of my dad's church in the South Bronx of New York City was family-central for my brother Ralph, who was ten years old, my little brother Howard, who was sitting in his high chair, my mom, my dad, and me. We joined hands. You could always tell when my dad was hungry by the length of the grace before eating. That night he was hungry. I was nine and full of new experiences and questions as a third grader. As we started to eat, I blurted out a question about a word I had seen written on the bathroom wall at school. In polite company, one might say "Sugar, Honey, Ice, Tea," but—not being aware of what's acceptable at the dinner table—I said the full unadulterated word in all its glory. Well, I still remember the look of shock on the faces of my mom and dad. Sensing I'd said something dreadfully wrong, I darted my eyes to Ralph, who looked amused that I might be heading for a spanking for saying such a forbidden word.

But instead of a spanking, and its painful aftermath, which would have come and gone, I received a lifelong lesson that I carry to this day. My parents looked at each other, and my mom very calmly said, "Have you ever heard your father or me say that word?" I confidently shook my head no. "Well," she continued, "if you haven't heard us say it, you shouldn't, either." Those words became the voice in my ear from that point on, because they provided me a guidepost to follow, even in my parents' absence.

In many ways, that experience helped me formulate a very important piece of my own parenting puzzle. In the same way that I looked to my parents for indelible markers, even in their absence, I promised myself that I would provide the same kind of out-of-sight guidance to my own children. And any partner in my parenting journey would have to feel the same way. We would have to back each other up, as the glances between my parents did that night at dinner. They were a team, and I was determined that one day I would be equipped to provide that kind of united front for my own children.

My parenting journey, however, turned out to have a very different trajectory. Through choice and circumstance, I would eventually carry the title "single mother."

The Pride and the Prejudice

I never imagined myself as a single mother. In addition to my parents, just about all my relatives and friends lived with both parents. So when I became a single mom, at first I thought I was heading into uncharted waters. But eventually I realized all the lessons my parents had passed on to me growing up had unknowingly helped prepare me for whatever my marital status would be. Their words of encouragement, their advice, and the survival skills they passed through my ears and into my heart proved to sustain me during my toughest challenges.

Probably first and foremost of their lessons on resiliency was not allowing society's expectations—in this case, of single motherhood—to define me as a liability. I thought back to how my parents had helped build community and a sense of family for anyone who needed comfort or assistance. They provided a presence for people in need, throughout the community or within our extended family. When someone had my parents' ear, they knew they also had their heart so they need never feel alone. In writing this book, I began embracing this presence of family and community taught to me by my parents and modeled in the animal world. I thought about how lionesses live in groups called prides—the only cats to do so—and how they help raise each other's cubs, share their food, and provide protection when threatened by outside forces. I realized that like a lioness, I too relied on a pride. I became determined that our family would not only survive but also thrive because I would somehow re-create the kind of community I grew up in and become the ever-vigilant, ever-present voice in the ear for my own children.

The obvious challenge for me and other single mothers is that we don't have a parenting partner with whom to share impressions or discuss options, never mind pick up the slack when children have conflicting schedules. We often have to work multiple jobs because we don't have a fellow wage-earner in the home. I like to think that these adversities increase the need for us to be stronger, wiser, and more resilient.

But unfortunately, what with being head of household, financial gatekeeper, social activities director, moral compass, maid, nurse, therapist, schoolteacher, and philosopher, all while fighting misguided public policy and the feeling of being crushed beneath the weight of stress and anxiety, sometimes it can feel like we are the butt of a sick, cruel joke. More times than not, we may feel less capable, less competent, and less deserving than other women of reaping the rewards life has to offer. The concern that lives right beneath the surface and never ceases to buzz us with fear and overwhelm is, "Are the kids okay? Am I enough? Is there enough?"

I know because I've been there—and yes, there is enough, and I took advantage of any and all opportunities presented before our family to make sure I was enough. Throughout the years, I built on the lessons I had learned as a child to be as present a parent as possible. But whatever measure of success I achieved in my parenting,

I also know there are many more examples of single-mother households that are rarely celebrated or consulted to give inspiration, parenting tips, or advice. There is a deep untapped well of knowledge in single-parent families that can benefit and inspire two-parent families, grandparents, mentors—all caregivers in the lives of children. I hope this realization begins with this book.

My Journey to the Present

I've been a single mom three times: twice by choice and once by tragedy. The first time, I left a deeply troubled, increasingly violent marriage, uprooted my two-year-old daughter, Nikki, and moved into a friend's basement furnished with only a twin-size bed and a portable crib. It was two weeks before Christmas. I brought along a bag for me and one filled with diapers and a week's worth of cold-weather clothes for Nikki.

The second time, single motherhood came in an instant. My second husband, William Westley Moore Jr., died suddenly after only five years of a blissful marriage, leaving me alone to raise Nikki; our three-and-a-half-year-old son, Wes; and our twenty-month-old daughter, Shani.

After the ER doctors admitted flatly, "There was nothing more we could do. He's gone," and sent me off with their condolences, I had yet again become a single mother.

My husband's death shook me so deeply that I wondered how my family would survive. Day by day, the enormity of suddenly becoming a single mother of three rose up like a flood. I couldn't even see straight, let alone remain steadfast in the present, as a lioness does, when I returned from the hospital a widow. Even in those moments when I was physically with my children, I couldn't stop worrying about their future. All the details associated with a sudden death, plus the everyday responsibilities like paying bills and taking out the trash, were pulling me in every direction. I could only see the have-nots of our situation.

The third time I married when the kids were teenagers, and I wanted to model a traditional two-parent family for them. He was a good man, a family friend whom I thought a safe alternative to single motherhood. But I soon learned that marrying for the wrong reasons never goes well, and I ended a union that was loveless and frustrating and turning me into someone I didn't want to be.

My children all had challenging moments, from academic problems to alcohol use to run-ins with the police. I faced the everyday, ordinary challenges so many single mothers face: from daycare issues to lack of male role models to, at times, extreme financial anxiety.

Despite all my mistakes and the obstacles placed in front of me, particularly as a black, single mother of three, my children's lives were filled with many more opportunities than my frightened mind could have imagined. It took me a while to notice them, to press the pause button on all the noise in order to assess the world around me, but when I did, I took advantage of as many opportunities as I could. Thankfully, all three of my children emerged strong, successful, and, most important, good people. Nikki channeled her creativity and keen attention to detail into founding a thriving event-planning business; Wes is a Rhodes Scholar, White House Fellow, president and CEO of the Robin Hood Foundation, and author; Shani graduated from Princeton and UC Berkeley before earning her law degree at Stanford and becoming an independent television screenwriter and legal and business executive at NBCUniversal.

When my son was grown, he retold the story of his father's death in his instant *New York Times* bestselling book *The Other Wes Moore.* He was critically acclaimed for his examination of, as he describes, "The story of two boys living in Baltimore with similar histories and an identical name: Wes Moore. One of us is free and has experienced things that he never even knew to dream about as a kid. The other will spend every day until his death behind bars for an armed robbery that left a police officer and father of five dead. The chilling truth is that his story could have been mine. The tragedy is my life could have been his."

As Wes traveled around the country raising awareness through his juxtaposition of his fate and the fate of the other Wes Moore, he encountered one recurring question that seemed to burn in the minds of the parents in the crowds:

"What did your mother do right?"

Soon the answer to that question, "What did your mother do," became like a Holy Grail mothers in the audience went in search of—the elixir for creating successful children, as if there is such a thing. And this question resounded despite my son's efforts to underscore the extreme social injustices that exist in our country that keep segments of the population trapped in a whirlpool of poverty. These mothers were desperate for just one thing—to get it "right."

Because of the focus on how my son was mothered, I was launched into a role of parenting expert seemingly overnight—a role I still reject. I am no expert; if anything, I'm an experimenter. I just did what I had to do, waited to see what worked, tossed out what didn't, and started all over again. Just as the lioness focuses on only one thing—survival—I fought hard to remain present in the moment. That presence helped keep my eyes wide open so I could snatch up the inner and outer resources I needed to raise bright, kind, and happy children. Though I sometimes felt ostracized, misunderstood, and completely alone, my dedication to staying focused on the here and now enabled me to see clearly the opportunities and support—the haves—that surrounded me, and put them to good use. Yes, I made a lot of mistakes, like worrying about the next day instead of what was happening at the kitchen table, and it certainly wasn't easy to stay grounded in confidence and strength, but I taught myself to keep asking the important questions: *What kind of people do I want my kids to grow up to be, and how can I model that despite the daily pressures that crush me? What do I have to do (or not do) to teach the values I learned as a kid even when I feel like I can't breathe, never mind be a role model? How can I inspire them to succeed without nagging and yelling?*

These guiding questions became my reset buttons when I felt a moment or situation getting away from me. During overwhelming days or just typical busy ones, I stopped and reminded myself of these questions because they pulled me back to what was important. In terms of what I *did* on a daily basis, I had no empirical examples to offer people who asked, so I turned to my children to find the more accurate answers. I've always believed children to be our guides, as they are wise and much closer to the truth than we think. Simply asking all three of my children, *What did I do that made a positive impact on you?* helped me remember moments I had either forgotten or not noted in the first place.

Wes: "The time we had two basketball games in two different states two hours apart and you made them both."

Nikki: "After Shani, Wes, and I argued, you pointed to the army of ants on our countertop, explaining that a family works together and always sticks together, or else nothing gets done." (Little did Nikki know I rushed to kill those suckers the minute she left the room!)

Shani: "The time you promised you would always keep my secrets, even from . . . *especially from* . . . my own brother and sister."

While the monumental stuff like working several jobs or stringing together loose change for a decent dinner came to mind as the "right" way to be present, my children's memories told me otherwise. Presence makes the little things much bigger; it takes a door that is ajar and swings it wide open.

Presence

Presence is the secret sauce of parenting, period. In fact, presence is what one survey revealed children crave most from their parents, married or not, and they get quite resentful when they don't receive it. According to one study, 54 percent of kids say their parents check their devices too often. And 32 percent describe themselves as feeling "unimportant" when their parents are sidetracked by emails, social media, online shopping, and texts. This reminded me of when my kids would tune me out, and I would demand, "Look at me when I am talking to you!" But do we look at our kids, *really look*, when they are talking to us?

It is easy to see, especially in our mobile high-tech world, how being present is difficult enough when there are two parents in the home. My mother used to say that she chose the relatively predictable field of teaching because if one parent travels extensively—as my dad did for work—the other parent can't "rip and run" at the same time. One of them has to stay close to ground zero. But once you are the sole parent, you lose your backup. There is no safety net at the bottom when you fall off the proverbial parenting cliff. Being a single mother doesn't come with the checks-and-balances approach you get when you have two parents on the case; nor do you have a different perspective or opinion to counterbalance your own, or, most important, the support and reassurance of the other parent when you make a hard call for your family. When you're tapped out at the end of the day, there isn't someone there to pick up your slack, able to be present for you when you need to check out. All that and more went out the window when I lost my parenting partner. So I had to be doubly present, and figure out a way to be present even when I wasn't anywhere near my children!

The voice in my ear was my consistent reminder that presence is more than simply being in the physical vicinity of my kids, or even providing for their basic needs. Presence is stopping in the moment with the intention of making a lasting impression of your own values, instilling them like pillars staked firmly into the earth. Presence is the "what" of successful parenting. The "how" is making sure there is a pride of people whom you trust and who can partner with you in the process. The "why" is that everyone needs help. The "when" is now.

Digging deep for this book, I thought hard about the pillars I incorporated to make our family work. Seven emerged. It is said that through necessity, we invent, and I believe that it was out of necessity that I frequently turned to my pillars as guideposts and reminders of what keeps me going. If these pillars represent my value system, then presence is the mortar that binds the pillars together, strong and erect, enabling them to be symbols of strength to this day.

I realize that telling you the secret to raising happy children is to simply be present in the moment might elicit one of two responses: an uncontrollable bout of belly laughter, or an eye roll. I wouldn't blame you. After all, chauffeuring kids around from activity to play-date to tutor, planning conference calls while paying bills and taking the dog to the vet, and having to take multiple trains or buses to accomplish all these things and more does not feel like a life conducive to "living in the moment," as presence is often described. But then I think back to what my grown kids have identified as being most impactful in their development, and I realize the irony: I *couldn't* have driven across the state line to two different basketball games, nor connected with my remorseful child by making an important promise, nor remained calm enough to turn an insect infestation into a teachable moment *unless* I was present in that very moment—the eye-on-the-prize kind of presence and, yes, much of the time the grasping-at-straws type of presence too.

My Guiding Pillars

Presence of Mind is about cultivating and adhering to the mindfulness necessary for being present in the first place. Presence of Mind means trusting your gut and acting with your wit. It is about the ability to connect with the voice in your own ear that encourages you to see a difficult situation in a new way if you want a different outcome. Mindfulness also allows you to be in tune with your children so you can anticipate situations rather than just reacting to them. It is the voice in the ear that keeps generations united through wisdom and experience.

Presence of Heart is what keeps you going despite all the ups and downs; presence helps the heart pump lifeblood throughout the family unit, keeping everyone focused on living their truth. Changes may have been made, but the family hasn't changed. Having Presence of Heart helps solidify this critical message and keep children feeling grounded and safe.

Regarding **Presence of Faith**, the Reverend Dr. Martin Luther King Jr. said, "Take the first step even when you can't see the end of the staircase." Presence of Faith lets you entertain the notion that there may be a staircase to better things even in the midst of great loss. It allows you to take an unknown path without knowing where you're headed. Faith allows you to quit a job and be confident that your next one will be better and more fulfilling. Faith allows you to leave an abusive marriage, leaving everything behind, and know that your life will be better when you walk out that door.

Presence of Courage helps us move out of our comfort zones. Heroes are celebrated for dramatic, daring acts and quick action in a crisis. If those are the criteria, all parents qualify! In hindsight I can see that some of the best choices I made came when I was acting out of desperation and seizing opportunities that were foreign and scary. Sometimes the most bravery we can show is to look within ourselves, admit wrongness, and make an about-face in the right direction.

Presence of Resources. Experts agree that one of the most predictable indicators of stress on a family is financial instability. But as I learned, there are ways to secure family financial freedom without losing the all-important connection to our children along the way. Learning to manage resources and accept limits, while teaching the wisdom of delayed gratification and embracing quality over quantity, decreases the financial anxiety that can threaten a family's well-being.

Presence of Connectedness has two facets: being physically connected to our kids and establishing the invisible connection that sends out our energetic presence in our absence. At some point, as your children navigate the world without you, they will make their own decisions about how to behave. It's critical that they have the tools to keep themselves out of harm's way in the moments when you're not there to guide (or chastise) them. Connectedness means that your voice will ring in your children's ears even when you're not physically in front of them. It is also about keeping the people and practices around you as a single mother that will give you the energy—both physical and emotional—to be all things: cheerleader, referee, coach, chauffer, tutor, understanding friend, and shoulder to cry on.

Presence of Values means passing down characteristics and traits that will carry your children for life. Instilling such values as honesty, trust, humility, compassion, generosity, and so many others is a great responsibility. The most effective way to teach values is to embody them ourselves. Children learn much more and much better by watching what we do than by us telling them what they should do.

For my family to succeed, I had to employ all seven of these pillars and call in all the resources I had at my disposal to amplify my presence. As a single mom, it wasn't always easy to remember to live by them, with all the myriad responsibilities facing me daily. Sometimes it was easier to just plop the food on the table without taking the time to be thankful for whatever it was that a limited budget could afford. Sometimes at the end of an exhausting day, it was just easier to send the kids off to bed without being present enough to read a book with them or say bedtime prayers. But these are tools of survival in a world that sometimes makes no sense or in a situation cruel beyond belief. We arm our kids with boots and umbrellas when it's raining, or sunscreen when they're exposed to the sun. A bag full of social and spiritual tools, like humility, empathy, kindness, high expectations, thankfulness, and faith in something bigger than themselves, is just as important to their well-being. While I relied on each of these pillars independently, it was the braiding and blending of all of them that propelled our family along a successful path.

While I share many stories about my family in this book based on these pillars, our success is far from unique. Therefore, I have also included the most striking and powerful stories I've heard from other single mothers. Some of these amazing women I've known for many years. Others I'd heard of or read about and couldn't wait to meet. From them I gleaned the essence of what single motherhood has meant to them and the moments that have most influenced their children's character. What were the crucial moments of presence in which they were able to see the world around their family with clarity and compassion? Some of these women had limited resources, some had plenty, but all had the intense challenge of balancing complex lives. All of them have made bold and sometimes heartbreaking choices and stuck by them with great discipline for the benefit of their children.

Throughout the book, you will learn the stories of these women. They add a new dimension to the conversation about single mothers, because this is not just my story. It is the pride's story. Their wisdom—highlighted by the heading "Lesson from a Lioness"—will inspire you to keep your sight and transform darkness into light.

Parenting in a World of Right and Wrong

When Mary Moore, the mother of a son named Wes Moore who is serving life in prison, and I appeared on *The Oprah Winfrey Show* to reflect on how we parented our children, I was asked the same question that audience members at Wes's speeches ask: "What did you do right?" I wanted to somehow make clear that the differences weren't in me doing something right and Mary doing something wrong. We all want to fiercely protect our children and want to see them exceed our own accomplishments. None of us set out to do anything wrong for our children. The differences are in the opportunities available to each of us as mothers to be present in our children's lives. The presence of sound family-supporting public policy cannot be over-stated. If Mary's education had not been cut short because funding for Pell Grants was drastically reduced, her life trajectory and those of her sons could have been decidedly different. I had the support of a pride—my parents, my husband's family, teachers, friends, trusted surrogates, my own education and career background—that I solicited to help me be present for my children. Because of all of that support, I experience the joy of seeing my children thrive today.

If you are a two-parent family, I want this book to shine a spot-light on often overlooked examples of resilience, resourcefulness, and sources of inspiration and parenting advice that come from the experiences, challenges, and successes of single moms. They have a story to tell and wisdom to share that can benefit all those with a child in their life. If you are a single mother, I want this book to be a source of celebration and proof that you are in no way a liability. I began to open my eyes to the many other single mothers in this world while journeying through my own singledom. The image of the lioness was a huge comfort and helped me change the way I viewed myself and my family's journey. Single mothers are hunting for food, caring for their young, fending off danger—they are able to do it by relying on one another. Lionesses' resourcefulness and power became emblematic of the spirit of single motherhood. If you think of yourself as one part of a larger pride, sharing ideas and champion-ing others, you will succeed in ways beyond your wildest dreams.

The metaphor of the lionesses' pride was popularized by author Lisa Bevere, who notes in her book *Lioness Arising* that lionesses are resilient and quickly able to set aside failures in order to do better the next time. They are said to see in the dark: "She can take the smallest light and transform it into sight." The women I have interviewed in this book come from all walks of life and became single mothers through all sorts of circumstances, but all embody the ability to see through the darkness, remain present, and bring their children and themselves into lightness.

As we move forward together to be present, mindful parents for our children, I hope you will take pride in knowing there is a vibrant, robust, and fierce community of like-minded competent women actively raising authentic, fulfilled, happy, successful, and, most important, kind human beings—who, through voices in their ears, have become recipients and providers of great joy and enormous pride.

Presence of Mind:

The ability to trust our experiences and inner voice to become in sync and in harmony with the energy, needs, and emotions of our children.

I

Presence of Mind

Introduction

Even if we're not literally in a state of emergency, we can often feel like our lives are a perpetual wheel of chaos, tests, demands, and letdowns. We feel like losing it most of the time, and who can blame us! Teachers call home to discuss a behavior problem, you are up most of the night because you forgot to bake cupcakes for a birthday party at school, and also did you tell your boss you'd be an hour late so you can make it to the classroom to sing "Happy Birthday"? There are the chores, the homework, the paperwork, the bills, the trying to get to the gym and lose a few pounds (yeah, right), the calls to your own parents, the doctors' appointments, the sports, the extracurriculars, the playdates! I swear my blood pressure is rising just typing this. To say to you this is all still not even the half of it would be preaching to the choir. You are well aware that your head feels like it's going to explode; that your mind reels with so much stuff that you forget where your glasses are (on your head); and that you are actually a year older than you thought you were.

To have Presence of Mind can be defined as being in a calm

state of mind that allows you to think clearly or act effectively in an emergency. During the early years of diapers and when the simple distraction of a cookie could appease your screaming toddler, your being "out of your mind" probably wasn't as noticeable to your child. But I remember when they were around eight years old, I could tell my kids began to wonder whether I had it together or noticed I was frazzled. Nikki, my oldest, would even call me out on it. I realized that if I seemed scattered and out of control it would make the kids feel less secure, less capable themselves. So I did what any normal mother would do. I got it all together and became perfect.

Ha! Okay, fat chance. I did exactly what every mother *really does* and does well: I learned to fake it!

But in all seriousness, while I was faking my way through being all things to all people, I also began to realize that I could put to use the parts of my mind that I still had intact. My resourcefulness and sheer will to see my kids succeed had never gone by the wayside. I also began to admit that Presence of Mind couldn't happen 24/7, simply because I wasn't with my kids all day every day. They were influenced by peers, by social pressures, by things beyond my control. Presence of Mind had to be something that I passed on to them with my influence by talking to them, sharing my ideology, and giving them things to think about. I called upon mentors to help me when I wasn't there. I utilized my big mouth to fight for my kids intelligently and respectfully, forming helpful collaborations that kept my mind at ease while expanding the minds of my kids.

But first I had to come to grips with my new normal, one that I'd never expected and—had it not been for the voice in my own ear—one that I might not have survived successfully.

Letting Go of What Was Supposed to Be

Open the window of your mind. Allow the fresh air, new lights and new truths to enter.

—*Amit Ray*

It was 1984, and I had settled the kids inside our powder-blue Honda Civic to make the familiar drive from our home in Takoma Park, Maryland, to the east side of the Bronx, where my parents bought a home once our dad left his pulpit full-time. North on Route I-95 to the New Jersey Turnpike, over the George Washington Bridge, and just off the Bronx River Parkway to our destination: a cheerful three-story red brick house where my parents, "Mama Win" and "Papa Jim," as my children called them, were undoubtedly already peering out the front window, debating exactly when we would be pulling up.

In the backseat, six-year-old Wes and his four-year-old sister, Shani, were comfortable with snacks, favorite books, and toys within easy reach. As I started the engine, I glanced over at their big sister Nikki, twelve, who was riding shotgun. She stared out the window, silently. This was unlike any other trip to see their grandparents, but only Nikki was old enough to realize this. We were moving, saying goodbye to our house in Maryland and letting go of the remnants of the wonderful life we had had there for five years with their father. We were headed back to my childhood home to start over.

Nikki had been my partner through my first two marriages, one ended by choice, another by the death of my husband. She was two when I left her biological father, who abused pot and was becoming physically violent. Seven years later, it was nine-year-old Nikki who dialed 911 when my beloved second husband, Wes, collapsed on the second-floor landing. And it was Nikki who stood guard by the front door and escorted the paramedics inside. Hours later Nikki was old enough to fully understood what it meant when the emergency room doctor said, "He's gone."

That day had shaken us all so deeply that I wondered how we would ever go forward. I'd lost the love of my life, and I was devastated. As the shock lifted, I felt the enormity of being a single mom: the definitiveness of my loneliness and the overwhelming sense of responsibility. My first experience of becoming a single mother had been so different from my second. The first time I was miserable in what was a sinking marriage, so I had saved my money and set out on my own with Nikki. I was terrified and sad, but also relieved during those first months on my own. This time my heart was shattered. I had no playbook for how to put the pieces back together again, no strategies directing me how the four of us would survive without our family's quarterback. My heart was merely performing its biological function, keeping me alive. I went into autopilot, closing the door on my emotions so I could devote whatever motion remained to keeping the house solvent and in order, getting the kids ready for school, fed, and transported. I refused to turn inward, fearing I would be lost in some kind of abyss of despair. I did not want my mind to take me to feelings of terror and sadness, compounded by overwhelming grief and the magnitude of my responsibility with not one but three children dependent on me. I didn't want to remain in that space, so I did what I could to ignore it.

The nights were the hardest. I didn't want to sleep in our attic bedroom alone. Every time I walked up those stairs, I pictured Wes on the landing, gasping, struggling, helpless, dying. I began to sleep on the brown leatherette sofa in the living room. At first, I told myself that from that perch I could more easily hear the kids yell out for me. When they clearly didn't seek me out night after night, a rash of break-ins in the neighborhood gave me a new excuse to sleep there. The bad guys would have to get past me first. I elevated myself to a first responder, but the truth was that I was miserable, eating poorly, barely sleeping, and I couldn't imagine being in the bedroom without my husband.

Guilt is a cruel companion to grief. When I finally got myself to close my eyes at night, I was tormented by the image of Wes in the ER. I had been shocked to see the man who lay on the hospital bed. He'd left the house that morning with a fever and a sore throat, complaining that an aspirin had lodged in his throat. He drove himself to the hospital. A few hours later, he seemed drugged and limp, unable to hold up his head or form a sentence. At first the doctor's solution had been for him to go home with a prescription for penicillin, to which Wes was allergic, as was clearly marked on his chart. After Wes died, the autopsy determined that he'd had a swiftly moving throat infection, acute epiglottitis, which if undetected can kill a person in a few hours because it cuts off the body's air supply. Of course, only a skilled physician could have discovered this. Nevertheless, the "I should haves" were my constant interior refrain. I should never have let him go to the emergency room on his own. I should have found someone else to drop the kids off at school and childcare. For weeks, I couldn't stop beating myself up. Whatever my heart had given to others throughout my life—empathy, forgiveness, compassion, or just the ability to listen with love—my mind forbade me to muster for myself.

Outwardly, I put up an amazing front of efficiency and effortless coping for the sake of the kids. I refused to burden them with my guilt, my feeling of inadequacy and failure. Inwardly, though, my survivor's guilt created a complete disregard for my own well-being, causing a twenty-pound weight loss, sleepless nights, and intermittent, uncontrollable crying. For weeks I refused to take a walk during the day, because the first time I did I saw an elderly couple walking down the street, arm in arm, and my tears flowed. That was supposed to have been us!

It took time, and I'm not sure exactly when or how it happened, but one day I looked into the eyes of my three confused children and a light pierced the darkness. They needed me to be present in their lives—more present than I had ever been before, and certainly more present than I had been since Wes died. I said to myself that while I would never understand God's choice to take Wes and leave me, the responsibility to raise the kids was now mine. I had to prepare myself to do that, and do it well. It was only when I was ready to become the parent that I knew I needed to be to raise my children that the voice of guilt began to soften, and I allowed myself to feel the full rawness of my broken heart. I felt the timing was right to stay put for a while, in the fear and grief; that somehow while I was vulnerable, I felt a little stronger. I began to see the direct link between the heart and the mind. What I was thinking about and tormenting myself with, causing literal physical pangs in my heart, caused my heart to feel weak—and my mind followed. It wasn't a conscious decision, maybe more of an instinct, that allowed my grief to evolve into a different phase: letting go of what I assumed would always be.

Our lives would never be the same without him, but we were safe and we still had each other. I just needed to figure out how to be a mother to them in a new way. I no longer had the luxury of saying, "We'll talk about this when your dad gets home," so we had to settle matters in the moment. I no longer had a co-signer on decisions I made regarding the kids, so I had to rely on past lessons to deliberate much more carefully. I wanted to feel confident that I was making decisions Wes and I would have made together. But most important, I had to make my heart take a step back so that my grief would not blind me to the deep sorrow the kids were harboring. They needed me more than ever, and the only way I could get up again, be a mother to them again, was to get back into my mind space, even though it hurt so much to be there. I wanted to put all that was human and maternal into my children—compassion, empathy, generosity, forgiveness, all of it. That is what helped me parent my children in a way that they could feel my presence and my own fight on their behalf, even when we were apart.

I had to face the fact that our new normal was going to be very different. Most of our savings had been depleted by the funeral, the life insurance payments were dwindling quickly, and the freelance money I was bringing in was barely covering the mortgage. The reality was that even a full-time job wouldn't be nearly enough to support us. Our modest house suddenly seemed a luxury we couldn't afford, especially if I was going to be present for my children the way I wanted to be, and I realized that I needed to accept that our path was going to diverge from the one that Wes and I had been on.

Presence of Mind means being aware of what's most important for the family and doing what it takes to make sure everybody's on board. I was acutely aware that the odds were against my family. My mind was saying that a thirty-two-year-old black woman wasn't likely to successfully support three children. I started a nightly ritual of looking back over the course of the day and deciding what decisions or actions were necessary and what could have waited or not happened at all; of assessing where the kids were in their healing journey and what I could do the next day to help them; and of searching my own heart to determine whether my actions lived up to the standards of excellence, patience, and caring that Wes and I had established together as family norms.

Even my college education and two degrees, which set me apart from some other moms, wouldn't ensure family-supporting wages. I'd probably have to get two or maybe even three jobs to make ends meet. And then there was the perennial question: If I wasn't there at night, who would watch over the children? If we moved from our familiar neighborhood to a small apartment, and I found a way to work from home or accept government support, I could plant my five-foot-five-and-a-half self at the front door every night until Nikki, Shani, and Wes grew out of their young bodies. But without a father, I feared the forces of confusion and distraction in the neighborhood could still slip in the windows and jimmy the locks on the back porch.

I kept hoping for a sign that would tell me what to do. One night I braved the stairs to our attic bedroom, turned on the light on the bedside table, and waited. I opened the door to Wes's side of the closet. His shirts and jackets were still lined up neatly on the top row, just as he'd liked, with the matching slacks slotted precisely on the rack underneath. I stepped into the closet doorway and held the sleeve of his favorite sport coat, inhaling deeply. His scent was still there, and rather than grief, I felt a part of him was still with me. I asked him, "Wes, what would you do?" One evening, after finally settling the kids down to bed, the house was particularly quiet, even peaceful. When I prayed my nightly questions, I felt a familiar sweetness around me and a mental picture of my parents' house in the Bronx appeared. I had an answer. I needed to go back to my childhood home. It felt like Wes had given me the push and permission to go.

My parents had suggested I move back home shortly after Wes died, but I hadn't seriously considered it. My heart was overshadowing my mind: I didn't want to leave the home that Wes and I had made together. There was also my independence (the gift of ego given to me by my mind). If I moved back home, wasn't I admitting defeat? I would be discarding the world of my own choosing to return to the one my parents had built. Standing in front of Wes's closet that night, I realized I was clinging to the illusion of autonomy—it was stubbornness keeping us there, not good sense. Staying in our house was not giving me independence; it was creating more burden, more debt, and more worry about how much longer I could manage. Moving home would allow me to give my children a life more like the one Wes and I had envisioned. What was truly important, what was truly my top priority, was doing whatever it took to best provide for my children. And at that moment, the simple, sad truth was that the plan Wes and I had of raising them in this house together was no longer an option. I couldn't be the family they needed or the mother I wanted to be, the mother who was present for them for their dance recitals and music lessons and swim classes, without Wes there to share the load. I needed a new blueprint for the new life that we had been thrown into, and as much as my heart didn't want to accept the change, my mind was finally able to consider new options for how to live by my priorities. I was lucky to have parents who wanted us to live with them; who had the means, however modest, as well as the fullness of heart to take us all in.

Author and spiritual teacher Allan Lokos explains, "To be mindful entails examining the path we are traveling and making choices that alleviate suffering and bring happiness to ourselves and those around us." Once I was able to truly listen to what my mind was telling me we needed to do, I was able to see my parents' offer as a path toward healing rather than a sign of defeat. I resolved to carefully plan our departure so as not to inflict yet another major disruption to the kids' lives, especially to Nikki's. She was doing well and loved her elementary school, so I decided that we would stay until she graduated.

With that decision made that night, for the first time since Wes had died, I slept soundly and fully in the room I'd been avoiding for months.

Two years later, as we turned off the Bronx River Parkway and made our way through familiar streets, Shani and Wes, who had been dozing, suddenly sat up. As we drew closer, they wiggled in their seats. Just as I had pictured it, when we pulled in front of my parents' house the front door instantly flew open and there stood my parents on the front stoop, arms open to receive us. As Nikki and I grabbed the suitcases from the trunk, Wes and Shani unfastened their seat belts and ran to their grandparents.

My father, now a retired pastor with a heart as big as his beloved Mets stadium, stood only five foot five, but his muscular physique more than made up for his small frame. He lifted both Wes and Shani up in one huge hug. Seeing him standing there, looking both old and incredibly strong, I found myself remembering his own story of a difficult homecoming.

Originally from Jamaica, my grandfather immigrated to the United States to attend Howard University, eventually becoming a minister and moving his wife and growing family, which would soon include my dad, to establish a church community in Charleston, South Carolina. A student of scripture, he had a difficult time reconciling the cruelty he saw around him with the word of God, and his pulpit became his megaphone against the discrimination and violence in the South. As stories of lynching became more and more prevalent, he became more and more vocal. This earned him the respect of his congregation but also a place on the watch list of the Ku Klux Klan. Eventually, under the cover of darkness, he was forced to move his family back to Jamaica to escape the growing threats of his own lynching.

Remembering my family's legacy in that moment put the angst of my homecoming in humbling perspective. It also reminded me that while change is a constant variable in life, no change is permanent. My father realized his father's dream decades later by coming back to America with my mother, becoming the first ordained African American minister of the historically all-white Dutch Reformed Church, building a dynamic church community in the Mott Haven section of the South Bronx, eventually buying his own home, and raising a family.

I awoke from my reverie to my mother's joyful West Indian lilt. "You go along now, children, and get yourselves settled. You know Papa Jim has been cooking for you all day!" She looked a lot younger than I felt, her slightly gray hair Jheri-curled beautifully and her smile radiant, as it always was when she saw her grandchildren. Now she would have them around all the time. I hoped she would keep smiling.

Shani and Wes rushed inside, while Nikki dragged her suitcase onto the stoop. "Oh my, Nikki, look how much you've grown," my mother said, even though she'd seen Nikki only a few weeks before at her elementary school graduation. Nikki smiled, a rarity these days, and I thought I even saw her thrust back her shoulders with pride as she followed her grandmother into the house. My mother knew how to lift your spirits like no one else I knew. I was looking forward to more of that. After my father helped me hoist the last suitcase up the steps, he gave me the longest, tightest, most loving hug I can ever remember receiving from him. "Joy, I'm so glad you're here." In that moment, I was beginning to think I might be glad as well.

My parents' house made up for its small size with the elasticity of its walls. Whenever family or friends needed a safe haven or just a place to stay, the walls of that little place expanded, and the food was always plentiful despite my parents' tight, carefully kept budget. As I entered the house I smelled the familiar scent of sautéed onions, green peppers, thyme, and garlic, which meant my father's trademark codfish dish was simmering on the stove.

While the children all started reacquainting themselves with their new home, I went upstairs to my old bedroom where I would sleep once again. I went to the window to take comfort in the familiar view of tidy rows of homes with barely a foot of space between them. I always felt our block was a little island of safety and stability, and it still felt that way. But now I was seeing those streets with the eyes of a mother whose children would be walking them every day. I'd felt a little uneasy on the drive in as I took in some disturbing changes in the neighborhood. The stores on Burke Avenue, the main shopping street, had metal security gates, and many of those gates were covered in graffiti. I saw encroaching signs of decay in neighboring houses, and on too many front stoops groups of idle young men. As comforting as it was to be home, I felt a twinge of doubt.

"Joy!" my mother yelled up the stairs. "Come join us while the food is hot!" I snapped out of it. No homecoming was complete without a Jamaican feast. My doubts would have to wait.

In addition to codfish, my father had cooked my favorite boiled green bananas, and mom's rolled biscuits were fried to golden perfection. As my father blessed the meal (it was a short grace, once again), I looked around to the faces of my three kids, one by one. Our family, with me at the helm, was starting a new chapter. I was not naive enough to think that our challenges were over, but sitting at the table, surrounded by my children and my parents, I finally remembered how it felt to be at peace.

LESSON FROM A LIONESS: *Do not fight against your pain.*

When we are in pain, we feel boxed in. When tragedy or misfortune forces us off the path we have been traveling, it can be extremely hard to find a new one. But as difficult as it may be, the only way to overcome pain is to journey through it, and to be open to the possibilities and new directions that are on the other side. And what I have learned is that we are never alone. Remembering that there are others struggling with the same questions or pain that we feel can help us let go of our isolation and begin to see a way forward. I'm not saying our pain or challenges will go away, but allowing our minds to embrace this notion of mutual suffering will help us avoid the quicksand of isolation and despair.

Decisions are best made when the mind and heart agree, but sometimes the heart is leading us to places the mind doesn't want to go. The heart doesn't guide us based on pros and cons and logic; it guides us back to our spirits, our true selves, the parents we were meant to be. Our minds tell us how we can get there by reconnecting logic and love.

I once heard someone say that she believes she suffered her trials in order to be able to help others overcome their own challenges. I found solace in that idea, and comfort in its truth, especially now as I share this with you through the writing of this book.

Mentoring Matters

Mentors are good listeners, people who care, people who want to help young people bring out strengths that are already there.
—Susan L. Taylor

Presence of Mind requires concentration and focus, following our instincts, and listening and observing intently. It is the ultimate awareness—of ourselves, our environments, what's right and what's wrong, how to create and how to think better, more sharply, more intuitively. Presence of Mind lives within your children when you can't be there, functioning as your voice in their ear whispering about values and choices. It helps to have a pride of others who share your values to reinforce them, but Presence of Mind is about finding ways to communicate with your kids about how to live their lives.

Whenever I had to make a big decision, I turned to mindfulness practice—clearing my mind of the day's clutter, breathing deep rhythmically, and focusing on the question at hand. The process was close to my "what would my late husband do" moments, because it helped me remember conversations we'd had or similar situations we'd resolved together and so provided the direction I should now take. Relaxing my mind prepared me to make more thoughtful decisions about what or who should impact the lives of my children.

Mindfulness allowed me to be more present for my kids because it made me more confident about my decisions. And when I made better decisions about the people who would mentor my children, it instilled my presence even when I wasn't there. The last thing I wanted, in the words of popular culture, was to be a helicopter mom who bubble-wraps her children so that nothing or no one else can get to them. As such, I had to learn to trust people whom I was confident really cared about my children, who held my values, and who could open my children's eyes, minds, and hearts to opportunities that I wouldn't have access to. Mentors had been part of my youth so I was sure they could and would fill in the gaps in our single-parent household. Long before I even became a mother, before my main concern was to find what my children no longer had after Wes died—other trusted adults, and alternatives to the male perspective—I believed in the power of mentorship. As the founder of the National CARES Mentoring Movement, Susan L. Taylor, says: "A mentor is an adult who along with a young person's parents or guardians provides support, counsel, friendship, reinforcement, and constructive examples of how to make choices that serve him or her."

My parents were always mentoring someone, as ministerial counselors to children in our congregation or to children from my mom's elementary school classes. They also became surrogate parents/mentors to young women coming to New York for school or work. That's how I, as an only daughter, gained three sisters during my teens. Zelma, or "BB," from Brewton, Alabama, was nineteen when she came to New York to go to dietitian school. Her brother, a Reformed Church minister, asked my parents to meet her at the bus stop and take her to the YWCA in Midtown Manhattan. My mom saw a young naive-looking girl coming off the Greyhound bus with a clock radio under her arm and said, "No, you are coming home with me." Today, BB is my godsister, godmother to my children, a grandmother to three, and remains an integral part of our family. Another "sister," Marlene, was the eighteen-year-old daughter of my parents' best friends in Jamaica who arrived in New York to go to cosmetology school. For more than two years she and I shared a tiny bedroom with two twin beds, two small dressers, and one closet before she went back home to Jamaica. She's a grandmother too. And there was eighteen-year-old Althea, a daughter of other friends from Jamaica who was coming to New York to work. She became a citizen, married, had children, and—before my mother moved from our childhood home in the Bronx to live with me in Maryland—made sure Mom wanted for nothing. And yes, she's a doting grandmother as well. Long before "It takes a village" became an overused cliché, it was standard practice in our house.

From my experience, there's a bit of a spectrum when it comes to finding the people who fill a child's life. You don't want to just welcome *anybody* to help provide opportunities you can't afford or access. On the other hand, and often with an only child, there are parents who refuse to let *anyone* become close to their child out of fear of an inappropriate mentor, or of losing influence. These are the parents who will go to extreme lengths to censor any budding mentoring relationship the child is attempting to have, like preventing phone calls, or scheduling something else during mentoring appointments, or insisting on being present during each mentoring interaction. For mindful single mothers, who must make these determinations alone, a good balance is to be cautious but aware of the benefits that an outside mentor can bring. Such a mom will thoroughly vet a mentor to make sure she and the mentor share the same values, that the mentor has the safety and best interest of that child at heart, and that the opportunities are potential stepping-stones to a more successful future. For these mothers, the mentor must become the voice in the ear when Mom is not around. This middle ground is where I tried to lower my anchor with my kids.

When I became a parent, especially a single parent, this mentoring philosophy was ingrained. I vetted any adult I allowed to interact with my kids. I thought about what my mother had told me about modeling behaviors whenever I met anyone who cursed regularly in conversation. Anyone who didn't respect the value of education or honesty or compassion for others, I kept out of my children's lives. I may not have necessarily ended my association with them, but I made sure that any interaction with them was mine alone. I adhered to the words of James Baldwin when he said, "Children have never been good at listening to their elders, but they have never failed to imitate them." I tried hard not to say or do anything unsuitable myself. I sure didn't want to have to worry about deprogramming my kids from other people's messes!

Even when they were adults, I did my best to curate the mentors in their lives. When Nikki graduated from college, for instance, I asked what would make her happiest when she woke up in the morning and was getting ready to go to work. Despite her sociology degree, she told me she was happiest doing event planning and personal shopping. So I called my longtime friend Helen Moody, who is one of Washington, DC's, premier personal shoppers, and asked if Nikki could intern with her for the summer. Two decades later, Nikki runs her own successful event-planning business. Sometimes when I didn't know someone personally, I turned to friends to make the connection. When Wes was at Johns Hopkins and looking for an interning opportunity, I had a friend who knew the executive assistant to then Baltimore mayor Kurt Schmoke. The executive assistant scheduled an interview with the mayor, and Wes wound up receiving an internship. A Rhodes Scholar, Mayor Schmoke took Wes over to a picture on his office wall of his class of scholars. The mayor asked Wes, "Have you ever thought about the Rhodes?" Up until then, Wes hadn't given it more than a passing thought. But that tiny spark of an idea put into motion the events that would impact Wes's life forever.

While I was essentially the gatekeeper of relationships in their early years, as my three got older they started identifying their own mentors, and they did a great job. When Nikki moved out to Virginia, she connected with college friends of mine, Judge Gerald Lee and his wife, Edna. Living just a few miles away from her, they have essentially become her godparents. As I witnessed their relationship blossom, I began to wonder why we don't encourage our children to select their own godparents when they come of age. When they are babies, we select friends who are in our orbit at that time. Those relationships don't always survive the years, so I was thrilled when Nikki's relationship with the Lees grew so organically, so importantly. Years later, Shani and Jamaar became the godparents of Eliza—the teenage daughter of one of Jamaar's former law professors—because of the friendship he and his wife saw her forming with Shani and Jamaar. Like me, Eliza's parents welcomed positive relationships with people who would echo our values when they weren't around. Great mentors become great friends.

A pivotal mentor in Wes's life was an American history teacher at Valley Forge Military Academy by the name of Lieutenant Colonel Michael Murnane (retired). Mike became one of Wes's favorite teachers in high school, providing a perspective on history that stimulated his mind and curiosity like no other teacher had done before. Wes recalls that Mike (who to this day he calls Colonel Murnane even though they are more like buddies, going to events and games together!) made history relevant, sparking ideas on how to use lessons from the past to affect today's outcomes. Wes loved going to class, and his grades reflected that. When Wes was about fifteen or sixteen, Mike told him about an annual American Legion competition on the Constitution. It was a two-part event that involves an eight- to ten-minute prepared speech and a three- to five-minute extemporaneous answer to a question on any aspect of the Constitution. Each January, the instructions and schedule go out to all the American Legion posts in the country. In February, competitions begin in the local posts in each state. The winners then go to the county, district, interdistrict, section, and finally state competition in March. At that point, the student will have accumulated $7,500 as a state finalist. Then the student can get an additional $3,000 for the next two interstate-level competitions. The three students who advance to the final national competition will get $18,000 for first place, $16,000 for second place, and $14,000 for third place. At the end of the day, the national winner would have amassed more than $40,000. Uninterested at first, Wes says hearing those numbers finally convinced him it was worth a shot.

I'd met Mike several times during the year, including during the trip he took with his class to visit Congress in DC, so I knew he wouldn't have asked Wes to embark on such a journey had he not had the confidence that he would do well. So when Wes called to tell me about it, I enthusiastically encouraged him to go for it. The next few weeks were intense as Mike worked with Wes, both preparing his presentation for the speech portion and practicing possible questions for the extemporaneous part of the competition. I collaborated with feedback on the phone, putting final touches on the speech. When Wes came home for two weekends before the first competition, he started to work with a speech coach I had found. Finally, the first competition in the Wayne, Pennsylvania, American Legion post commenced. Wes began with an impassioned examination of why, even though the Constitution began with "We, the People...," it was never written with his ancestors in mind. His speech ramped up when he described how the authors had the foresight to make it a living document:

The Fifth Article to the Constitution ensured that if ratified, additional amendments to the Constitution could be added because they anticipated that times would change, opinions would change, America would change. My parents and grandparents worked long and hard so they could be called Americans . . . and despite the obstacles of slavery, Jim Crow, and Separate but Equal, they persevered. Because they persevered, I am as American as anybody in this room.

Wes won that first leg of the 1996 competition in that small room. Mike Murnane was there, as he was for each of the weekly competitions for the next month and a half. As Wes advanced victorious through the various levels of the competition, different groups of people were also there to support him. At the state championship, my brother, his wife Pam, her sister Toni, my parents, and the girls were all there to cheer Wes on. The next level of the competition, the district, was held the following weekend, in Annapolis, Maryland, and as I walked in I saw the president of Valley Forge, Admiral Virgil Hill, and his wife, Kim. I was so touched that they were there to support Wes, as mentors and as cheerleaders. Wes was thrilled they were there as well and was delighted they could go back to school and report that he'd won that level too! While Wes lost the next regional round in Virginia, I was so proud of how much the experience changed him. Even in his disappointment on the day of the loss, his mind refocused on using this as a character-building experience and what he would need to do to win his next competition, and the next, and the next after that. And remembering he had already earned more than $10,000 in scholarship money, the defeat stung a little less. None of it would have happened had Mike not been attentive to my son and recognized his potential. I'm so grateful that Wes was able to blossom under Mike's tutelage.

Mike continues to epitomize the true meaning of the word *mentor*, which derives from the Greek word meaning "enduring." When Wes received his commission as a second lieutenant, it was Mike and I who secured Wes's army pins on his lapels; he was there when Wes and Dawn got married, and whenever their schedules allow, they get together to share Mike's favorite pastime, watching any University of Maryland team game. I still speak with Mike fairly regularly. He recently revealed that Wes was the first student he ever encouraged to go for the American Legion competition, and he was the last. What he saw in Wes was a promising orator and enthusiastic student of history. I guess Wes's current success as a highly successful public speaker and television commentator has borne out his faith in my son.

When I clear my mind to express gratitude for our family's blessings, I think of mentors like Mike Murnane, who epitomizes the words of William Arthur Ward:

> *The mediocre teacher tells. The good teacher explains.*
> *The superior teacher demonstrates. The great teacher inspires.*

LESSON FROM A LIONESS: *Don't be afraid to share your child.*

I have seen how my sharing of my children has developed them into people who now share themselves with the world. When you're validating a mentor for your child, whether it is to address an academic endeavor, a struggle, an athletic interest, or a more specific or sensitive need, your mind will be reeling with questions and concerns. Calm your mind and use its more efficient resources, like analysis, judgment, and intuition. You can also incorporate some of the following tips, inspired by the Davidson Institute for Talent Development, into choosing—or helping your children choose—the other adults in their lives.

- **Define the relationships specifically around a tangible goal.** Wes and Mike had a relationship built on a shared interest in history and a focus on the competition. It gave them a shared focal point and also was a way for Wes to have a relationship with someone outside of the family who valued his mind. After that, the relationship grew organically; at its heart, though, was Mike's interest in helping Wes develop as a thinker, which in turn gave Wes the confidence to think big.

- **Define the role each party should play to achieve the ultimate goal.** The parent's role is to supervise the child's interaction with the mentor and provide support as needed, while mentors provide direction and advice on completing the project. Make sure your child knows that you're not ceding involvement in his or her interests to the mentor, and be sure to ask questions and keep tabs on the big picture even if you're not part of the day-to-day.

- **Assist your child in identifying potential mentors.** An effective mentor should share your child's interests and your values. Professional and religious organizations, universities, and community groups are all good sources for potential mentors. Contacts you have may be helpful. You can also check out the following programs: National CARES Mentoring Movement, National Mentoring Partnership, Boys & Girls Clubs of America, and iMentor. Information on all of these can be found at www.power-ofpresence.com. What's important is that you assess early on that your child's mentor is going to be amplifying and supporting the values that you're already working to instill in him or her. You also want to make it crystal clear that as much as the mentor will be valued, *you* still have the biggest influence over your child.

- **Make sure your child knows that mentoring is a two-way street.** If a mentor-mentee relationship is to be enduring, your child must realize that at some point his or her skills, time, or talents may become of use to the mentor. Encourage them to know that relationships are give-and-take and that whenever possible—even an issue such as helping the mentor with social media or providing some research assistance—they should provide their talents in the same unselfish way their mentors have provided theirs.

Minds Are Masterpieces

*Sibling relationships outlast marriages, survive the death of
parents, resurface after quarrels that would sink any friendship.
They flourish in a thousand incarnations of closeness and
distance, warmth, loyalty, and distrust.*

—Erica E. Goode

One of the projects I worked on during my decade in television production was a four-part series called *Images and Realities*. We looked
at the myths around and realities of life for African American men,
women, families, and children, respectively. The late Gene Davis,
the supervising producer of *Essence: The Television Program*, produced this series under his own production company and drew our
crew from colleagues at *Essence* and other shows he'd worked on.
I was fortunate enough to become one of the writers for the four
productions.

In each of the pre-production meetings, we sat down as a group
and Gene asked us to make suggestions about whom we should pro-
file. For the families episode, we wanted a family who would challenge the prevailing image that black families undervalue education.
Through some great suggestions, we were referred to the James family. Clarence L. James, residing then in Atlanta, Georgia, is a very
popular minister with six amazing, high-achieving children. They
fell between the ages of seven and sixteen and they all said they were
heading in only one direction—college and beyond.

From the moment our crew walked in the front door, everyone
knew the James family was one that valued and celebrated children
and all their possibilities. With enormous pride, Reverend James
escorted the crew around his family's compact home and pointed
to framed honor roll report cards and certificates of excellence that
decorated their refrigerator and hallways. There was little doubt in

any of our minds, in large part because the kids said it themselves in one way or another, that the parents' verbal and visible appreciation of their accomplishments and attitudes toward each other helped fuel their desire to achieve. Education was clearly a value that this family firmly adhered to: To breathe is to learn and grow, they believed; to use your mind and use it well is a duty. The brag walls and curio cabinets around the James house were so much more than gold and silver medals, trophies, and straight A's. They represented the characteristics that come along with children who apply themselves in any way, shape, or form. Reverend James highlighted all the things and attitudes I wanted to one day see in my children. Resilient, check! Inventive, check! Supportive of each other, check! Committed to excellence, check! I locked away that moment, imagining the walls of my own home similarly decorated with ribbons and certificates of honor. *This*, I said to myself, *would be a great way to show the impact of their hard work and what happens when they commit their minds to something.*

Taking the time to collect, collate, and celebrate my kids' achievements would also be, I calculated, a way for me to show that I could value, love, and celebrate each of them as much as any two parents. My challenge was to celebrate each of them as an only child so that each would feel favored but none would feel that I favored the others. If I could accomplish this, I surmised, it would let them know that even when I can't be with them individually, I appreciate each equally, living and lifting up our family values in regard to education and extracurricular activities. The reward? Recognition. The only problem was that unlike the James kids, my three kids weren't marching the trail of achievement at the same pace. Shani was my reader. There was hardly a moment that you wouldn't find her on the couch, in the car, on her bed, or in a corner somewhere reading something, anything. Her love of the written word provided a strong academic foundation that formed the basis for solid grades. Then there was Wes, who finally found his footing in the structure and discipline of Valley Forge. But for most of her tween and teenage years, my challenge was Nikki.

She always had a big personality, which, as she grew older, became a mask for the hurt she felt having essentially lost two fathers. After our move to New York, her grades started slipping, and for the rest of her tenure in junior high and high school, going to school became for her a necessary evil. It wasn't until she began taking classes at the local junior college that she started believing in herself and realized she could measure up academically. She got all A's in her first semester at Mercy College. When the second semester yielded the same results, I could see her sense of accomplishment and self-esteem blossoming.

That was all the opening I needed to try out the tool I had kept in the back of my mind since visiting the James family years before. While Shani was always getting commendations for academics or gymnastics and Wes was starting to bring academic and athletic recognitions home too, I never wanted to display their achievements as overtly as the James family did because I didn't want to draw attention to Nikki's late achievement. Of course I congratulated Wes and Shani individually and let them know how proud I was of their successes. But because keeping our family as a tight unit is one of our core values, I knew that comparing the kids in any way, even unknowingly, would cause a rivalry that could threaten their relationships with one another.

When Nikki's first semester brought her first set of all A's, I bought a sixteen-by-twenty-inch frame and gathered up the certificates and commendations Shani and Wes had earned their first semester. In the very center I put Nikki's full transcript, and I made a collage of pictures of all of them and of the various commendations that Wes and Shani earned throughout that semester. Next semester Nikki had the same results so I put both transcripts center stage in a larger, poster-size frame and created a collage of the report cards, articles, photos, and special messages teachers had sent home from all three kids throughout the year. I wanted them to see how relationships and respect are formed and earned through hard work, collaboration, and tenacity. So much more is gained than a degree, and those messages from people outside the family were quite effective in showing that point. We all worked on creatively cutting and pasting together the various parts of the puzzle, and at the end we decided to call it "The Best Of." I hung the frame in the entryway by the front door so anyone who came in or out could see how well all three were doing.

Without a doubt, visitors were very impressed, but more important I wanted Nikki, Wes, and Shani to see that with their individual achievements they had created a bold and beautiful visual statement about their combined strength as siblings. If any of them secretly counted how many of their achievements were included versus the number of someone else's, it was never said. As we put up the poster on the wall, the children celebrated each other—especially Nikki, because she'd excelled and was where Wes and Shani wanted to be someday—in college! Some months later Nikki confided in me that she was really proud to have become a role model for her brother and sister, and that their affirmation of her that day made her want to maintain that status. "The Best Of" became our win-win, all the way around.

That was the beginning of Nikki's college experience. A month later, in an example of the importance of social networks and the power of the pride that has always been present for our family, with the assistance of a friend of my brother's, Tony Aponte, she was able to transfer her first-year grades to the New York State University System at Purchase. She was accepted into a special program that was created to identify students who had demonstrated the ability to do college work but lacked the high school grades for admission the traditional way. Nikki commuted the half hour to Purchase, New York, for the next three years, majoring in sociology and loving her college experience. Nikki had launched!

As a full-time college student, armed with a self-confidence that had eluded her throughout most of her academic career, Nikki said she no longer felt the need to be included in "The Best Of" posters. But since Wes and Shani asked me to keep it going, I continued collecting what they gave me throughout the year. "The Best Of" became a source of pride and friendly competition between the two of them. Eventually, because there were so many certificates and newspaper clippings, I had to give them their own individual poster-size frames as they progressed through high school.

I am so grateful to that little voice inside me that told me to wait before throwing a spotlight on Wes and Shani's honors. I really felt vindicated when Adele Faber and Elaine Mazlish's *New York Times* bestselling book *Siblings Without Rivalry* came out and one of their main lessons was that when parents make comparisons, we heat up rivalries. I'm convinced that had I made that poster earlier, it would have caused Nikki shame that I never wanted her to feel. She was harboring enough self-doubt on her own without me using her siblings to pile more on. When she had earned the right to brag, after finding the joy in her own talents, we all were there to brag right alongside her.

To this day, the three of my children are incredibly close. They talk, tweet, or FaceTime all the time. When Wes's first book came out, Nikki was his very first assistant, handling his social media, making travel arrangements, and scheduling speaking engagements. Shani remains their editor and legal adviser, and Wes is an amazing brother to them both. They remain my greatest joy and are on the way to fulfilling my fondest wish, as expressed by an unknown writer: *A mother's prayer is that her children will love each other long after she is gone.*

As for "The Best Of," like fine works of art, these framed poster-size montages that documented their hard work so many years ago still hang in the hallway of my home. Gratefully inspired by the James family, they are now a daily reminder for me and an occasional one for my grandchildren when they visit of a few things:

I have three amazing children;
my grandchildren have an amazing dad and aunts;

hard work can yield amazing results; and

whatever good is done in life—small or big—has value and should be appreciated and preserved.

LESSON FROM A LIONESS: *Make it a celebration, not a competition.*

One of the things I remember taking note of when I saw the brag walls of the James household was the celebration of small victories as well as the big ones. Research has shown that praising children for little achievements goes further in increasing their self-esteem than big stuff like making captain of the cheering squad or a high score on the ACT. Remember to reward things like kindness, sharing, or trying to achieve something out of a child's comfort zone. Having the versatility to celebrate all kinds of positive outcomes enables moms to find ways to highlight one particular child's strengths—not *over* the others', but as a way to show the cumulative genius and talents of the whole family unit. Not every person in the family could be every color of a rainbow, but together you are vibrant and awe inspiring.

Remember it's not what you do to celebrate, just as long as you remember to celebrate! Whether it's the gift of your time, or a brag wall of your own, or even something larger, like a dinner out or a small celebratory slumber party, the recognition and validation is what this is all about. A friend of mine removes a special tiara from her curio and places it on her daughters' heads when they have done something worthy of royalty!

Finally, remind your children, it's not the perfect score or the Eagle Scout award that you are celebrating; it's the fact that such achievements represent the result of a commitment the child has made to the values that mean the most in your family.

Presence of Heart:

The ability to achieve and dispense unconditional love, compassion, and guidance—to yourself and your children— creating an enduring safety net that allows the family to discover and live out its truth.

II

Presence of Heart

Introduction

A good head and a good heart are always a formidable combination.
—Nelson Mandela

As I dug deep inside my memory bank to write the stories in this book, the many different idioms about hearts played through my head. "Have heart," "save heart," "from the heart," "listen to your heart," "broken heart"; even the song inspired by *ET*, "Turn on Your Heart Light," melodically got stuck in my head. When I identified my own experiences of having Presence of Heart, I realized they were the times when I felt like some powerful parenting reserve tank had been activated. These were the moments when I believed miracles were really happening. I was somehow getting my children and me through life despite the sporadic nature of my wisdom and courage, my limited finances, and sometimes my limited faith. When the going got tough and I felt I was falling short on everything that was important to me, my heart stepped in and carried us through.

Having heart is easiest to see in sports. What fuels a fatigued beat-up body at the twenty-fifth mile of a marathon? What keeps a boxer getting up on the count of seven to face more pummeling? What makes an Olympic skater pick herself up off the ice after missing the landing of a triple axel? Sports psychologist and blogger Eric C. Stevens explains, "Heart transforms our lives, knowing that we are fighting for what we love. Heart is what gets us to compete authentically with our true nature. When we see real sportsmanship and those competing at a level far beyond their athletic prowess, that is heart." Remember Michael Jordan's herculean effort during the 1997 NBA Finals against the Utah Jazz? He played forty-four minutes, four minutes short of the entire game, and scored thirty-eight points. All this while he was fighting debilitating flu-like symptoms! Or gymnast and Olympic gold medalist Kerri Strug, who delivered a spectacular run, cartwheel, and springboard to the vault, ending in a near-flawless dismount that she stuck on one foot, only to be carried off the mat by her coaches with two torn ligaments in her ankle? That performance helped clinch the first-ever gold medal for the US woman's gymnastic team in 1996.

Stevens continues that having heart does not always lead you to the win column. "Having heart means accepting failure with grace, and being willing to accept it, grow from it, and try again. Even in defeat, no one can take true heart and love away from you."

My favorite definition is actually from the dictionary. "Have heart: to showcase compassion, empathy, humility, forgiveness, putting all that is human in someone or something." That begs repeating: *Putting all that is human in someone or something.*

I just love that.

We all strive to be present for our children, but it's easier said than done. The reality is that being present demands a special kind of attention in a hectic world—a world that forces you to jump from one task to the next, from one worry to another, all with the nagging dread that you'll never be enough, or be good enough, and that there's no way you can get this right on your own. I found that my own feelings of inadequacy surfaced most in that moment when I first approached my front door, already drained from the frustrations of the workday and uncertain that I had enough in me to face any challenge on the other side of the door.

What I hope you will discover when practicing Presence of Heart is the art of forgiveness and compassion for yourself. Presence of heart, more than any of the other pillars, must be available to you first. Dr. Kristin Neff, a pioneering self-compassion researcher, author, and teacher, describes self-compassion as translating the compassion we may feel for someone we see in pain, physically or mentally, to ourselves. When we are experiencing inner conflict or pain, Neff advises, "Instead of ignoring your pain with a 'stiff upper lip' mentality, you stop to tell yourself 'this is really difficult right now,' how can I comfort and care for myself in this moment?" We must remember that if we don't tend to the heart, the muscle itself weakens and we'll have no heart to pay forward.

A research study from Israel has noted that mothers and infants can synchronize their heartbeats simply by looking into each other's eyes and through vocal cues. Through our ability to offer such comfort, stability, security, and consistency from those first moments and throughout their lives, we as mothers can be comforted in knowing that small acts of pure love are enough to anchor our family. When it came to the loving connection and unconditional love I had for my children, those moments of a hug or a tender wiping of a tear gave me hope that the light that existed in my heart was still there.

Learning to Breathe

In all kinds of ways—if we are willing—our children take us into
places in our heart we didn't know existed.
—Dr. Shefali Tsabary

I remember the evenings when I'd drag myself home, my arms weighed down with groceries, my briefcase, and usually something

I had to bring home for one of the children: shoes I'd had repaired or some special supplies one of them needed for a school project. On the ride home, I'd imagine the kids waiting for me at home: hungry, feeling neglected, and lashing out at each other. I could feel my own resentment rising: They were old enough now to feed themselves a snack, to do their homework without prompting, to support each other if one felt sad or neglected, but somehow I knew these things and more were all going to be loaded onto my plate as soon as I walked through the door. I remember feeling the events of the work-day buzzing around my head, and in my exhausted state, the familiar pull of my worries about the future was impossible to resist. And then there were the decisions that had to be made before I arrived, like what to make for dinner. Would I be a bad mother if I ordered pizza *again* this week? I would reason that pizza is the perfect food: carbs, fiber, protein, good fats, lean meats, lots and lots of veggies. But how easy it was for me to rationalize something I wanted to do!

When I finally got home, I'd open the door and be welcomed by my children pretty much the same way every evening. Shani wanted to talk right away about everything, before I could set my bags down and get my bearings. Nikki almost always left the living room as soon as I entered, and most of the time Wes kept his eyes glued to the television screen, acting as if I were invisible.

I would notice everything that was wrong. Why was there a wet towel on the sofa? They had closets for their shoes and drawers for their sweaters, but it seemed like all three of them had forgotten those minor details. Wes probably had a paper due the next day. I doubted he'd finish it—and I doubted he cared.

It was tough to suppress the swelling part of me that wanted to start barking orders at my children. Most of the time my words were on repeat: "You know I work hard all day to put food on the table and the very little I asked of you, you can't manage to do!"

There are a hundred variations on this daily homecoming sce-nario, and when I speak to fellow mothers, they give me their version of what I've come to call "the Not-Welcome Home Refrain." We want to feel welcomed and grateful to see our kids after a long day apart. Instead, we are exhausted and irritable and feel taken for granted. We may run a familiar script in our head every night: "My kids don't appreciate me, I sacrifice so much, would they please just leave me alone?" It's a paradox of sorts. We want to give everything we can to our children, but feel burdened when we are doing just that.

Essence magazine once did a spread on the fashion sense of working women during pregnancy, and the television staff was invited to bring our young children to be a part of the photo shoot. What a fun experience for Shani and Wes, I thought, so off we went the next morning to the *Essence* offices downtown. They had their turns in wardrobe, hair, makeup, and then met with the photographer and model. There were about four or five other kids of the magazine staff and they all had a ball acting like real live models. I knew I was earning mega brownie points in my cool mommy account. But the next days were back to normal, the kids taking on an air of business as usual and ingratitude for an experience so few kids get to have. That's a lesson I'd relearn time and time again—do what you do for your kids because it's the right thing to do, not because you expect some giant show of gratitude in return. It won't happen, at least not at first. The reality is that kids learn gratitude from observing how we respond, and often do not express it in the moment. But as long as we're consistent with expressing our gratitude to others and to them for the things we are able to accomplish together, they'll learn gratitude in time. As I became more confident in my parenting skills, I hung on to the belief that by twenty or so, their gratitude gene would finally kick in, along with all the other civilities teenagers seem to bury when they are thirteen. Thank goodness, I wasn't wrong!

When we are in the thick of it, in real time, carrying the stress of the day and the burden of our worries into our house, it's hard to play the long game. We turn on our children and lose our hearts as well. During those maniacal times, I wasn't fully present because my head was swirling and my pride was telling me I was losing. I was so caught up in where I was trying to get us that I wasn't focused on where we were as a family.

Dr. Shefali Tsabary, clinical psychologist and author, says, "To parent consciously we have to become astute observers of our own behavior when we are with our children. In this way we can begin to be aware of our unconscious scripts and emotional imprints as they arise in the moment." My moment of reckoning with my own actions came when I was doing my regular writing for *Essence: The Television Program* and a friend asked me to help with a short-term writing project. At the time, I was also working on a fairly regular basis with the furrier James McQuay in his downtown salon and alternately in his Mount Vernon salon with his wife, Doris. I was stretched razor-thin. I saw the kids in the morning when I took them to school and kissed them when they were fast asleep when I got home at ten o'clock or so. My brother and his wife, Pam, lived right next door so Wes and Shani would usually do their homework and eat at their house and stay until I got home; if it got too late, one of them would come over and stay with the kids until I arrived. Years later Wes would say that his only comfort during that period was the smell of my perfume when I kissed him good night as I got home. While I thought I was handling this juggling act adequately, I began noticing that the morning routine was getting harder; tempers flared more easily, there was more bickering in the car on the way to school, and collectively my kids just seemed angry—at each other especially. One especially rough morning, after I dropped the children off, I sat in my car for about half an hour and put myself on pause to answer these questions. *What am I doing to them, and to myself? Are they just trying to get my attention because they know this is the only time of the day they can get it? Is the reality that they aren't angry at each other but are really angry at me?* I realized that the precious few hours

I had with them were being wasted on tension and resentment. I was pushing them away rather than bringing them closer. And in the end, my outbursts would change nothing—that wet towel would still be on the couch, the paper unwritten. I needed to reconnect with my top parenting priorities and spend more time enjoying them—I needed to remember that my most important job was raising children ready for the world and that couldn't always include saving all the wet towels from mildew!

I wanted to provide for my children and was going about that by working myself to the bone. But it was at the expense of my relationship with each one of them. When I took a step back and examined what was at the heart of the situation, I realized it was my time that my children were craving. That day I stopped everything but my job at *Essence*. I was worried that we'd hurt financially if I cut back on the extra work but I actually ended up having more money for the household because I cut down on parking fees in the city, eating out, babysitting charges when Howard and Pam weren't available, and on taxes. Sometimes I did miss some of the interaction I had with folks on those other projects, but it didn't compare to the satisfaction of being with my kids and their happiness at having me home more.

After that morning in the car, I made a habit of literally catching my breath on my way in the door. It got me back into my heart space and out of my overcrowded head space. And when I could connect with my heart, that place where I loved my kids unconditionally, I could parent with greater effectiveness.

Every evening before I put my key in the door, I put down my bags to settle myself. Yes, I embraced the mindfulness practitioners and concentrated on being aware, eyes closed, feet planted firmly on the ground, and taking a deep breath. When I turned the key and heard the click of the lock opening, I took another big breath and put—or sometimes forced—a smile on my face and envisioned my large exhale expelling all the negativity I had endured throughout the day. That simple ritual made a difference. Today we have science that proves putting on a smile, even when we don't feel like it, can trick the brain into thinking we are happy. I know from experience this is true! My smile, while put on, became genuine as the hours ticked away toward bedtime.

I felt a little more present for my kids' needs and less reactive to their behavior. And I was more open to making a connection, even in those messiest of moments at the end of a long day.

We can all relearn to be present by shifting our perspective and making a conscious effort to leave our negative thoughts behind. Psychologists call this boundary work: devising routines and rituals that provide a mental space between the day's challenges and the evening's gifts. Boundary work does just that—sets boundaries so that work doesn't invade your home and home doesn't invade your work. The end result is absolute presence. Drawing the line in the sand begins with you, and doing so can save your heart—and your home—in the long run.

LESSON FROM A LIONESS: *Dedicate time to building your boundaries.*

Figure out how you can make a smooth transition from your working self to your mommy self in order to be fully present for your children. Some people create a sort of buffer zone during their last thirty minutes at work, not taking calls or scheduling meetings, to begin to slowly transition out of "the zone" and into the home. Other people like to stop at a store before going home, creating a physical transition space, while many find visualization a helpful mindfulness technique, such as mentally picturing work concerns being dropped into a box and then shutting the lid. This can be helpful whether you're leaving a boardroom, a classroom, or a factory floor. One thing I used to do if I was unable to decompress prior to walking through the door was to say, after I kissed each of my kids hello, "Okay, it's been a tough day so I need a time-out for myself—just for a little bit. I'll be a much better 'me' when I come out of my room." I didn't do it often, so they took it seriously when I did; they knew to give me the space I needed, and I would emerge mind and heart ready to be present for and with them.

A Heartbeat Away: The Rama Chakaki Story

Do nothing out of selfish ambition or vain conceit. Rather, in humility value others above yourselves.
—Philippians 2:3

Rama Chakaki was sixteen years old when her parents decided to make America their home. Following the American dream and an opportunity for Rama to begin college, she and her younger brothers and sister immigrated to the United States from their adopted home in Saudi Arabia. Having escaped the escalating tensions in their home country of Syria years before, the family moved to a suburb of Washington, DC, where Rama's father began a successful career as a real estate developer. Rama, a recent graduate from an all-girls high school in Saudi Arabia, started classes at the then all-women Marymount College in Arlington, Virginia.

Eager to pursue a medical degree, after one year at Marymount Rama transferred to and eventually graduated from George Washington University. She then went on to earn a master's degree in engineering management. As she was about to start her studies as a medical doctor, Rama's father suffered his second heart attack in ten years and died. She abandoned the decision to pursue a medical career and continued to work in computer engineering.

It was traumatic because my brother Omar was very young and my other siblings were not much older. After his death, I felt I shouldered a lot of the responsibility of the family, not financially but more emotionally. I was trying to keep things moving along as best as possible.

Perhaps the weight of that responsibility pushed her into the arms of a man who would share and help ease her responsibilities as firstborn. When Rama was twenty-one, she and Emad married, and out of that union came two children, daughter Tala and son Aboudi. She immediately embraced the joys of motherhood, staying home to maintain a physical presence with them, much as her own mother had done. But a few years later, Rama began having heart problems reminiscent of her father's. She says trying to maintain a presence as wife, mother, sister, and attentive daughter took its toll and almost cost her life.

I was diagnosed with cardiac sarcoidosis and that year was really difficult because my heart was just all over the place. I was in and out of Georgetown University Hospital. In one episode that I had, my defibrillator fired seven times, and I felt almost paralyzed by the electrical current it was pushing. I was taken to the intensive care unit at Fairfax Hospital, and I literally couldn't speak to anyone for about a day or two because I was just so stunned by what was happening. Then I remember, one of the nurses came in and said, "You have to think what matters most in your life. What's most important, and let go of everything else."

The only vision I had in my mind at the time was seeing Tala in our backyard wearing a white graduation dress. I thought, that's it. That's the image I had to maintain in my mind, to see her and Aboudi at the age of eighteen. A stillness fell over me and I absolutely believe that those visions and the love in my heart for my children is what settled my actual heart and pulled me through.

She survived that health episode. Within a few years, though, another big shift happened when Rama and her husband accepted that while they both loved their children deeply, the love between them was gone.

> *By twenty-nine years old I was divorced with two kids. We moved back with my mother, who was now living in Washington, DC. There was pressure to remarry because in our tradition and culture a woman can't live alone; or at least my mom thought I couldn't live alone even though we were in the States. The idea was, you can't stay unmarried for long. The first guy that came along, I remarried even though emotionally, I don't think I was prepared. It wasn't like we loved each other. It just became expected.*

Expedient yes, forever no. Within a year they divorced.

A single mom for a second time, Rama moved back in with her mom. But now, with her sister and brother graduated from college and the last brother almost finished, her mom followed the call of her old life and friends and returned to her native Syria. Her children and grandchildren were left in the United States to provide support to each other.

Things went fairly smoothly for a while but then tensions began to escalate between Rama and her children's father. They ended up in court, in a bitter custody battle over Tala and Aboudi. Rama won full custody and her ex-husband moved to Dubai to join his family and pursue a career in real estate investment. By now the children were approaching middle school, and Rama saw that every time his father's name was mentioned, Aboudi's eyes would tear up. He loved his dad, and as he neared his teens, Rama knew that despite the anger between the two of them, their son needed his father in these critical years. This was the true test of her unconditional love for her children and her determination to maintain a presence roared.

> *I thought, How do I make a bad situation for me work well for my kids?*

They all moved to Dubai, and she rented an apartment close to their father.

> *I went from demanding full custody to conceding, "Okay, the kids can stay with you during the week." This meant the hassle of having to see my ex-husband every morning when I picked them up for school and every afternoon when I brought them back to his apartment. If that was the only way I could have him be involved as a father, I had to do what I thought, as a mom, was best for my kids.*

I could so empathize with Rama as she recounted her decision-making process. I too had to make the choice between what felt more comfortable for me and what my heart was telling me my children needed; I too had reached the sobering realization that my life was no longer mine, and my responsibility toward helping my kids build theirs was in my hands, if I could somehow find the heart. Author Roy T. Bennett has said, "You can have everything you want if you can put your heart and soul into everything you do." Well, Rama definitively did that, despite the discomfort or compromises it caused.

> *Whatever job I took in Dubai, I always had to put this disclaimer forward: I'm a single mom, which means I have to sometimes leave work early. I need flexibility. I want to be there for their soccer games and whenever as needed. That was always a compromise with work whether it was pay, long-term commitments, taking on jobs that required more travel. I was getting a lot of other offers that I would decline despite much higher pay and a much higher position, but they would have required more travel or longer hours. Not being present for my kids was non-negotiable.*

Socially, while she found that being a divorcee carried somewhat of a stigma in Dubai, it ironically became her ex-husband who was the most helpful in getting her beyond the isolation and into a true support network in her new country.

When I got settled he introduced me to a few of his friends whose wives I became very close with, and they became my support, my rock. One of them was an educational psychologist whose kids and mine were the same age, and we did a lot of things together. She's a very strong and opinionated woman who's always there for me. She connected me to a few other women in a similar situation, who were either married or divorced like me and who really became my network. I remember one instance when my disease recurred in Dubai and I had to have surgery. I texted one of my girlfriends, and for the next two weeks there were these five women who were taking turns sleeping over and doing whatever the kids or I needed. They truly were my rock and, in the words of the metaphor, my pride.

Rama stayed in Dubai throughout Tala and Aboudi's high school years. When it came time for college, both were accepted into US universities and Rama followed them back to the States.

The day I dropped Tala off at college, she slipped a letter in my purse that I found later. It read, "I know it's been difficult for you as a single mom. I know that it's been difficult for me, a child of a divorced couple, but I also am so grateful for having you as a mom because of what you've done. How you've managed to do adventurous things, but always be there for us. Even though it was really difficult to deal with certain families, the cultures, you still managed to pull through. You've always modeled what it was like to be a working mom, and I'm really happy to have seen you do this. I know that it wasn't easy. I love you."

Now, almost a decade later, Rama works remotely as a principal with a tech venture capital firm in Dubai as well as with a nonprofit organization that helps young adults connect with economic growth opportunities outside their conflict-torn countries. Being in the States also helps her stay close to her children, both of whom are thriving.

While feeling fortunate and content with where her life has taken her, like most immigrants she still yearns for her birthplace. But at this moment in its turbulent present, she knows returning to her native Syria is an impossible dream. As she prays for peace so that her children will one day know Syria too, her heart remains full with the knowledge that she has kept its rich culture alive for them. And she knows in her heart that she was only able to accomplish this through maintaining physical presence and presence of a forgiving heart they needed from her to grow into strong and productive citizens of the world.

LESSON FROM A LIONESS: *Love your children more than your pride.*

Divorce can bring out the worst in parents. After years of battling inside the home, divorce brings animosities into public spaces where each side is trying to emerge the winner. When we determine the true winners must be our children, handling the process with civility becomes easier. Rama and her ex-husband were able to put the needs of their children front and center in their lives, and the kids emerged whole. No matter what we are dealing with, we have to prioritize the emotional well-being of our kids. When the welfare of our children becomes the guidepost for our lives, making choices about what we say, what we do, how we do it, and when we do it becomes easier. That means it's important to do regular self-checks to make sure that your actions are pointing you toward the goal that you truly want to reach. And that goal should be emotionally secure and content children. So no matter the circumstance, if you feel stuck, ask yourself, *What is my endgame here?* The answer will most likely be about enhancing your child's welfare, and that reminder will set you back on track.

Sisters from Other Misters

Some women pray for their girls to marry good husbands.
I pray that [my daughters] will find girlfriends half as loyal
and true as the Ya-Yas.

—Rebecca Wells

The day I walked onto the campus of American University in 1968, I found sisters I never knew I had: Mary Braxton from Plainfield, New Jersey; Pam Higgins from Teaneck, New Jersey; Gail Black from Washington, DC; and Vicki Pinkston from Greensboro, North Carolina—all of us eighteen years old and bound and determined to make a difference in the world. A year later, Linda Allston from Darlington, South Carolina, joined our core group. What we didn't know then was that whatever contributions we would make to the world in our adult lives would pale in comparison with the impact we would make in each other's lives, for the rest of our lives.

Probably the first thing that pulled us together was cultural connections. We were young African American women on a predominantly white campus, at the height of social unrest over the Vietnam War and the murder of Dr. Martin Luther King Jr. We bonded soothing each other's eyes when police tear-gassed our campus amphitheater, Woods-Brown, during a demonstration. "Remember Woods-Brown! Remember Woods-Brown!" became our battle song for weeks afterward. We locked arms fighting perceived injustices, on campus and in the streets of Washington, DC. We tutored cafeteria and grounds workers so they could get their GEDs, the route to better-paying jobs, or even being able to take classes there. My girlfriends and I wrote articles together and took photos for the newspaper published by our black student organization OASATAU, the Organization of African and Afro-American Students at the American University. After the initial random pairing of roommates by the university, most of this core group and a growing number of other women elected to live together on the Black Cultural Floor of Letts Dorm. We truly became sisters, as Pam's parents noted during their fortieth anniversary celebration, in which we all participated. "We never worried about Pammie being an only child," remarked Dad Higgins, "because of the caliber of loyal friends she is blessed with... and for that we are eternally grateful." They knew, like all our parents knew, that no matter what we would always have each other's backs.

We were there for each other as study partners and cheerleaders during final exams. We were there to talk out every new romance, or to provide a shoulder for each inevitable breakup. We were in each other's weddings, witnesses for each other's divorces, anxious bystanders for the births of each other's children—and then unofficial aunts. Our group expanded and contracted with other amazing women during the years but the core, no matter where we lived in the world, remained essential, connected, and intact.

Never was this more evident to me than the night my husband died.

Linda and her family lived a couple of blocks from us in Takoma Park, Maryland, so we were frequently back and forth between each other's houses, doing activities together with our kids. Our husbands got along great because both of them worked in the news media— Wes was in local radio and television news while Linda's husband, Bernard Shaw, was the senior anchor for CNN. So when the doctor confirmed that Wes had died and I regained my coherency, I made two phone calls from the hospital. First, to my parents, who fought back their own tears and said they would fly down first thing in the morning. The next one was to Linda. I left a message, and then Nikki and I went over to Wes's parents to pick up Shani and little Wes. Within five minutes of our getting home, Linda and Bernie were there. Then Mary, who had heard the headline on the eleven o'clock news; Pam and her husband, Ty; then Gail and her husband, Bill. I was particularly surprised when I saw Gail and Bill; Gail had recently given birth to their daughter, Lauren, and I knew they hadn't yet left her without one or the other being at home with her. But they were all there for us, and in the midst of my grief, seeing them provided a momentary stillness where I could sit in gratitude for my circle of friends. My pride.

Snatches of memory are all I have left from that night: looking up from a chair in the kitchen and seeing Mary picking up and washing the cast iron skillet I had dropped to the floor when I heard Wes gasping for air on the landing; Linda putting the kids to bed and then feeling a cool washcloth tenderly applied to my forehead as she was saying through her own tears, "It's okay, we're here"; hearing the almost constant ringing of the phone and Pam and Ty, fielding each and every one with the words, "We'll give her the message." At some point, I recall that Gail and Bill, both lawyers, huddled with everyone to discuss what each could do to help us get through the next few days. My only crystal-clear memory is Bernie offering to go to 7-Eleven to pick up milk and cereal for the kids' breakfast the next morning, as well as bread, eggs, coffee, and then he said the word that brought the weight of the moment crashing down on me, "cigarettes." Bernie and I both shared the habit so he made the offer with no bad intent. What he wasn't aware of was the deal I tried to strike with God to give up smoking if He let Wes live. Still furious over God's perceived abandonment, I took it out on Bernie. I looked at him and with glaring, angry eyes blurted out a loud and hostile "No." As it was coming out of my mouth I wanted to shove it back in, but I couldn't even muster the strength to do that or explain my moment of rage. Weeks later when I tried to apologize for my reaction, Bernie didn't even remember the incident (or so he said).

For the next few days before the funeral, my family and pride of sisters had a constant presence. The college circle expanded to include Vicki Davis; Jackie Flowers, whose rendition at the funeral of our favorite song, "Endless Love," brought tears to everyone's eyes; and Helen Moody, who brought outfits for me to wear to the funeral and who made sure the kids' clothes were ready and in order. And even my college guy friends came through those first days, like Gerald Lee, who brought cases of soda and water and who reminded me of the words I needed to hear at that moment, "Let Go and Let God."

At the grave site, my virtual circle that began coalescing that first day on American University's campus and their husbands formed an actual circle. With our arms stretched across each other's shoulders, we lifted our heads to the sky to signal Wes's ascension. As we moved our heads toward the center of the circle, Ty offered a prayer, wishing Wes safe speed and thanking God for Wes's time on earth and the ties that will continue to bind and connect us.

The year 2018 marks our fiftieth anniversary as friends. As my core sisterly pride sat around, listening to the music of our youth and reminiscing on all we've done together and meant to each other over the years, I shared what I think is one of the best tributes acknowledging the power of our friendships. It came from my son, Wes, when he and Dawn were starting to get serious in their relationship. He came to me one day and confided that one of the reasons he thought she just might be "the one" was because she had a circle of girlfriends, "just like yours." With that as a touchstone, I was sure that theirs would be a relationship built on solid ground.

LESSON FROM A LIONESS: *Create a sacred sisterhood.*

Psychologist and author Randy Kamen says that research has indicated time and time again that the strongest predictor for a fulfilled life is building healthy relationships with others. Among the most durable are relationships between women. The emotional connections, he says, are actually based on science, as revealed in a landmark study by Laura Klein and Shelly Taylor, which noted that "women are genetically hard-wired for friendship in large part due to the oxytocin released into their bloodstream, combined with the female reproductive hormones. When life becomes challenging, women seek out friendships with other women as a means of regulating stress levels. A common female stress response is to 'tend and befriend.' That is, when women become stressed, their inclination is to nurture those around them and reach out to others."

But the same life transitions and stressors that signal us to seek out support may also be what interrupts the momentum or intimacy of our friendships. At first, I feared that as a widow, I'd be a third wheel among our sisterhood of married women. I can truthfully say, however, that in all these years I have never been made to feel that way. Yes, true friendships in adulthood can be much harder to make and maintain than was the case when we were living together in dorm rooms, but time and concerted effort have proven there are ways we can remain connected. Inspired by clinical psychologist and author of *The Friendship Fix: The Complete Guide to Choosing, Losing, and Keeping Up with Your Friends*, Andrea Bonior, PhD, here are some suggestions for preserving our friendships.

DEVELOP MOMENTUM.

Staying connected is key to maintaining lifelong friendships. Our group, like many in this modern age, has lived all over the country and some in foreign countries since we graduated. But no matter where we are, we've tried to connect at least once a year in person and numerous times by phone or Skype during the year. We've come together for special concerts or annual fashion shows in DC or even for a week at a spa resort in California. We have always believed, as Dr. Bonior says, that if you want to stay close, you had to stop letting schedules contribute to the deterioration of your relationships. Sometimes someone will send out a quick text to someone in the group and say, "Pick a time so we can do a catch-up phone date!" Sometimes it is just our core group; other times it may be another group of amazing women from work. But if relationships are important, then don't let getting disconnected be an option. Once a day is agreed upon, get together for dinner, then go around the circle and share what each person has been up to for the past six months. If schedules allow, set regular get-togethers—the second Sunday of every month for brunch, for instance, or every Wednesday afternoon for a phone chat during your commutes—or let it work spontaneously. What's important is that the friendships remain a priority in your lives. Then the magic of seamless connections will happen, as it has for our core pride for the past fifty years.

END POISONOUS FRIENDSHIPS.

Sometimes we hang on to a friendship out of habit or because we feel obliged to, even though we know it just doesn't feel right. Some common scenarios are: When you have to see or talk to that person, is there a sense of dread because you know the conversation will be dominated by constant chatter about things that no longer or maybe have never interested you? Does this friend feel that her opinion is the only one that matters, and is she disrespectful of anyone else's point of view? Do your other friends bow out of getting together if they know that this person will be coming? If any or all of these things ring true, then you have a toxic friendship and should end it. It doesn't have to be a confrontational breakup. Not returning calls or being too busy to get together sometimes is enough to get the message across. But if you do elect to have a conversation, then explain that the two of you are just in two different places now, and rather than continuing to be frustrated with your changing priorities and interests, it's better to end the friendship. Dr. Bonior says, "The inertia of unhealthy friendships can be strong: Guilt, fear, and familiarity can keep us in them much longer than is good for us. But if you can bring yourself to make some real changes, you'll have even more room for healthier relationships."

REMEMBER THE LITTLE THINGS.

I love roaming around the card store and picking up "just because" cards. I'll send one to a girlfriend just because its picture reminded me of her, or the words inside almost exactly mirror a conversation I had with her at some time. Expressions like this—"Just because I'm thinking of you"—can mean so much. And who knows, maybe that person really needed that little boost at the moment your card arrived! Dr. Bonior warns, "We often get so bogged down with perfection that we sabotage ourselves, like the person so focused on 'owing' their friend a nice, long email response that they put it off and fail to respond at all. But done is better than perfect."

AVOID TECHNOLOGY TRAPS.

Most of my girlfriends have kids or aging parents, so our standing rule has always been that when we get together we will only answer the phone if our kids or parents call. Smartphones, social networking, instant messaging: All those things are great when you are not face-to-face with your friends. For the friend who is tethered to her smartphone, Dr. Bonior has a cute suggestion. "The next time you're lucky enough to be sitting across from a friend over coffee, pile your phones up in the middle of the table, and the first one to reach for theirs pays the tab."

Moving Beyond the Heartbreak: The Mary Ann Boyd Story

Great mothers build bridges instead of walls.
—Reed Markham

The finicky sun played hide-and-seek through the oversize picture window. It provided the perfect frame for the kidney-shaped front-yard swimming pool, protected from prying eyes by gray wooden privacy gates. Inside, Mary Ann Boyd and I sat near the baby grand piano, a focal point in this midcentury modern corner house in California's prestigious Orange County.

Looking at her surroundings, it's hard to imagine her growing up in extreme poverty as one of eight children in Milwaukee, Wisconsin. Her father left the family for another woman when her mother was pregnant with twins and Mary was only two. Five of her siblings were under the age of eight, and all were eventually raised by their single mom, Dorothy Elizabeth. A high school dropout, Dorothy was unable to find a family-supporting job that paid more than babysitters' costs, so their primary source of income when Mary was growing up was welfare.

We were extremely poor and reliant on social services and the church, because we were raised Catholic. You know, getting free turkeys every Thanksgiving, and eating that turkey carcass for what seemed like a month, down to boiling the carcass in a pot to get any remnant of meat on the underside. My mother thought public housing would be a move up for my family. She was very excited to be one of the first families to move into the "new" projects located on 6th Street in Milwaukee.

Mary recalls that even though the family was poor financially, they were rich in so many other ways. Theirs was a house full of love, with her mother instilling her commitment to learning in all her children. By three years old, Mary could read, and as she grew older she got a library card and transported herself out of her neighborhood into other destinations through the books she read. Always keeping the words of her mother in mind as motivation—"You can do anything in life if you utilize your brain"—Mary became obsessed with education and determined to work her way out of poverty.

As I got older I became keenly aware of the political climate of the haves and the have-nots. I worked at the neighborhood Malcolm X Center where I helped serve dinner to neighborhood children. The money I earned helped pay my tuition at the private high school I attended in the suburbs and helped my mom pay for extra clothes. It became really important to me to be as good as I could be, as a child. I wanted to please her, I wanted her to be proud of me. I didn't want to be a problem.

Mary sailed through high school academically and without the typical mother-daughter conflicts that almost seem like rites of passage in most families. She was easily accepted into the University of Wisconsin–Madison, and that's where, in her freshman year, she fell in love.

Robert and I fell in love really quickly. We met when I was eighteen, and soon after we decided to live together. I just knew we would be together forever, so for about a year I tried to get pregnant. Yes, it was intentional. I wanted to give Robert what I considered to be the greatest gift of love, his child.

Unfortunately, that was a gift he wasn't ready for. About a month after her pregnancy was confirmed, Robert told Mary he was too young to be in a relationship and moved out. He didn't totally abandon her, but he began to date other people, which broke Mary's heart.

A difficult pregnancy coupled with long cold Wisconsin winters and the pressures of her academic life forced Mary to consider a different option.

I was on my way up Bascom Hill to drop out of school and go on public assistance when a little voice inside me said, "Mary, turn your tail around. Don't you dare do it. You've got this child inside of you, and who else does he or she have? Who is going to take care of the two of you?" So I turned around and I went to the library and I sucked it up. I pulled off 4.0 that semester. I was doing it, not for me, but for this baby. That was my inspiration then and has been ever since.

For Mary, connecting with her intuition helped her focus on what was most important to her. Opening her heart and listening to her mother's voice in her ear about the importance of education strengthened her resolve about what she needed to do to create a blessed life. As her pregnancy became more and more difficult, Mary's mother came up from Florida and moved in. She was there three months before the baby was born and then stayed about four months after Jamaar Maurice Boyd was born that September.

And when it was time for her to go back home, I cried like a baby but I knew she had to go. She left me with the confidence I needed to not only raise my son alone if I had to, but to finish my education too.

And that's exactly what Mary did, and then some. She finished her undergraduate studies, then worked for a year to raise her son and save enough money to go back to school. With the help of University of Wisconsin scholarships and fellowships, she not only finished law school but went on to earn an MBA.

Motherhood had intensified her desire to settle down, but fatherhood seemed to have the opposite effect on Robert. He never shied away from his responsibilities as a father. He helped support them when he could and occasionally dated Mary, but marriage was a bridge he just could not seem to cross.

That is, until Mary moved to California, where her mother had relocated. Mary wanted to fulfill the promise she had made to her mother to take care of her when she needed it, in the same way Dorothy had taken care of Jamaar and Mary in Wisconsin. Robert refused to leave Wisconsin so Mary packed up their son and left. Within a year, Mary heard the words she never thought she would: Robert called to say he was getting married. Mary was devastated and spent many tearful days and nights. But as the fog of disappointment lifted, she became determined to get past the piercing pain in her heart and finally accept the fact that Robert was not hers to have and she would not let this episode in her life determine the rest of her life.

The one thing that remained constant was Robert's commitment to Jamaar, who was now eight years old, and Mary put aside her own needs and emotions and opened her heart to support their relationship in every way possible. Despite the fact she missed her only child desperately, Jamaar spent summers in Wisconsin, and Robert and his wife, Brett, became his midwestern parents in every sense of the word. Robert and Mary agreed that Jamaar would go to elementary school in California but because the middle school years were so critical for young males, he would attend middle school in Madison. Then he'd come back to California for high school.

The plan worked great through junior high school, but what we adults didn't factor in was that Jamaar had a voice of his own. He said, "Mom, I want to stay here. I don't know anyone in California. All my friends are here and I want to stay." Now, I don't know whether I was so looking forward to him being back in California with me or what, but that same little voice that told me not to quit college was screaming at me again. In my heart I knew he needed to come back with me. I told him to just give it a year. If he still felt that way after his freshman year he could go back to Wisconsin. He eventually agreed.

Back in California, within a few weeks Mary knew exactly why her inner voice had been on high alert. With all the back and forth between the two school systems, Jamaar had missed some really critical and fundamental grammar work. Because his English composition skills were so poor, he was testing on a third-grade level as he entered high school.

Once again, my mom and I sprang into action. I chose a school where he could take two English classes, English composition and English literature. I also arranged for him to have a private tutor to

*bring his writing skills up. We're talking, every extra dollar I had
and that my mom had we invested in his education. The tuition
was very expensive, so my brother Thomas made a very large
donation to our effort. If you're talking about the pride working
together to survive, you'll know exactly how we worked together
to accomplish so much that year. By the end of the year Jamaar
was back on track and on grade level. His success, though, wasn't
enough to make him change his mind or forget his friends. That
September he went back to Wisconsin to finish high school.*

By now Robert and Brett's family was expanding. First a son and
then a daughter. Mary said that even though there were some initial
adjustment issues, it was good for Jamaar to share space with siblings. They adored him and he blossomed in the role of big brother.
The relationships among Mary, Robert, and Brett evolved as well, so
much so that Mary became the unofficial godmother to the newest
members of the family, Robert Jr. and Kara.

*As soon as I was able to admit to myself that I would always love
Robert as the father of my son but I was no longer in love with him,
I was able to break down the wall I had built and normalize the
relationship between our two families.*

*Now, that's not to say that there weren't conflicts during those
high school years. Jamaar emerged as a serious basketball player
at about six foot four, and by his junior year, he was considered
one of the top players in the state. So between his basketball schedule and his friends, disagreements emerged with Brett and Robert
about chores and times spent with his studies. By his senior year
his grades had slipped, as did his prospects as a college basketball
player. Jamaar realized he was in trouble if he wanted to get into
college so he called me up. "Mom," he said, "I'll sign a contract
with you. I'll do whatever you ask me to do, but Dad says that if
I'm college-bound, I'm on my own. Will you believe in me again?"*

I said, "Jamaar, when have I ever stopped? At what point in your life haven't I believed in you? We'll figure it out."

Mary got on .the phone with an old friend of her brother's, who was the coach of a basketball recreational league that Jamaar played with one summer. He added Jamaar to the roster of players in the Easter tournament, which was only a week away.

Jamaar ended up having a great tournament, playing so well that by the end he was recruited by Cal State Polytechnic University, Pomona. It was a partial scholarship that paid three-fourths of the tuition, but because he was coming from Wisconsin, out-of-state tuition rates made the balance still somewhat steep. Her family rallied again and came up with the rest.

Jamaar was well aware of the sacrifices being made on his behalf, and that seemed to give him the inner drive to put his own heart into everything he did for the next four years.

I've never seen an eighteen-year-old with such drive, such determination. I mean, it was like maybe he had something to prove— that he was in fact worth an investment. I don't know because we never talked about it but he earned a 4.5 average his freshman year. I didn't even know that was possible. He was a man on fire. He was president of the philosophy club and a starter on the basketball team. He actually took a year off from playing basketball so he could do a judicial internship. He went on to graduate magna cum laude from Cal Poly.

In 2000 Jamaar became the only African American male in the first-year class of Berkeley's Boalt Law School, the consequence of the end of the state's affirmative action policies. Three years later he graduated. On that beautiful day in May, the California and Wisconsin families converged to witness an amazing graduation ceremony in Berkeley's iconic amphitheater and to share in a weekend of family celebrations afterward. Mary, Robert, and Brett were beaming parents as they witnessed Jamaar receiving his degree. That weekend he became the younger generation's standard-bearer, the example of what's possible if only you keep your eyes on the prize and your heart's desires in front of you.

This was only possible because long ago Mary swallowed her pride, asked herself hard questions about what she wanted for her child's life, and opened her heart to help build an enduring bridge of family support around her son that spanned from Orange County, California, to Madison, Wisconsin. I can attest to the authentic closeness of these families now because I was a witness too—at the graduation and celebrations of my future son-in-law Jamaar Boyd Weatherby, Esq.

LESSON FROM A LIONESS: *Commit to your top priorities, and let the rest go.*

Classical pianist Arthur Rubinstein once said, "Of course there is no formula for success except, perhaps, an unconditional acceptance of life and what it brings." In Mary's case, this is especially true. It's so easy to try to ease the pain of a broken heart by cutting out the source of the pain, like you cut out a diseased part of the body. No one would have questioned Mary's decision if she had vowed never to see or communicate with the man she had pinned all of her hopes and dreams on for so many years. Instead, through intuition and observation she was able to set her personal feelings aside and look into her heart to admit her son would benefit from a meaningful relationship with his father. By accepting that, she was able to help her son grow into a well-adjusted man.

Presence of Faith:

The ability to pursue an unknown or
untested path with the confidence that there
is something greater than ourselves leading
us to better days.

III

Presence of Faith

Introduction

Faith is the strength by which a shattered world shall emerge into light.
—Helen Keller

When something bad happens, we are harshly reminded that we aren't in control. At least not of the big stuff, like a spouse asking for a divorce, a lover not wanting to be in his baby's life, or the death or illness of a partner. In the face of this helplessness, some of us turn to existential questions, such as who is in control, and why has he (or she or the universe) allowed such an injustice to happen. It is at these times of unforeseen grief or crisis that many people find comfort in their faith to make sense of things, or at least to come to grips with the fact that what has happened cannot be undone.

Faith, however, needn't be relegated to religion or doctrine, although many people turn to their houses of worship and clergy leaders in times of great need. Faith is a deeply felt trust in something good—in ourselves, our loved ones, our community, and our spiritual life—and the confidence that keeps us moving forward. Faith allows us to acknowledge the bad, but believe that better days are ahead. Faith allows us to move past fear and keeps us from being crippled by doubt. When we are present in our faith, our options are more open and we can creatively take chances, which comes in handy as we experiment with solutions to unexpected challenges.

Your relationship with faith is very personal, not to be judged by anyone. But the one thing I am very sure of is that all of us benefit when we believe and operate under the assumption that *something* exists to help ensure that things will turn out okay. The late spiritual teacher Dr. Wayne Dyer said faith is a "positive belief in the universe," which doesn't have to be necessarily tied to any sort of deity, though often it is. Faith can be a buoy that keeps you from sinking when things get difficult. It can act as a beacon when you don't know where to go next and provide support when you're feeling alone in your circumstances or decisions. Even if you haven't connected with your spirituality in a long while, maybe not ever—and admittedly, there are many who may fall into this category—I am convinced that believing in a power greater than yourself will be a lifesaver and a game changer.

Faith can also be a comfort partner when you are traveling the parenting path alone. It provides the confidence to make a decision without feeling that it was arrived at arbitrarily. It provides the courage to make bold moves because you know a higher power has your back, even if a partner is not by your side. Faith prevents us from waving the white flag when we are feeling intense pressure and rising heat. Without faith, the heat is relentless, the pressure unforgiving, because faith provides the safety valve that lets you know that whatever you are going through can be released.

"When faith rests in the foundation of a mom's life," says the Reverend Dr. Suzan Johnson Cook, who served as ambassador-at-large for international religious freedom under the Obama administration, "it is easier to cool that rising heat and prioritize solid values for the good of the family." Dr. Cook is a former White House Fellow under President Clinton, a New York City police chaplain, an author, and a motivational speaker. Having advised dozens of single mothers while raising her own two sons, Dr. Cook stresses that grounding our children in faith at home is the key to raising them emotionally healthy. She and her ex-husband successfully co-parented their sons into two amazing young men, who both graduated from tier-one colleges and are now heading to graduate school. "I had to love them enough to let them know what true nurturing feels like—to mother, not smother—and to provide enough boundaries to frame their understanding of the world and to appreciate the possibilities awaiting them. Grateful for our many blessings, as a family we embrace the words of the gospel song, 'We've come this far by faith.'" And as the song asserts, "this far" is the progress made, the fact that we keep moving, inching forward, fueled by our faith, and never stop trying to further our families or achieve equality.

But let's get real here. Presence of Faith is hard to sustain at times, so how do we remain on high ground when something bad happens and faith just slips away? What happens when your faith, trust, and love for your maker, in yourself, in your child—or whomever or wherever you tend to put your faith—is replaced with anger, resentment, deep doubt, or pessimism?

According to the American Psychological Association, life events can shake and shatter people spiritually as well as psychologically, socially, and physically. People may struggle spiritually with their understanding of God, with inner conflicts, or with other people. A growing body of research has linked these spiritual struggles to higher levels of psychological distress, declines in physical health, and even greater risk of mortality. In essence, you lose much more than your relationship with your God—you lose your sanity! I was no different.

My commitment to God was shattered after the loss of my husband Wes. Depression and anger leaked into my life in the place of prayer. Even though I made sure the kids ate, I didn't. I guess Wes's aunt Mildred saw my weight loss and gave me vitamins especially designed to help relieve stress. I had no idea there was such a thing! But despite that, I couldn't sleep in our bed. I was angry that the future I had envisioned so clearly had been taken away. I was betrayed, confused, and in agony with grief. Finally, I had to admit that I was lost in my emotions. I had to throw my hands in the air, saying, "God, I don't know what to do, so you handle it." And when I let go of ownership of my anger, I was able to slowly begin to heal. With faith, you can have the confidence that a higher power will handle what is too much for you alone. And as my faith grew stronger, a higher power did, in fact, intervene.

Mine was a circuitous journey back to my faith, not only in the religious sense or even back to a brick-and-mortar church building, but back to a deeper belief in the resiliency of my children, myself, and the power we all have to help each other, to believe in each other, to trust that our pride will protect and support us. I learned to never doubt that my child would come around, does truly love me, and would eventually understand that I needed to be a mother before I could become a friend, which I am now to all of my children. One thing I am most proud of is successfully equipping them with access to faith as a tool to help them navigate life's uncertainties. Tests of faith only prove to us what we're really made of. After all, without intense heat and pressure, a rock cannot become a diamond.

This is precisely why, for me, Presence of Faith has been my go-to more than any other pillar. Being present in faith, while difficult for many in the thick of a life challenge, means much more than staying spiritual or religious; it is a matter of sustaining the mental and physical health of yourself and your children.

Returning to God in the Middle of the Night

The Lord replied, "The times when you have seen only one set of footprints, is when I carried you."
—Mary Stevenson

With an ordained minister of a conservative denomination as a father, I grew up embedded in a spiritually rich, faith-saturated environment. There was Sunday school, Bible class, choir rehears-als, youth group, summer Bible school, catechism classes, and of course Sunday services. Once I could officially taste the consecrated Welch's grape juice and the small, square-cut pieces of bread my dad carefully cut on communion Sundays, no one could tell me I wasn't God's chosen child.

Faith was my constant companion when I rode New York City trains from the Bronx to Harlem throughout high school; it com-forted me when my grandparents and other family members passed; it bolstered my confidence when I had to make a decision about which college to go to; and it strengthened my resolve when I ended my first marriage. There was never a doubt in my mind that all would be well, even at moments when all logic, circumstance, and reason indicated otherwise.

But the night my husband died, the faith that had always blan-keted me with confidence and comfort became my shroud.

I'll never forget the night that I heard Wes stumble down the steps and collapse on the second-floor landing. I ran to him and saw he was gasping for air. As I positioned his head to begin my failed attempts at CPR, I began my silent prayers to God.

"God, help me. Please don't let him die. He can't die. He's too good a man...too good a father. You can't take him."

My prayers intensified after the EMTs came, moved me aside, and did their best to open his airways. And as I followed the whirling red lights of the ambulance in front of me, my pleas for God's interven-tion became even louder and more desperate. The only thing I could think to bargain with was the habit both of us had been trying to conquer for years, smoking. "God, if you let him live, I will give up smoking forever." I remember at that point a certain calm came over me. I was sure that with my faith, Wes's goodness, and my agreement with God, my husband would live. I even imagined the next day he and I would be laughing about all the drama that had unfolded dur-ing the course of the day.

But an hour later, when the doctor came in the waiting room and said, "He's gone," my knees buckled, blood rushed to my head, and for the first time in my life I fainted. As I regained my bearing, I remember as clearly as if it were yesterday, I said, "God, how could you do this?" My faith was shattered. God had failed us, and the love of my life was gone.

I didn't set foot in a church for the next two years.

It took much longer to give up smoking. It became my tool of defiance against a God who had forsaken me when I needed Him most. All those religious greeting cards I received were hollow reminders that I was now walking alone. There were no footprints in the sand. The children were without a father, and I was without the man I loved and wanted to grow old with.

I had hoped that moving back into my parents' house would help me feel myself again, to at least become reacquainted with if not regain the faith of my youth. After all, I was living once again with the two most spiritual people I had ever known. I hoped I'd snap back, eventually find a great job, ease the kids into new schools, and take comfort in family and familiarity. The warmth and support of my parents and their help with the daily routine were blessings, but my nights were still sleepless and full of anxiety. The streets of my old neighborhood in the Bronx had grown darker and more dangerous. The crack epidemic had created an uptick in street crime, and safety gates on graffiti-stained buildings were now the norm. It scared me to picture my children walking the streets now, despite knowing that they were the same streets I had walked carefree decades before.

It had been two years since his death, and yet the hole in my heart for Wes was as big as ever. I couldn't put the grief behind me. Why? I had changed locations and magnified my support system, which should have been all I needed for a fresh start. But eventually, I had to admit that what was missing was the relationship I had been avoiding the most.

I could finally admit to myself that it wasn't just Wes that I missed;

I missed God too, and I needed to believe in something bigger and better than the world I could see around me.

As I had hoped, being back home reminded me of the authenticity of my parents' faith: We all said grace at every meal, morning and evening prayers bracketed each of my parents' days, and though my father had retired from his pulpit, God was a constant presence, weaving His way into many conversations. As I lay in my childhood bedroom, I began a new middle-of-the-night practice. I closed my eyes and summoned up images of my father in front of his beloved congregation, back when his church was filled to the brim every Sunday. I'd return to being that little girl in the pews, completely safe in the warmth of my father's voice and the strength of the God he spoke of with such love and conviction. I envisioned my mother, always supporting my dad and hanging on to his every word while establishing her own legacy as the church's First Lady. Phrases and stories from my father's sermons would come back to me, and I would say them aloud in the dark to myself. Somehow, I could summon them at night, though I couldn't during the day. I could access a deeper part of myself—a kind of peace in the silence, a comfort in my aloneness.

Sometimes I would even find myself rocking back and forth like he had when he preached. I would clasp my hands in front of my face, trying to block out my despair, saying over and over, "Have faith!" Other nights, that wonder-filled voice of my father lulled me to sleep, and I felt that sleep alone was God's grace.

There was a simple message woven throughout all my dad's sermons: Take one day at a time, put one foot in front the next, and keep going with the faith that the Lord will guide you. Those words became my nighttime mantra, and by remembering them I found my own praying voice.

That was probably the beginning of the resurrection of my faith. I had to realize that the hole in my heart had been left not just by the loss of my husband, but also by my loss of faith. In order for me to heal, I had to find a way to let God back in my life even though Wes was gone. Letting go of my anger and inviting God in forced me to consider that I might be stronger than I knew, more resourceful than I could see, and more loving than my broken heart seemed to allow. It also fostered faith in my children, in their resilience and ability to believe in something greater than themselves during good times and bad. So although this began as a personal effort to help myself move from a paralyzing place, I realized that Nikki, Wes, and Shani had been watching me all along. Their spiritual journey would have been compromised had they not seen me authentically walking back along faith's path with them.

LESSON FROM A LIONESS: *Find a spiritual anchor.*

When our days are darkest and our nights never ending, sleepless from unimaginable grief, believing in a power greater than yourself is oftentimes the only way to release healing light. But the question that most of us ask—I know I did—when we are caught up in this cycle of pain is, How does faith break through? Most theologians agree that anchoring yourself in a set of action steps that may or may not be spiritually based will be helpful until you decide what formal steps you can take back to a specific religion, if ever. Among some of the suggestions I found most useful were:

MAKE THE MOST OF YOUR SITUATION.

Crediting Albert Einstein, the late spiritual leader Dr. Wayne Dyer said the most important question you'll ever have to answer is, "What kind of universe do you want to live in?" If your answer is different than the universe you currently exist in, then be prepared to ask whether you have been attracting the wrong things in life. Instead, begin looking at things that may feel boring and routine, seeking opportunity in them. This will start helping the universe work for you.

START LOOKING FOR RAINBOWS.

Once I began to emerge from my initial heartbreak, I knew the first step to my healing was to begin forcing myself to embrace the positives around me. First and foremost, I looked to my children, the ultimate salve for my broken heart. Bolstered by the presence I needed to help sustain them, I started looking for rainbows, flowering meadows, the changing leaves, cooing newborns, and, yes, aging couples holding hands. Once you can appreciate the positives around you, experts say the obstacles in the path of healing begin to fall by the wayside.

CREATE AFFIRMATIONS.

As important as it is to have a positive worldview, it is even more important to put that worldview into active practice on a daily basis. A good way to do this is through affirmations that remind you to put your faith forward:

- ✓ I will get the job that's right for me.
- ✓ The people I need in my life are on the way.
- ✓ All things are possible when I decide I have faith.
- ✓ I will not be defeated.

Dr. Dyer said to start looking at the world in terms of what's right instead of what's wrong. Then you can look at what made you lose faith in the first place and say, "What's the lesson I needed to learn?" or "Why did things have to happen the way they did?" After time has passed, he promises, you can look back and say, "Okay, I get it."

LOOK BEYOND YOUR OWN PAIN.

One of the most inspirational moments I have spent was with former vice president Joe Biden when he spoke with such eloquence about loss and faith. Speaking about his unbelievable family losses, he held my hands and said, "But there are so many others who didn't have the resources I had, the support I did." In an amazing display of his humanity, he is able to look beyond his own pain to feel the anguish of others. That's faith. In the words of Dr. Maya Angelou, when you soar above your own pain, you become "the rainbow in someone's cloud." That's when your own faith can resurface.

Moving Forward with Grace: The Una McHugh Story

Your hardest times often lead to the greatest moments in your life. Keep going. Tough situations build strong people in the end.
—Roy T. Bennett

Una McHugh is one of the thousands who lost a loved one on September 11, 2001. Her husband, Dennis, a firefighter from Engine Company 22, Ladder 13, was one of the first responders on the scene. Their children were five-year-old Chloe and ten-month-old twins Joe and Sophie. A teacher, having just returned to school after her maternity leave, Una saw her status change to single mother of three as her world spun off its axis in ways she never ever saw coming.

> *I was only back working a couple of days. I don't even think it was a week. Dennis came to meet me with the twins at lunchtime. We walked around together outside the school and I just remember him saying we were so lucky. We both had jobs we were passionate about. We felt that way. Him being a fireman, he was able to be around a lot more with me and the kids, which is what he wanted.*
>
> *Off he went to work for his twenty-hour shift.*
>
> *As he walked out the door, I turned to look at the kids to get them ready to take them to the park. Dennis popped his head back*

in one more time. He said, "I love you." That would be the last time I saw him. A few hours later, into the night, when the twins were already asleep, he called to say good night to Chloe and see how the twins were doing.

I remember chatting on the phone and then hearing Chloe chatting with him and laughing. He was asking what her favorite part of school was and like usual it was recess.

The next day, my sister was there to help with the twins while we were both at work. I left and soon after I got to work, I don't remember how but we knew something was going on. As I watched the scenes unfold on the library television, the school became more chaotic.

With each hour passing without hearing from anyone at the firehouse or without receiving a call from Dennis, Una's fears mounted. Glued to the television, she saw the death toll climbing, as was the number of those missing. She prayed as she never had before that Dennis was just too busy doing his job and would call any minute. She prayed for a miracle that she finally knew would never happen when the phone rang and a voice from the firehouse said that Dennis was among the missing.

In the beginning, my Catholic faith was very intense. I remember being in church praying. When the collection basket came around, I took all the money that I had and just dumped it in thinking, "That's going to bring him back." As I drove home, I saw the members of the local fire department outside with buckets, collecting donations for the victims and families of 9/11. I was mortified. I had no money. I just opened my window and said, "Sorry. I have no money. I just gave it to the church. Don't worry. My husband's missing." Sometimes I look back on things I said. I felt bad I couldn't give any money. I wanted them to understand me, as I meant to say, "Don't worry. I'm one of them!"

I would go to church every Sunday, and at first, it was comforting. When reality sank in that he was officially dead and a little shock started wearing off, hearing things like "He's in a better place" enraged me. I'm left raising kids and babies on my own, so my response was always hostile: "He's not in a better place. A better place would be here with the kids."

I couldn't go to church. It wasn't bringing me peace. I felt guilty that I was failing in that area. Even though Dennis wasn't here, I thought I was disappointing my devout Irish Catholic in-laws. But God bless my mother-in-law. When I did finally mention it one day, she said to me, "Una, Chloe knows all her prayers. The twins will too. Your kids will be wonderful kids. You don't need to be in a church to pray." It was such a gift for her to say that. I still feel her love for me in the moment to this day.

But she and my father-in-law did something else that I was very grateful for. Even though my faith faltered, I wanted the kids to have the anchor in their lives that faith provides. My in-laws took the twins and Chloe to mass for me when I didn't take them. They liked doing that, and the children liked going to church with them.

In the years Una spent reassessing her relationship with her faith and the actual church building, she looked at a potential family endeavor that would send a transformative message to their children about presence, something that would reinforce the need to share experiences, like reading with your children, and about legacy.

I just looked at my kids and thought, "How will the kids look at the death, destruction, and hatefulness of that day? How will it jade them?" I thought of Dennis and how he would have handled it. He always looked at life optimistically, so we were trying to focus on the positive. I, my siblings, and the people around me asked ourselves, "What can we do?" We turned our eyes a few miles from our house to the village of Piermont.

Piermont is where Dennis, the kids, and I spent all of our time, whether at church, dining out, or going to boutique stores. The town has undergone a massive restoration thanks to the passionate people who wanted to preserve the history and beauty of a special place. [But] the library was still not built. Dennis just loved reading and believed in the importance of books and all of the gifts they give. He often took our five-year-old daughter to the library. One day we had seen the Friends of the Piermont Library were selling shirts to raise money to build a new, state-of-the-art public library. Dennis said, "They're never going to build a library if they're charging so little for shirts," so we bought five of them, using whatever money we had on us. That is the kind of man Dennis was.

It just seemed to make sense that we start a foundation. The first project was helping Piermont build the library.

We pledged $500,000 and asked the library to be named for Dennis. The first few years we did two fund-raisers, one a comedy night and the other a silent auction, and we thought, "He loved to laugh and he had a good sense of humor."

All these years later we still organize a 5K run and people of all ages come and we have a little family fair. It's always right here, in Piermont, overlooking the Hudson River and the Tappan Zee Bridge. It is about bringing people together and having some fun and laughter and enjoying our community spirit.

In 2007, the Dennis P. McHugh Piermont Public Library was born. After this pledge was met, Dennis's relatives and Una went on to raise money to do other things in the community. They raised money to build parks; to support a local hospice and Homes for Heroes, which provides apartments for veterans; and to help local families falling on hard times. Una found her calling in giving back and having her faith manifested through acts of kindness throughout the community. She came to believe that faith can be everywhere and wherever you are.

Looking back over the years, she recalls the words of a favorite aunt, drawing from her own heartbreak after losing a husband, who told her following Dennis's death, "Your kids will see you through it." And they have, says Una. The beauty of maintaining presence for your kids does as much for the single mom as it does for her kids. It also allowed Una untold opportunities to keep Dennis's memory alive for their kids, especially when her own sorrow started to surface.

> I would think, "What would Dennis do if he was here?" He would laugh because he had a great sense of humor and start to do what he called "tickle time." So I'd say tickle time and they'd run over and I would lay them on the ground and I would go and tickle each one of them and they would just roll around and laugh and laugh. I'd think about what Dennis would want for us and I know he'd want us to be happy.
>
> In addition to tickle time, I always tried to carve out time for us to maintain little traditions. Often, we'd come down to Piermont and have a picnic by the water and things like that. Every Christmas our routine is to go see a play and then go out to dinner, just the four of us. In more recent years, obviously when everyone is becoming more independent, having that time together remains incredibly important, although the kids fought it at first. I remember saying to them, "I hope as you age and when you have your own families, you think at least once a year to come together as siblings with your families."

Establishing family traditions, and feeling guided by thoughts of what Dennis would do, helped Una find something she could believe in. For now, she is content with the way her single-mother life has evolved and the way the kids have fared. Chloe graduated from Villanova, where she majored in nursing. She is now working at Sloan Kettering hospital. Joe and Sophie will also graduate this year with stellar high school credentials and are weighing numerous college options for the fall. Una is grateful to have had support from the 9/11 fund and pensions. But to those around her it is clear that despite her unbelievable loss, Una is living out the teachings of Luke 12:48—To whom much is given, much is required.

LESSON FROM A LIONESS: *Help your children find their spiritual base, even if you are reassessing yours.*

Presence of Faith can feel elusive in the midst of tragedy. How do you find your joy when grief has stolen your heart? Sometimes, however, as a single mother you must help your children remain grounded in a spiritual base. Just as it will in time help you re-anchor your life in something bigger than yourself, believing in a higher power will provide your kids with the armor they need to deal with life's uncertainties.

When you know that your own spiritual practice is a struggle, call on your pride to help. For Una, having Dennis's parents continue the ritual she and Dennis started of weekly church with their children was a godsend. Without judgment, they stepped in when she needed them the most. That provided Una with the comfort of knowing that even though her faith was in a reassessment stage, her children would not lose the anchor that faith provides. But even more than physically going to a sanctuary, the words that Dennis's mother said to Una—"Chloe knows her prayers"—I think provided the clue to what Una had already instilled in Chloe: spiritual strength through prayer.

Much of what is written about prayer is based in Christianity. But I wanted to provide some tips culled from my own family plus numerous sources that can be applied to those on all faith journeys, be they Catholic, Protestant, Jewish, Muslim, Mormon, or—according to a 2017 Gallup poll—the substantial percentage of people who claim no faith preference at all.

INSTILL THE BUILDING BLOCKS OF GRATITUDE, TOLERANCE, AND
KEEPING AN EYE ON THE PRIZE.

- **Teach your children to be grateful for what they have.** This
  doesn't mean "things." In the American Indian culture, gratitude begins with Mother Nature. A Tecumseh prayer begins,
  "When you arise in the morning, give thanks for the morning
  light, for our life and strength. Give thanks for your food and
  the joy of living." When children see the struggle of a single
  parent, be it financial, the inability to buy certain clothes or
  go certain places, or sometimes the social isolation caused by
  small-minded people or living far away from a support system,
  teach them that you are grateful for what you do have, the fact
  that you have each other, and the hope that things will turn
  around because you have faith.
- **Teach your children there is a spiritual being that is bigger
  than themselves.** I once addressed the Valley Forge Chapel
  on Mother's Day, understanding that not all of the cadets and
  their family members were Christians like me. Part of what I
  said was, "Another lesson that I know cadets will learn at Valley Forge is to always have God front and center in their life.
  But that part of learning is learning tolerance—accepting
  that the deity of one's classmate may be called Allah, Shiva,
  Yahweh, Theos, Adonai, or Jehovah. The name's not important. What is important is believing that with faith, you will
  never stumble too far before Divine Intervention will lift you
  back up."
- **Help your children keep their eye on the future.** Authors and
  spiritual advisers Dennis and Barbara Rainey, in their *Family
  Life* newsletter, suggest that keeping kids "mission-minded" will
  help them understand that they are part of a divine plan and
  that they have been given abilities, personalities, and qualities
  that will help them fulfill their life's mission. Truly embracing

this and understanding that they have a higher purpose in life "will compel them to seek after God and His calling in their lives rather than to follow the herd after the lesser gods of popularity, selfishness, etc."

- **Teach kids to be their brothers' and sisters' keepers.** All kids go through a selfish stage. As parents, it is up to us to teach them to share when all they want to do is to hold on to that toy or food. Showing them that whatever we have can be shared with others who may have less than we do is a critical job for parents. And it can't be a "Do as I say, not as I do" kind of thing. Children will learn by interacting with you. It can be through volunteering at a soup kitchen with your kids, raising money for a special cause or charity, or letting them help you make posters for a charitable event, no matter how young the children. My daughter-in-law Dawn recently had the kids on the floor with her, handing her stickers and stars to put on posters. This is how kids learn selflessness—show, don't tell.

Faith Not Fear

Feed your faith and your doubts will starve to death.
—*Debbie Macomber*

Mahatma Gandhi once said, "Faith is not something to grasp, it is a state to grow into." Without question, thanks to my parents, that process of growth defined the faith journeys that my brothers and I have been on since childhood. Growing up, we balked at the numbers of hours we had to spend in church activities, so we really didn't always appreciate the cornucopia of spiritual tools they made available to us—Sunday school, Bible class, morning worship, vacation Bible school, choir, youth group, church revivals, helping to prepare food baskets for struggling families, and other experiences that can only be categorized as enrichment. In our home, there was not a morsel eaten or a sip taken before we gave thanks for what was before us and the hands that prepared it. Prayers on our knees at bedtime were mandatory, and a short morning prayer, thanking God for allowing us to see the morning light, was encouraged. But even though we grumbled about it, my parents instilled a spiritual foundation that grounded us in the belief that there is something bigger than the eye can see, more powerful than we can imagine, and more reliable than we can reasonably hope for.

As is quite typical, both the practice of religious faith and developing a deep trust and faith in oneself became a top priority once I had children. Whatever faith I had learned, I passed on to my kids through storytelling, prayer, church, and, most important, through my behavior in day-to-day life. By the time we moved to New York, their spiritual foundation was evident by the way they treated each other (most of the time), the way they embraced spiritual rituals, like saying grace before eating and prayers before bed, and the enthusiasm they showed hearing stories of faith and resilience. This was particularly true for Shani and Wes, but it was Wes who clung closest to this spiritual foundation as a result of the growing closeness he felt for my dad.

In Wes's book *The Work*, he says: "My grandfather and the way he lived his life inspired me to be better. To never be afraid of difference or of being 'different.'" My father was Wes's hero. Dad was a scholar and lifelong learner. There wasn't a room in the house that didn't have books prominently displayed, and he was quick to go to them for reference whenever the need arose. He didn't flaunt his own intellect; very few people knew, for example, that he had four degrees including a doctorate in adult education from Columbia University. But it was his faith and theology that really connected him to Wes. Dad was always referencing passages from the Bible when he and Wes shared quiet moments. I remember one day Wes came home from school and asked Dad, who was sitting in his favorite tattered corduroy recliner, if he had a minute. Wes then told him about one of his classmates who was being bullied by some other boys in class. Dad quoted Matthew 7:12: "So whatever you wish that others would do to you, do also to them, for this is the Law and the Prophets." "Let me say that another way," Dad continued, telling a story about empathy and its role in our lives. I, who was eavesdropping from the other room, had to smile because I knew he was going to tell Wes one of the stories I'd loved hearing him repeat from the pulpit in my own youth.

"There was a little boy named Billy who was diagnosed with a ruptured appendix," he began. "After his surgery, the doctors told his parents that he would be fine and they, in turn, called the teacher. The next day she explained to the class that Billy was sick but doctors were taking care of him and he would be back soon. A week later the teacher noticed that the class was really upset. One by one the children started crying. She asked what was wrong and one student finally blurted out, 'We hurt because we have a pain in Billy's stomach.' What this means, Wes," Dad continued, "is that you need to put yourself in the place of the boy being teased. If he is pained by being teased, then so should you be. Is there something you can do to help?"

As it turned out, Wes's birthday was coming up and I had planned a big party for him. I told him he could invite whomever he wanted, and he invited the little boy he'd told my dad about. His mother called me a week later and told me what an impact that day was making in her son's life. While he still wasn't the most popular kid in class, the fact that he was included gave him some credibility that he didn't have before. Wes's act of kindness, she said, was helping to turn around his experience at school and that made Wes a very special young man.

Lessons learned at my dad's knee were exactly the kind of character-building tools I had dreamed my kids would get when we moved in with my parents, the same kinds of lessons that I had valued so highly growing up. To Dad, spirituality was about building a community of people who walked the path of kindness, achievement, and dedication to contributing to a better world. Dad didn't believe, nor did he teach, blind allegiance to religious dogma. It was always faith, coupled with an intellectual and realistic assessment of a situation that informs a decision as you take that leap of faith to make a difference in your life and, ultimately, the world.

Wes made that first commitment to service when he talked to me about joining Valley Forge's Early Commissioning Program in its college. A moment of fear gripped me. It would mean that he would be obligated to join the service upon graduation from college; paintballs and blanks would be replaced by real bullets in hostile situations. But it was something he was passionate about. That is how, in May 1998, with his favorite teacher, Colonel Mike Murnane, and I on either side of his dress green service uniform, we affixed the official officer pins of the United States Army to his shoulder straps. Wes then took his Oath of Enlistment: "I, Wes Moore, do solemnly swear that I will support and defend the Constitution of the United States against all enemies, foreign and domestic; that I will bear true faith and allegiance to the same; and that I will obey the orders of the President of the United States, and the orders of the officers appointed over me, according to regulations and the Uniform Code of Military Justice. So help me God." Wes was officially in the US Army and could one day be in the line of fire with real bullets and bombs.

That possibility became a reality seven years later.

After finishing Oxford, Wes began a banking career in London in 2005. But then his friend and mentor, Deputy First Brigade Commander of the 82nd Airborne Major Michael Fenzel, called and said, "Wes, so, we have some fights going on. Are you ever going to jump in and help?" Wes was making lots of money and living the good life of a young American at Deutsche Bank, so he had to seriously consider trading that life for an uncertain and dangerous one in Afghanistan. Major Fenzel didn't sugarcoat what he was asking Wes to do: "You will see combat and be surrounded by people who want nothing more than to kill you and your soldiers. It will be tough, uncomfortable, and dangerous." Wes's first thought was *Man, does Mike know how to make a pitch attractive!* But then he asked himself, *Is there something I can do to help?*

This would be Wes's first combat deployment since he'd received his commission as a second lieutenant at Valley Forge. Because of his paratrooper training and other qualifiers during the time he was a full-time student, he had advanced to the rank of first lieutenant when Major Fenzel called. Wes and I had many transcontinental conversations during his decision period as he weighed the pros and cons and the what-ifs and the what-fors. While the lioness in me wanted to say, *Hell no, you won't go,* and hold him close and out of any line of fire, I listened intently to his lists and rationales, and I could clearly see which side was winning. Wes was never one to take the easy route. His passion to make the lives of others better, sometimes over his own comfort, was one of his core values. Another was a deep and abiding belief that once a decision is made, based on all available facts that have been thoroughly informed by his values, faith will guide the journey.

A few days before his deployment, my parents presented Wes with a worn, vinyl-bonded Bible. On the inside page, yellow with age and written with all the love and precision of an eighty-seven-year-old man, were the words: "Have Faith, Not Fear, love always Papa Jim and Mama Win." That Bible was one of my dad's first acquisitions as a twenty-seven-year-old newly ordained minister, about the same age that Wes was then. When my dad handed his inscribed Bible to his firstborn grandson, my dread of saying goodbye to my son resurfaced. But as I considered those words in the Bible—Have Faith, Not Fear—I knew my dad was sending a message not only to Wes but to all of us, particularly me, the first in our family to send a child off to war. In a sense, it was a warning that my faith would be seriously tested over the next year, but fear must never overtake it. I needed to have faith that Wes had the strength he would need as he journeyed into war. The Bible became Wes's prized possession and constant companion from Kabul to the mountain ranges of Kandahar and the plateaued regions of Khost. He tucked it inside his Kevlar vest whenever he left for combat, and although the Good Book was not a shield against the bullets, the words within were a source of inspiration for the task my son was doing. When not engaged in armed conflict, Wes's specific assignment was to organize and conduct reconciliation meetings between Afghan insurgents and government representatives. When the stakes were this high, Wes told me he held that Bible close to his heart, figuratively and literally. It would guide him as he made decisions that impacted that side of the world.

Have there been instances when he's feared he's made the wrong decision or he had no power over one? Of course. One that was particularly poignant, and that I know he labored over, was when it was clear my dad was in his last days of a two-year-long battle with cancer. At that point, Wes had been in Afghanistan about eight months. I called the American Red Cross to explain the situation, and it immediately notified Wes's unit. When Wes called, I knew his only thought was to jump on the next flight to try and reach his grandfather while he was still here and could hear him: to hold his hand as he had done so many times while growing up; to tell him how much he meant to him, how much he had learned from him, how much he appreciated his stepping in as a surrogate dad. By then, Dad couldn't speak, and Wes asked that we put the phone to my father's ear. As I watched a single tear fall from my father's eye, I imagined that Wes was able to say all the things he would have said in person. Three days later, Dad was gone and Wes was on his way home, along with the Bible tucked in his bag.

When I look now at that Bible and the shaky inscription, I am reminded of my intense fear when I heard the proposal of now General Mike Fenzel. But because of faith, I was able to put aside my anxiety and fear and instead support Wes's decision to join the fight.

Because I decided not to become a barrier of tears or anger at his decision, I now see what God's plan was all along. Wes, now a captain following a battlefield promotion, stood shoulder-to-shoulder with his troops, in the battlefield and in rooms where the United States was trying to build bridges of reconciliation between the rebels and the government. He learned how to lead his troops with strength and compassion. He set clear objectives and devised strategies to achieve them. These are all qualities he now employs as the CEO of New York's largest foundation devoted to eliminating poverty—the Robin Hood Foundation.

This was the real fight he was being prepared for and was meant to have.

LESSON FROM A LIONESS: *Faith is a tool. Make it a family rule.*

As single moms, sometimes our must-do lists seem endless. But one thing that must never fall off is providing the spiritual tools of survival to our children. Finding faith is a process that takes time to cultivate, if the end result will withstand the inevitable challenges life brings. It doesn't necessarily mean spending every waking moment in a house of worship. But it does mean setting an example by living a life according to the teachings of your faith. Again, faith does not have to be religious; it is about something bigger than yourself that you can point toward, trust, and rely on to help you make choices for a life oriented toward good. Without faith, Wes would never have left the life of a young international banker in London. Without faith, he wouldn't have taken up the gauntlet to join the fight. Without faith, Wes wouldn't have believed his mission was not just to fight, but to build the hope of better futures for people halfway around the world. Without faith, I would not have slept a moment during the time he was deployed.

Because I instilled faith as an essential and non-negotiable element in our family's toolbox, my children have been able to access it throughout their lives. As I experienced when their dad died, faith doesn't always give us the outcome we hope and pray for, but it does provide the calming belief that there is a purpose and a plan and things always work out the way they are supposed to.

Blind Faith

Faith is seeing light with your heart when all your eyes see is darkness.

—*Anonymous*

The fall of 2009 marked almost two years since I had—in the words of educator Johnnetta Cole—"re-wired" from my position at the Annie E. Casey Foundation and formed my own media consulting firm. I was leisurely enjoying my newfound morning routine— savoring my first cup of coffee, catching up on Facebook's overnight posts, and listening to the morning headlines on cable news. While I was casually dressed and enjoying the comforts of my own home, as a retired person might, I was wired up, ready to work with the clientele I had acquired since starting my own business. At about 8:30 AM, the phone rang and I saw it was my youngest child Shani's cell phone number. It was 5:30 AM in Los Angeles, unusually early for her to call, but to hear her voice, no matter the time, was a day's bright spot. I answered with a huge "Hi," but the moment she replied, I knew something was wrong.

She began by saying that she didn't want to worry me but two days before she had woken and realized that she couldn't see out of her left eye. At first she'd thought it might have something to do with the contacts she had fallen asleep with, but removing them made no difference. She was working for a downtown law firm then so she had called in, explained what was happening, and said that she would be in after going to the hospital. There the doctor gave her a single corticosteroid treatment and told her to see an ophthalmologist. After that she'd gone to work and put in a full day. She'd asked her husband, Jamaar, not to let any of us know, because she was sure her sight would return.

It did not. On day three, as her dawn was breaking, Shani finally called me. As calmly as she could, she recalled the events of the past two days. I tried not to sound panicked. My heart, however, was beating at warp speed. She needed to make an appointment with an ophthalmologist and my instincts—or maybe it was my distrust of doctors, which I developed after what had happened to her dad—told me she needed a specialist she could trust. As I put down the receiver, up went the first of my many, many prayers over the next few months. "God, please don't let this be something that will take Shani from us or that will fundamentally change her from the active, athletic, gregarious woman she's become. Help me help her as best as I can."

I so wished at that moment I had a partner to lean on, to strategize with, to hold my hand, to reassure me that everything would be okay. I knew this was not something I would or could keep to myself or handle on my own, so barring a husband, I gathered the best action corps I knew—Nikki and Wes—to help figure out our next steps. Within the hour, a plan was in place: Nikki had set up what we still call our family conference line; Wes, who at the time was a Johns Hopkins board member, called fellow board member Howard Mandel, MD, a prominent gynecologist and obstetrician in Los Angeles and one of Wes's mentors, who immediately contacted a friend and one of the most renowned ophthalmologists in Los Angeles. Within thirty minutes Shani had a name, a cell phone number, and an appointment for the next day. We pledged to hold a weekly family call for the foreseeable future.

Rather than make an exact diagnosis, the ophthalmologist

ordered tests to (hopefully) rule some things out. While waiting for the results, which would take about a week, Shani decided to go ahead with a previously scheduled business trip to Chicago. During our next family call, I told her that I would meet her there. I had to be in her presence, see her myself, better sense her mood, hold her tight. She arrived in Chicago first and went to the hotel. When I arrived and she opened the hotel room door, I searched her face, especially her eyes, to see if I saw any difference. I saw none. Instead, she greeted me the way she has always greeted me: "Mamacita!" We hugged longer than usual. She was trying so hard to keep the atmosphere upbeat for my sake that I did my best to reciprocate. But when I went to the bathroom and thought about how scared she must feel inside, I broke down. I didn't know she was doing exactly the same thing on the other side of the door.

For the next three days, in between her business obligations, we laughed as often as we could; cried together when we couldn't hold back the tears; and prayed together that this trip would mark the return of her sight. We even took one of those architectural river cruises through the city, hoping that a Hollywood moment would occur and her sight would miraculously return as the sun began to set in the western sky. It did not, and she returned to Los Angeles as she'd left, unable to see from her left eye and not knowing why.

By week three, the sight in her right eye was starting to fade as well, but test results showed that her eyes were not diseased. Based on her symptoms, she was advised to see a neurologist. After Shani researched potential physicians on the internet, she made an appointment with one of the highest rated. After undergoing a series of tests and a MRI, she learned that what she was experiencing had a name—multiple sclerosis.

MS? My first thought was that it couldn't possibly be MS. Wes's wife, Dawn, had been diagnosed with it years before, so lightning couldn't possibly strike the same family twice! Dawn first presented with double vision and loss of taste. Shortly after that, her balance was affected, so it couldn't be the same thing. Or could it?

Shani once again searched on the internet and found a specialist who was given high marks in MS treatments. This doctor prescribed a course of action: Shani was to give herself shots, rotating around her body every other day with Betaseron, a drug designed to reduce the number of MS-induced relapses. The doctor then said this particular medication might cause depression, so she prescribed Prozac. Then she said it might also cause insomnia so she gave Shani a script for Ambien. No further directions or cautions about dealing with the side effects of combining these drugs were given. This was a completely different course of action than Dawn's (who injected herself once a week with an entirely different drug), which is why I suspected Shani's case might be a little more progressive but hopefully as manageable as Dawn's seemed to be.

Almost all of Shani's eyesight returned by the following June, but prior to that she experienced a growing numbness on her left side, which she compensated for by increasing her exercise schedule to keep her muscles as strong and agile as possible. She pushed through her every-other-day drug regimen while continuing to go to work every day, trying to keep up with the required billable hours and even joining voluntary office committees. We continued our weekly family check-ins so all of us could keep track of how Shani was feeling and how Jamaar was coping. Both of them reassured us each week that Shani was making progress; her vision, while not back, didn't seem to be getting worse; and Jamaar was able to work uninterrupted but still be responsive to anything Shani needed. We didn't see them that Christmas because it was their turn to visit his dad's family in Wisconsin. Not hearing otherwise, we entered the New Year thinking Shani was living with MS relatively well. We suspended the family's weekly check-ins.

Near the end of January, however, Jamaar called and said that

Shani hadn't slept in three days and she was hallucinating. He had called the doctor but was told she was on vacation. No other contact information was given. I tried calling, to at least speak with someone who was filling in for the doctor, but got no response at all to my messages. I was pissed, panicked, and prayerful all at the same time. My journalism training reminded me that HIPAA laws prevented the doctor's office from disclosing any information to anyone other than the patient. The lioness in me, furious, thought, *How the hell are people supposed to know what to do with a patient in crisis if we can't get any directions or referrals?* My instinct told me this couldn't wait so the next day I was on a plane to California, lifting up a silent prayer that I would know what to do once I got there.

When I arrived, there was no "Hi Mamacita." No hug. No warm smile. There was an uncharacteristic, first-time-ever mistrust in Shani's eyes. She was agitated and combative, acting paranoid and answering questions with short, curt responses. But as alarming as this was at first blush, I no longer felt panicked, just anxious to figure out what was going on. I knew my child and had faith that no matter how loudly she snapped at me or glared while I was speaking, I hadn't lost the real Shani forever. I thought back to an incident from my college days when my mom, who has been asthmatic since childhood, was prescribed prednisone to treat an asthma attack. She followed the instructions listed on her bottle, taking three pills three times a day. By day three she'd become incredibly paranoid, even mean, not wanting to speak with anyone on the phone or see anyone except my dad. Knowing that the only new variable in my mom's life was the medication, he called the doctor, reported what was happening, and read the dosage indicated on the bottle. The doctor was horrified: The correct dose was one pill three times a day. She swore up and down that the mistake was on the pharmacist's end. She told my dad how to safely wean my mom from the overdose, and within a few days her state of mind returned to normal.

I never lost faith that what was wrong with Shani was something we could fix. I believed every moment, deep in my heart, that we just needed to work hard and we would find a solution. My anxiety was tempered by my faith that, as with my mom, somehow everything would be okay in the end. But oh, did I wish I had a trusted doctor to talk with! Turning to our family network once again, I called a neurologist friend of my brother's in New York. She said if I could get Shani to New York, she would do a full evaluation. The challenge was getting Shani there.

She started sleeping on and off, so Jamaar and I tossed around the idea of driving her cross-country. He was exhausted, however, after working and staying up with Shani at night over the past few days. Even if we were both fully rested, driving the three thousand miles would probably take three to four days, us taking turns without stopping overnight. The fastest way was flying, but airline security was at an all-time high; given Shani's agitated state, we feared that if she got nervous on board, air marshals might overreact. The only other option was the train. It would take three days to get back east, but that seemed to be the safest option. At first Shani agreed, but then at the last minute she refused to go.

It was a phone call with my mother that finally achieved the impossible. My mom told Shani that she had a dream the night before that my dad, who had died four years earlier, was walking into the room Shani usually stayed in when she visited their home in New York. She asked him why. "You know Shani's coming and she needs to sleep there." I heard Shani reply, "That wasn't a dream. Papa Jim wants me to come." They got off the phone and Shani calmly said, "I'll go."

The next morning, without any resistance from Shani, Jamaar drove us to the airport and we boarded a Southwest plane back east.

The next morning we had an appointment with Carolyn Britton, MD, an extraordinary neurologist who became Shani's lifeline to normalcy. With the demeanor of a grandmother, the gentleness of a spiritual counselor, and the knowledge of a renowned practitioner, Dr. Britton explained that test results would have to confirm her diagnosis but in all probability the combination of drugs Shani had taken had created a toxic cocktail that caused her insomnia and psychosis. Shani and I stayed in New York almost two months while she underwent the initial weaning process with both neurologists and psychiatrists. Jamaar flew in every other week to see Shani, and when the doctors determined that she could return home to continue her treatments, he flew in to escort her back. It was a relief to see my daughter had a partner she could rely on unconditionally to help her recover. Jamaar was indeed a part of our pride, and I was so grateful to have him standing by Shani's side while we were all figuring out the next steps.

It was by no means easy, and it would be months more before Shani could rid herself of the drugs that had gripped every fiber of her being. But when her mood was no longer being dimmed by the drugs, Shani came back with a vengeance, determined to take control of her own care and well-being.

Advances in modern medicine are getting closer to a cure that will allow Shani and the estimated 250,000 to 350,000 people currently diagnosed with MS in the United States to live mobile and pain-free lives. Until then, Shani continues to keep up with the latest research, following what years ago became one of our family mantras: All you can do is the best you can do, and the rest you have to leave to faith. It's not a blind faith, but faith grounded in informed decision making, constant vigilance, and an active pursuit of wanting more, of wanting better.

As a family we embrace the Presence of Faith, grounded in the teachings and examples of my parents and bolstered by many acts of kindness from friends, mentors, and good people who walk with us. Thank God, Shani is thriving and an inspiration to anyone who meets her. With her deep faith and spirituality, she's determined to live her best life, no matter what direction it takes.

LESSON FROM A LIONESS: *Faith and medicine work, but it won't hurt to give them a boost.*

Physicist Edward Teller said, "Faith is knowing that one of two things shall happen: either you will be given something solid to stand on, or you will be taught how to fly." Once Shani was able to focus on her faith, she could return to the prayers that buoyed her in her youth. For her, prayer was a personal and spiritual conversation with her God. But not everyone has this faith connection or feels comfortable with the classic definition of prayer. The reality is that prayer can come in many different forms, and over time Shani added meditation to her daily spiritual regimen.

She, like millions of others who have embraced meditation, found that it provides a way to calm the mind, identify her greatest need—in her case wellness—and visualize the best possible future. Emma Seppala, PhD, director of Stanford's Center for Compassion and Altruism Research and Education, says that there are twenty scientifically proven reasons to consider meditation, including these: It increases immune function and decreases inflammation and pain; it increases positive emotion and decreases depression, anxiety, and stress; it boosts self-control, improves productivity, and changes the brain by increasing cortical thickness in areas related to paying attention.

There are many different approaches to starting a meditation practice. One that inspired me is by Wendy Koreyva, a certified instructor in meditation and yoga, who advances an easy six-step approach to getting started:

1. **Choose your mantra.** A mantra is a word or phrase that you silently repeat to focus your attention on something other than your thoughts. It can be any word, but Dr. Koreyva suggests using a Sanskrit mantra, *So Hum*, because it is not English and will not trigger additional thoughts.

2. **Find a comfortable place to sit.** You need a place that is quiet and where you will not be disturbed.

3. **Gently close your eyes and begin taking deep breaths.** These first few breaths are called cleansing breaths. After a few deep ins and outs, continue to breathe at a normal relaxed pace through your nose.

4. **Begin repeating the mantra in your head.** The repetition of the mantra should become almost effortless. Sometimes it is helpful to imagine that rather than repeating the mantra to yourself, you are actually listening to it being whispered in your ear.

5. **Do not try to stop your thoughts or empty your mind.** As you continue with this process, Dr. Koreyva says you will inevitably drift away from the mantra. It is human nature for the mind to wander, so she advises *not* trying to stop your thoughts or empty your mind. If you find that your thoughts are drifting, simply return to silently repeating the mantra.

6. **Stop repeating the mantra.** After approximately twenty to thirty minutes, you can stop repeating your mantra and continue sitting with your eyes closed. Spend a few minutes relaxing with closed eyes before resuming normal activity. (You can use a kitchen timer; there are also smartphone apps available that provide a gentle tone to mark the end of a meditation session.)

If a walking meditation regimen is preferable, health psychologist Dr. Kelly McGonigal suggests a ten-minute walking meditation involving one minute of paying attention to each of these: (1) the feeling of your body walking, (2) the feeling of your breath, (3) the sensations of air or wind on your skin, (4) what you can hear, and (5) what you can see.

Follow this with five minutes of open awareness in which you allow anything you can observe or sense to rise up into your awareness. Don't go looking for things to hear, see, or feel. Just let whatever rises up into your awareness do so and be naturally replaced by something else whenever that happens.

In the Spirit

Seeds of faith are always within us; sometimes it takes a crisis to nourish and encourage their growth.

—*Susan L. Taylor*

It was a steamy July in 1984 when the kids and I moved back to New York. Feeling for the first time in a long time that I had control of my schedule, I began the process of mapping out our next couple of months: get us all settled in our new, albeit cramped, space within my childhood home; research schools in the Bronx or nearby Westchester and get the kids enrolled; go shopping for school clothes; and finally, around September, start my job hunt. After Wes's death, instead of going back to work full-time, I did freelance writing for publications in Washington so I could be more available to the kids. Writing radio or brochure copy is what I had been trained to do, so one day my girlfriend from college, Mary Braxton, called and said *Essence* magazine was developing a weekly television show—*Essence: The Television Program*—and needed a writer. Immediately, my insecurities got the best of me. I had written and produced for radio, not television, and news was my thing, not the lifestyle content the magazine was known for. I figured I wouldn't even have a chance at getting the job. But Mary convinced me to at least check it out.

After meeting with the director, Alexis Revis, whom I learned during the interview had also graduated from my alma mater American University, I submitted my writing samples. I was called back to interview with Susan L. Taylor, the editor in chief of *Essence* magazine and the show's host. If you are not familiar with Susan, she had joined *Essence* the year it was founded and was instrumental in not only its growth and success but developing its unique brand. She is what Dame Anna Wintour is to *Vogue*—iconic and extremely influential. I was terrified to meet her because back then for a writer, it was like having an appointment with the queen, except this queen had been called "the most influential black woman in journalism today." The job I was applying for was not just important but actually groundbreaking in television. It was my chance to stretch out of my comfort zone and contribute to the beautiful booming voices the magazine was already sharing.

After all this buildup in my mind, of course my stomach was in knots when I walked in to meet Susan. I was so afraid that my clothes weren't right, that she'd notice my worn shoes, or that I'd sound like I had no idea what I was talking about. I tightened my stomach to keep it from growling. But Susan couldn't have been nicer nor our meeting any more cordial. We talked about the show and its needs, but we also talked about our West Indian backgrounds, our children and our hopes for them, and the country as a whole. I walked out with the job and into one of the most exciting chapters in my expanding career. But what I didn't know then and would learn over the next five years as the show's head writer is that Susan's dominance in publishing and everything else she conquers stems from a deep spiritual place that she unearthed when leaving an abusive marriage.

The path to single motherhood for me had to do with infidelity, disrespect, and disregard. The night it descended into physical violence, I fled. I'm not a woman to take beating. I was twenty-three, and knew I would be in one of those prisons that I often visit women in—women serving life sentences because they murdered their abuser. That could have been me.

I am just grateful that I had the good sense to pick up my Shana and leave when she was six weeks old. Mommy welcomed us back into the home I had left at seventeen. The challenges of living with my mother—I inherited her bossiness—made me vulnerable to my ex begging his way back into my life. The following year, for a short period of time, I gave the marriage another chance. But again, there was infidelity. It didn't weigh on me this time because the magic was gone, the trust was gone, and it was just a matter of time before I left for good and became a single mother for good. I went from being a middle-class, well-supported wife to a poor single mother overnight.

Susan faced her single motherhood head-on, often calling her daughter Shana "my anchor," who provided her the power to keep pushing through poverty, loneliness, and an unrealized career. She tried to keep up with her growing cosmetics company, which she started years before, but the products were in her husband's beauty salon. Susan hadn't yet gone to college, but her knowledge of cosmetology led to work as a part-time beauty editor for *Essence* magazine. Her salary at the new magazine was $350 a month, and her rent alone was $368!

I was so stressed. I had a pain in my chest and difficulty breathing. I thought I was having a heart attack and went to Columbia Presbyterian Hospital in New York City, where the emergency room doctor said, "You're not having a heart attack. It's an anxiety attack, and you need to relax." I left the hospital and started walking up Broadway thinking, "How can I relax, with the world shifting beneath me?" It was a gray October day, and misty. I was now twenty-four, relieved I wasn't having a heart attack but so fearful of what was going to happen to Shana and me. My mother was struggling too. And Daddy had passed away. I kept asking myself, "How am I going to keep the roof over our head? How am I going to feed Shana?" My car was broken down. I had no money. I literally had $5 in my pocket that day!

I started walking but for some reason in the opposite direction of my Bronx apartment. I look up and saw a marquee—Church Service 3 PM—on an old, grand movie theater in Washington Heights north of Harlem.

It was what is now known as the United Palace cathedral, the creation of charismatic Evangelical minister Reverend Ike. His weekly radio sermons were carried by hundreds of stations around the country, and he became famous in the African American community for his prosperity theology, flamboyance, and slogan: "You can't lose with the stuff I use." There were numerous services throughout the week but the one that Susan stumbled upon was going strong that Sunday afternoon. Her restrictive Catholic-school training might have made her keep walking past the Palace, but not that day.

I'd been trained to dress up for church. That day I was wearing jeans and a leather jacket. But some force that I didn't understand then pulled me into the back of the sanctuary, where I heard a sermon that changed my life. The Reverend Alfred Miller, Reverend Ike's assistant minister, whose memorial service I just spoke at last year, was speaking passionately to the congregation. "The Holy Spirit is alive in you! God is alive in you!" he shouted continuously. "With your mind you can change the world!" He continued saying that our minds could change our world. He said that no matter what our troubles, if we put them aside for a moment, focus on possible solutions, and imagine a joyous future and work toward it, we would find a peace within, and positive experiences would begin to unfold.

What I began to embrace after that sermon is that life will sometimes bring you to the edge in order to make you wake up. Sometimes we think we're being punished for our mistakes. Our God is not a punishing God. By whatever name we may call the Divinity, all the pain that we endure is an awakening for us to understand that we're more than we seem, that we're human and divine. We really do have the power to do what needs to be done as single mothers. I'm not saying it's easy, but it's possible if we don't fold within ourselves, but go within ourselves for where the illumination and light are. After that service I gathered up the little pamphlets, walked home with the $5 I needed to buy milk and cereal so I could feed my little Shana that week. Five dollars could stretch that far back in the day!

The next morning, rather than lying in bed, or getting up reluctantly with fear grabbing me, I just said, "I'm going to do what that minister told me to do. I'm going to get up, I'm going to have faith, I'm going to sit in quiet for a moment and allow God to speak to me." I don't know if I sat there for three minutes or thirty minutes, but something just said, "Why don't you call the Ophelia DeVore School of Charm?" Ophelia DeVore was a very well-known woman who trained want-to-be models.

After nine AM, I made the phone call. To the woman on the other end of the phone I said, "My name is Susan Taylor, and I'm the beauty editor of Essence magazine. I'd like to know if you'd be interested in my teaching your students how to put on makeup and fix their hair." I was transferred to a woman named Jackie Wellington, who said, "Well, we don't know you, but we surely do know the new magazine Essence." She said, "We'd love to have you."

With that one phone call, my life changed. My monthly income increased 40 percent. Reflecting on that experience over time, I saw clearly that Divine Order is always at work. So if I'd had a little more money that Sunday, I would have taken public transportation and not set out on foot. If not for the pain in my chest, the blessing of an anxiety attack, I wouldn't have gone to the emergency room, where I learned that I wasn't dying. If my car wasn't broken I wouldn't have stumbled across that church, but driven past it as I had many a Sunday. In time, I would come to see that the breakups, the shakeups, the fears that continually bite at our heels—and that some say unhealed, are the cause of all of our crises and those in the world—these are a natural and important part of life. They teach us to look beyond the physical world for information, to turn within to our spiritual world for confirmation. Realizing this is how I began to change my life, how, as a single mother and still today, I manage to keep overwhelm and fear at bay and

practice having faith and looking for the larger spiritual cycles that
are always at work.

Susan embraced practicing daily gratitude and the belief that our thoughts create our reality, and faith is an active partner in shaping that reality.

With her reawakened reliance on her faith came the blossoming of her career at *Essence*. Within months, then editor in chief Marcia Ann Gillespie recognized her drive and talent and Susan went from part-time beauty editor to full-time fashion and beauty editor. In 1981, at age thirty-five, she was named editor in chief. She also enrolled in college and earned her degree at night from Fordham University—all while working full-time, hosting the television program, becoming a sought-after public speaker, and dating the man who would become the love of her life. While some called it an unconventional and meteoric rise to the top, Susan said her goal was to continue growing a world-class magazine while maintaining her personal and spiritual life as well as a presence for her daughter, no matter what else was going on.

But with her increasing fame came a reminder of what was missing in her formal spiritual training. A Catholic-school girl, she read her catechism every day and in elementary school, attended church seven days a week. She believed that sanctity rested in the beautiful statues of saints in the sanctuary, and that the nuns and priests had a direct line to God. Until that day in the United Palace cathedral, she never really connected to the understanding that the power actually resided within *her*. An incident one night when Shana was about twelve years old brought this realization into sharp focus, and it marked the beginning of Susan's new approach to single mothering.

One Friday night, I was working at my desk and Shana's calling every few minutes, wondering when I was coming home. "Sweetie, I'm coming, sweetie, I'm coming," was my rote response to each of her calls. Our offices were in Times Square and it was very seedy then. "Coming, sweetie." It's eight o' clock. Nine o'clock. "I'm coming, sweetie." It's ten o'clock. I arrived home at about ten thirty that night and my Shana was putting on her coat and on her way down to Times Square to meet me. I was horrified and said, "Shana, what are you doing?" She responded, "You're Susan Taylor and you have fancy stuff, and I thought somebody might hurt you. Nobody was going to bother me, so I was just coming to get you."

Whatever it was that I was doing at my desk could have waited. Or I could have brought the work home and attended to it with Shana doing her homework right by my side. After that incident, I had to teach myself to come home from work and focus on Shana first. I had been arriving and complaining about Shana's undone chores and stepping out of my heels and into the kitchen to fix dinner. I remember asking her one evening, trying to focus more on my daughter, how her day in school went. "You don't really care, Mommy," she responded. It hurt and also woke me. I started coming home from work differently, ignoring things out of order in our apartment. I'd go into the bathroom, close the door, sit on the edge of the tub, and let go of Essence. I'd take some breaths and just resolve to be present for Shana. Our children need our presence. They don't need the presents, more stuff. They need our listening ear, our affirmation, to know that they are important and loved.

Soon it became a habit, taking a few minutes to resettle my mind, sitting with her and just saying, "Tell me about your day." At first, she didn't believe I cared. "Mommy, you don't really want to know. Come on." With my consistency, Shana began to trust that I cared about her, and both our lives changed. My beloved went from being a failing student to the valedictorian of her high school graduating class. The change needs to happen in us as parents first.

Susan realized that she needed to apply the same focus and listening skills that elevated her faith to her parenting. She became determined to create a work environment where there would be no conflict between doing a good job and being a good parent. She brought toys and books into the office so that when the staff's children came to the office because of minor illnesses or days off from school, they would feel welcomed.

In many ways her experiences at home and in the workplace are what helped fuel Susan's passion for mentoring, which began as Essence Cares while she was still editor in chief. Following Hurricane Katrina in 2005, she saw so many children suffering, so many single parents profoundly stressed out, not having the support they needed to provide the presence their children required to rebuild their lives and sense of security. In 2006, she transitioned Essence Cares into the National CARES Mentoring Movement so local CARES affiliates could begin building the movement in under-resourced communities.

From improvised single mom to legendary editor in chief to founder of one of the nation's preeminent mentoring movements, Susan L. Taylor has chartered her own spiritual journey and ministry—a lifetime of excellence, grounded in her faith. She has been presented with thousands of honors and awards in appreciation of her efforts, but not surprisingly, there's one recognition she treasures above all others.

There's nothing more important, or that I take greater pride in, than a daughter who has raised her own daughter well. As I say to Shana, "We survived me," a single mother, who wasn't highly educated, who initially wasn't making a lot of money, and who didn't always make the right choices. My granddaughter is now in college and our extended families have emerged into a great loving and trusting unit where we take care of one another in ways that are needed. That gives me permission to keep doing the work that I have to do in the community.

LESSON FROM A LIONESS: *Have faith in your inner resources; they are there to be tapped if you believe in your own skill set.*

Sometimes the pressures and challenges of today make thoughts of tomorrow mind numbing. With faith, however, we know that a force bigger than ourselves will guide us beyond today and into a brighter tomorrow. And if we can get beyond tomorrow, and the next day, and the day after that, we can start thinking about what our strength, resolve, and resiliency mean to our children.

Susan says sometimes, when stresses come all at once and life becomes overwhelming, even she forgets what she knows is true. Even though, as she admits, "I have written four books and twenty-seven years of editorials about this, still I forget under stress and forgo practicing my ritual—taking quiet time, time to listen in, time to exercise, time to remember these truths." She concludes that this is when we can begin to focus again, find the light deep within ourselves, and "see the things needed to care for ourselves and our family, to live our lives fully, all at our fingertips. Call this synchronicity! Divine Order! Truth!"

Presence of Courage:

The ability to boldly move out of a comfort zone to respond to emergencies, seize opportunities, or take unexpected risks to ensure better and brighter futures for our children.

IV

Presence of Courage

Introduction

Believe in yourself. You are braver than you think, more talented than you know, and capable of more than you imagine.
—Roy T. Bennett

Many people, especially single mothers, are just like the Cowardly Lion from *The Wizard of Oz*: braver than we think. Presence of Courage is not only about finding ways to talk yourself into something you are afraid to do, or jumping in with both feet without a life raft. Yes, there are times for blind bravery, for when our adrenaline takes over and we lift cars like superhumans or run faster than a gazelle to save a child. The true essence of courage, though, is to discover that it already exists inside us; to learn that the foreign, uncomfortable circumstances delivered to us are there to help us remember our courage and exercise it for the betterment of our lives and our children's.

If you are a mother, I presume you have been in situations that found you freaking out over something—maybe a mouse or traveling by plane or even leaving the closet door open at bedtime (it still bothers me)—but when it comes to how you act around your child, you put on that brave face, calmly explaining that "there's nothing to be afraid of." Then you might silently scream in the bathroom later or scratch yourself silly after killing a barrage of ants, but you grow a little, because c'mon, that brave face was pretty impressive, and (1) you worked through your own fear, and (2) you helped break a cycle or at least tried to not give your baggage to your child. That intent alone is brave; putting a strong example in front of our kids ahead of our own fears is the definition of Presence of Courage.

The Courage to Let Go

Success is not final, failure is not fatal: it is the courage to continue that counts.

—Winston Churchill

The year was 1968 and the country was still smoldering from the assassination of Dr. Martin Luther King Jr. and subsequent explosion of urban rage. I spent that summer before college working for the National Council of Churches (NCC), headquartered in what was affectionately called "the God Box"—the Interchurch Center in New York City. My job each morning was to clear the reams of Telex reports sent in by ministers around the country about the unrest in their cities the night before. Once I condensed the individual reports, I disseminated the summary throughout the NCC network before day's end. It was a sobering summer, as I read reports of communities burning and destroyed by rage, disinvestment, hopelessness, neglect, and indifference. When I walked onto the campus of American University that fall, I was highly politicized and eager to prepare to make a difference in a nation that I saw imploding before my eyes.

I had been on the campus a little over a week, but had quickly learned that the hub of student life nestled in Mary Graydon Center.

That's where everyone hung out between classes, where you could always find a bid whist card game going on, where lifelong friendships were started, and, in my case, where romances began. One day I walked in and saw a bunch of students clustered around four guys who were in an animated conversation about the state of affairs for black students and workers on campus. I soon learned that they were the leaders of the Organization of African and Afro-American Students at the American University, commonly called OASATAU.

Out of respect for the private lives they now live, I'll simply call them the Magnificent Four, all seniors and icons on campus. Even though they were the strong and vocal proponents for black history classes, equal distribution of student affairs activities dollars, and greater recognition of the need to recruit and retain more professors and students of color, they were still friends of the administration. As the fall of 1968 heated up, when the more radical students who were against the Vietnam War took over one of the buildings, the administration asked the men of OASATAU to help keep the peace and make sure the building wasn't damaged. I loved the fact that they could fight for a cause but still maintain a working relationship with those who could actually change policies. That was a skill I wanted to learn, and one of the four—whom I'll call Bill— became my willing teacher. With him as my inspiration and partner, I jumped into the movement with both feet. I helped start and began writing for the OASATAU newspaper, *UHURU*, organizing strategy for budget hearings and running a Saturday-morning breakfast program for kids in Northeast Washington, DC. With him, I felt like I was making an enduring difference. Activism for the cause on campus evolved into our personal passion at home, and by December we were engaged.

But like many women in love, in the year and a half before our wedding, I ignored the red flags. I looked past the fact that a good part of Bill's popularity was linked to the ease with which he scored weed. Let's face it. It was the late 1960s and there was always the distinctive smell of marijuana in the air, in the dorms, in the stair-ways, and on the quad. My classes were going well and I was hav-ing an impact on things bigger than myself, so having a joint with him and friends occasionally was fun and made me a full member of the influential inner circle. But as time went on, I found myself becoming more and more concerned by Bill's increasing and more regular drug use and the impact it was having on his moods. When he was high he was the life of the party, full of jokes and conver-sations ranging from the state of world affairs to the newest Jimi Hendrix album. In between joints he was controlling, demanding, and almost OCD—going around the apartment on cleaning binges and demanding that nothing be out of place. Even more disturb-ing was that his moods were affecting mine. When he was up, I felt down. When he felt down, I was up. We were on two totally different tracks, and rarely did we intersect.

In the months before our wedding I often thought about calling the whole thing off, but I felt trapped. The invitations were mailed, the bridesmaids had their dresses, and my mother was almost finished making my wedding gown. Besides, I reasoned, as other graduates were faced with the reality of having to find jobs and grow up, most of our friends were moving on from even occasional drug use. I con-vinced myself that he would too, that somehow a marriage license would make him the man I needed him to be.

I was wrong.

Neither a license nor the birth of our daughter Nikki a year and a half later made any difference. If anything, it emboldened him to be even more controlling and entrenched in his ways without regard for the impact on our young family. There were still people coming in and out of our apartment regularly, and I found myself escaping to our bedroom and shutting the door as soon as I heard the front door ring. He wasn't dealing drugs in the menacing traditional sense, but he was always ready to share what seemed to me and others a bot-tomless supply of joints of grade-A grass.

Today marijuana has become acceptable, and even legal in many states, but back then it was called the gateway to harder drugs and the best way to land yourself in jail. I kept begging him for us to go to counseling, but he refused. I should have had the courage to go to counseling myself, but I didn't want to do it without him. Then I did what probably most women do when they are in a bad situation—I threatened to leave without being willing to actually go. I lacked the courage to face my truths: I'd picked the wrong man; I was used to a two-income family, even though Bill kept the purse strings insultingly tight; we shared the same friends and I feared my circle of girl-friends might be disrupted; and what I feared most was telling my parents that I had made a mistake. Over and over I threatened to leave. But he assumed I didn't really mean it because after each argument he'd apologize, and I'd end up staying.

Most important, though, was Nikki. She was still too young to know what was going on, but she wouldn't be a toddler forever. And then what? Would I just keep holding on and standing by my man in a marriage crushing under the weight of unhappiness, not to mention illegal activity? Would her future have to become more important than the fear of disrupting the so-called security of the present? As I looked at her sleeping peacefully in her crib, at the end of her day of exploring and embracing a brand-new world, I wondered how I would feel if I stayed and years from now Nikki became hooked on drugs and said she'd learned it at home. That terrified me. As I was coming to grips with that possibility, an incident the third year into our marriage sealed my resolve that our union couldn't be fixed.

My first job after graduation was at WMAL-AM radio in Washington, DC. I was hired as a news assistant for the 5 AM Monday-through-Friday shift and had been there for about eight months. My days began at three. Nikki's weekday babysitter lived in the same high-rise apartment building we lived in so I'd make sure her diaper bag was stocked for the day, her clothes laid out, and her lunch made and in the refrigerator before I left the apartment at 4 AM. All Bill had to do was wake her up, dress her, and take her down the hall to the sitter before he left for work. Technically, I was off at 2 PM every day, but within a couple of weeks I began doing some research and writing for the public affairs department as well. That extended my day to about 4, which gave me just about enough time to pick up Nikki by 5 PM.

During the week, each evening was a carbon copy of the evening before—fix dinner, feed Nikki, leave dinner on the stove for Bill if he wasn't home, give Nikki a bath, read her a story, and put her to bed. Then I'd wash the dishes, get her bag ready for the next day, pack her lunch, and go to bed so I could get up again to leave by 4 AM. It was a grueling schedule, but I loved being a mother and I loved my job in the newsroom. What was wearing me down was my marriage.

One night in early November 1974, I was exhausted after I put Nikki to bed so I decided to take a quick nap. I was still asleep by the time Bill got home. He stormed into the bedroom and told me to get up and wash the dishes. I thought he was joking at first so I just turned my back to him. Then I felt the covers pulled from me.

"Get up, I said."

"I'll take care of everything later."

"You'll do the dishes now."

By this point, I was fully awake and aware that he was serious.

"I said I'm not doing it now," I said, getting increasingly angry that my husband was treating me like a child.

He grabbed my arm, pulled me up from the bed, and pushed me into the kitchen.

"Get off of me," I screamed as I pulled away and ran back to our bedroom.

Then he grabbed me again, this time by my hair, and pulled me back into the kitchen.

I wanted to scream at the top of my lungs but I was acutely aware that Nikki was in the other room and I didn't want to wake or scare her.

This was the first time that Bill had actually become physical with me. I knew women who had been physically abused by their husbands, but I'd never thought it would happen to me. Something had set him off before he'd gotten home, and I was determined it would be the first and last time I would be treated like this.

By the time we got to the kitchen, I looked for the first thing I could find to defend myself. I saw the knives in the butcher block holder on the counter and grabbed the first one within reach.

"Get the hell off of me now," I said between clenched teeth. I surprised myself with the intensity of my words, but I was also terrified at what I'd do if he didn't back off. He must have been as surprised as I was, because he let go and moved back immediately.

"Don't you ever, ever touch me again," I said through my tears, holding the knife like an exclamation point.

I went back to the bedroom and locked the door. That was my moment of clarity, when I knew I had to find the courage to do what I had been avoiding for far too long. Nothing would deter me this time. That night was the beginning of the end—or in hindsight, the beginning of my new beginning.

He apologized over and over, promising never to get physical with me again. I'd always excused and forgiven his behavior, but this time he crossed a line I just could not forgive. When I threatened to leave before, something always came up that made me stay—he was having a hard time at work or he'd had a fight with his dad or there was an event we really needed to go to together—there was always something. But this time there were no second chances. I spent the next couple of months planning my escape. As disturbing as that pivotal and violent night had been, I knew I needed to take time to make my move in the right way. I knew I wasn't going to quit my job, which I loved, and run back to New York and into the comfort of my parents' house. I opened up my own bank account and arranged for automatic deposit for my paycheck. I started looking for a subsidized childcare center, one that I could afford and was close to my job.

Fortunately, the extra work that I had been doing paid off and I was given a promotion, with more money and regular hours.

Feeling confident that I had figured out a budget that would work for us and meet Nikki's childcare needs, I chose to move before Christmas, figuring that if I could actually leave before a major holiday, nothing else could come along that was more important, or problematic, or symbolic, that would make me change my mind. My reasoning now seems a little odd but at the time it was what I needed to cling to in order to keep my resolve. Two weeks before Christmas, on a Friday night when he went out with friends, Nikki and I left with only two suitcases and her portable crib. I was stepping out into the unknown but I was determined that my new year would be different.

For the next six months, we lived in the basement apartment in the home of my friend Rae Carole and her mom, Barbara. I met Rae Carole at the hospital the day Nikki was born. She was a spunky and sweet high school candy striper who became a dear friend and my weekend babysitter. I also began seeing a therapist, thanks to a very good health insurance plan at the radio station. I told my parents that I was going to try to save my marriage. But I knew the truth was that I was trying to figure out my new world and my place in it. I'd never, ever thought I would become a single mother.

At the six-month mark, Nikki and I moved into an apartment of our own. This was the first time in my life I had ever signed a contract in my own name. I had gone straight from my parents' home into a marriage. Before Rae Carole's, I'd never been tested to balance a checkbook or live on a budget. I never gave myself a chance to know what I could do myself or if I could even survive on my own. This was my chance. I was now solely responsible for Nikki and myself. Now, with eyes wide open, I had chosen single motherhood. I had chosen the courage to find my own strength.

While it was a relief not having to deal with Bill's erratic mood swings and abuse, it was an adjustment dealing with just one paycheck. Staying with Rae Carole those few months had enabled me to save some money, and when I moved a little bit deeper into suburban Maryland, rent became more affordable. Also working in my favor were those extra dollars in my paycheck. I was learning to live on a budget, and everything started falling into place. I had a newfound confidence that I could actually make a life for us, and it felt really, really good.

As I began basking in my newfound liberation, I realized how much better I felt—about my life, about my job, about my role as a mother, about me as a woman. I thought about the Maya Angelou quote, "Courage is the most important of all the virtues because without courage, you can't practice any other virtue consistently." How right she was.

After a few months of being on my own, I unexpectedly found myself drawn to one of the up-and-coming reporters in the newsroom. William Westley Moore Jr. had cut his reporting chops in Florida and North Carolina, and everyone loved not only his professionalism but his easygoing manner and infectious smile. He had been hired as a street reporter but our news director, Ted Landphair, recognized Wes's talent for more long-form reporting and began assigning stories he could spend a couple of days on and really dig deep. He was promoted to director of public affairs and since I was now the public affairs researcher, Wes and I started working more closely together. I felt like I was thriving in my independence as a single mother, but eventually our respect for each other's talent turned to love. But while it was the work that connected us, it took Nikki to seal the deal.

When she first met Wes and took to him immediately, I made a note that this guy just might have a future in our lives. We gradually came to know and eventually love his family—his mom, dad, and three sisters Evelyn, Dawn, and Tawana. Living halfway between his apartment and mine, they were always willing babysitters and became an incredible support system for breaking news days and our date nights.

I was determined not to make the same mistake I had made before by jumping into a relationship too quickly and too intensely. My therapy sessions, along with the struggles and eventual satisfaction of single motherhood itself, helped me find the courage to recover from a bad marriage and pace myself on the road to a better one. Two years later, when I walked down the aisle that second time, each step was sure and fearless.

LESSON FROM A LIONESS: *Learn to let go.*

If you look really hard, as I have, at why we stay stuck for way too long, you might notice it is the fear of change that's at the heart of the matter. We can fear a lot of things, but fear of change is one of the most debilitating. Change means uncertainty, and who has ever been in love with the unknown? Tony Robbins says that our need for certainty is what keeps us stuck in the past, even if the past is as horrendous as my first marriage. "Certainty is fundamentally about survival," Robbins says. "We all need to feel certain that we can avoid pain, and, ideally, find some comfort. Continuous pain means continuous damage, and that eventually leads to our demise. It's frightening to step into the unknown. It's difficult to be vulnerable. And it can be overwhelmingly uncomfortable to have that sense of uncertainty about what lies ahead. So we hang on to the past—because even if it's steeped in pain, it's what we are familiar with and what we have certainty about."

The courage to change is not easy to muster, and this type of change does not come overnight. Here are some thoughts to help you as you get comfortable with the idea of getting a bit uncomfortable.

Step 1: Say Yes to What Is.

Author Eckhart Tolle says, "Whatever the present moment contains, accept it as if you had chosen it. Always work with it, not against it."

If you feel like a failure because you couldn't make your marriage work, don't resist the feelings. Give them permission to exist, and then let go as a natural part of the growth process. I went into my first marriage thinking it would be like my parents', but I had to admit that I was ending a marriage devoid of the core value of a loving two-parent family. I had to say yes to my feelings that the relationship wasn't right for me. The recognition and acceptance that each relationship is unique and deserving of forging its own path gave me the strength and courage to later build a union with Wes that was enormously rewarding.

STEP 2: LET IN INSTEAD OF LETTING GO.

Inviting in the new comes after we have achieved acceptance.

"Change is always scary, especially when you don't know what's coming next. That's why you might find yourself clinging to the unwanted because that's what's familiar and known to you," says author Maria Stenvinkel, who wrote about this in her article *A Surprising Way to Let Go of Painful Feelings and the Past.* "To make sure that doesn't happen, consciously decide what's coming next. Let in instead of letting go. Rather than pushing away the unwanted, invite the wanted."

When I decided I would find a new home in a suburb of Maryland that I could afford on my own, I realized I didn't have to fear being homeless. When I replaced my fear of not making enough money with the goal of getting a promotion, I created something new to fill the void. And of course, letting love into my heart let in hope, instead of the dread of feeling I had to let love go for good.

STEP 3: FOCUS ON WHAT YOU DESIRE.

It's time consuming and energy sucking to replay mistakes in your mind. It's frustrating to live in the past. "Instead of trying harder to let go, accept fully where you are," says Stenvinkel. "Embrace it completely. Say yes to all worry, shame, and guilt. Confirm all the negative thoughts and feelings so that you can release yourself from their grip. Simply, give up the battle."

It's what I did with Bill; my white flag rose a little more slowly, but wound up waving nevertheless. I had to admit that I was ending a marriage when I'd grown up with the core value of a loving two-parent family. I had to allow myself the shame of being the divorced one in my circle of friends. I had to accept that I would live in the basement before I allowed my daughter to have a life less than what I knew I was capable of giving her. Then, and only then, did my negative feelings start to disperse and make room for empowerment. Saying yes to those feelings gave them less power. It was like facing kryptonite and realizing it wouldn't weaken me after all; that it was all in my head.

Profile in Courage: The Terrie M. Williams Story

You cannot swim for new horizons until you have courage to lose sight of the shore.
—*William Faulkner*

I first met Terrie Marie Williams in 1984, walking through the halls of *Essence* magazine. Talk about presence! As we were walking toward each other, I saw a tall, beautiful woman with close-cropped hair, sporting palazzo pants with an oversize jacket, carrying a briefcase-size pocketbook, with bright welcoming eyes and a huge smile. As we met mid-hall, she extended her hand and said, "Hi, I'm Terrie. I understand you are part of the TV crew. Welcome to *Essence*." With that began a friendship that, for me, has been one of the most inspiring examples of what courage and true grit look like.

Terrie provided public relations assistance to both the magazine and our show, so that's how I got to know her after our brief encounter in the hall. She was great at what she did, always able to get interesting tidbits of information about the guests that I hadn't seen anywhere else. Guests could sense that Terrie genuinely cared about them, so they became forthcoming with information that eluded most other public relations professionals. That she was able to marry these two very different professions was my first indication of Terrie's intellect and courage when it came to taking risks. It was only one of her many courageous milestones.

She became so successful at *Essence* that in 1988 she took a huge leap of faith and started her own public relations firm—The Terrie Williams Agency—and landed one of the biggest box-office stars at the time, Eddie Murphy. I asked Terrie what it took to leave the security and stability of *Essence* and branch out on her own.

I look back and say, "Who did I think I was?" I'm trained as a social worker, took a PR course or two, and then land one of the biggest stars in the world! Who does that, you know what I'm saying? I don't think I had a whole lot to do with it. It was Divine Intervention. I guess I was able to connect with people and who they were underneath, regardless of what they were presenting to the world, and I guess they trusted me not only to help them with their skill set but to reach them on a personal level.

Eddie Murphy was just the beginning. Miles Davis, whom she had met years before as a social worker and who encouraged her to one day start her own business, was next. As one of the country's fastest-growing public relations firms, Terrie became a highly sought-after public speaker for conferences and lectures all over the country. In one of these presentations in New York, she met a young man. He wasn't famous; nor did he have the next great idea. All he had was a heart that Terrie couldn't resist. She had the courage to make a life-altering decision.

I don't even remember what the conference was or what I was speaking about but at the end of it this young man, this beautiful soul, came up to me. He had a light force about him that I had never seen in a young person before. It was part of God's plan that we met. We talked for a long time, long after everyone else left, and I just felt compelled to give him my number. It clearly wasn't a romantic thing or anything like that. Damn, he was only about sixteen years old! But there was just this connection with this beautiful, beautiful soul. I think I knew that day that Rocky Ephraim would always be part of my life.

We started talking fairly regularly, and I found out that his parents were divorced; his mother had moved down south and Rocky and his three brothers were pretty much left to fend for themselves. They lived in Brooklyn but he was always in Manhattan because that is where he went to school. One night he was in the city really late and since I had a spare bedroom I invited him to stay there so he wouldn't have to ride the trains so late at night. He started to do that really frequently, going to school straight from my apartment.

I was pretty shocked his father never tried to contact me. After about a month or so I called him and he had no problem with it. So Rocky literally moved in for good. I never thought I would be a parent because I never saw myself raising an infant but it became clear that Rocky needed me and I needed him. He became my son, with no formal papers, only the intervention of a higher being.

Terrie racked up dozens of awards and honors, ranging from the Public Relations Society of America Mentoring Award to being named in *Woman's Day* as one of the Fifty Women Who Are Changing the World. But the recognition that meant most to her was when she finally met Rocky's birth mother at his high school graduation. Terrie says they hugged, with Terrie saying, "Thank you for birthing Rocky," and his mom saying, "Thank you for raising him and taking such good care of him."

Her world, though, came crashing down in 2005 when she couldn't get out of bed one day. One day turned into two, three, and then four. Finally, a couple of her girlfriends, concerned that they hadn't been able to reach Terrie, went to her apartment and found her in a dark room, curled in a ball and unable to get up. They encouraged her to get up, shower, and get ready for an emergency session with a therapist that one of them had managed to secure. The therapist told Terrie that she was in an "emotionally dangerous place" and that she needed to see a psychiatrist immediately. With the therapist's cell phone number in one hand and an appointment with a psychiatrist for the next day in the other, Terrie's friends took her home for what she later described as one of the longest nights of her life.

The next day her friends took her to see the psychiatrist, who took her blood pressure, asked lots of questions, and began the long process of trying to find the right mix of medications to treat what she diagnosed as major clinical depression. Terrie says it took a couple of weeks for the medication to kick in and the next six months to admit, with clarity, that she needed help that she could never have admitted to before. As she explained in her book *Black Pain*:

> *When I think back on that time, I'm stunned. Here I was, a mental health professional, and I couldn't bring myself to admit that I was suffering from major clinical depression. I had been too paralyzed by my feelings to recognize the whole range of symptoms. All my energy was going into just functioning, doing the work things I "had to do"; and because I was hiding my feelings, the only guide to my well-being became my own confused perceptions.*

Even while Terrie battled to gain control over her depression, she continued to parent Rocky. She helped support him as a co-signer as he worked his way through and eventually graduated from college, and then helped as much as she could while he earned his MBA; he introduced her to the woman he would eventually marry and when she went to the wedding, out of respect for his birth mother she stood proudly but quietly on the side; and now she once again stands proudly, but this time as "grandma" to Rocky's two children.

Unfortunately, this was not the end of her challenges nor her need to seek help. In 2015, Terrie began forgetting things. For most people of advancing age, that's no big deal. But it was worrisome for Terrie because she was known for her computer-like memory. She never forgot anything—no one's name, face, where she met them, how she met them, and why it was important to remember them. Suddenly that skill was gone. She finally admitted to herself that this was beyond the usual aging process and she needed professional help again. While she feared she was developing the dementia that both of her parents were experiencing, it took a year to get the correct diagnosis of mild cognitive impairment (MCI).

According to the Alzheimer Association, *mild cognitive impairment* is a condition involving problems with cognitive function (mental abilities such as thinking, knowing, and remembering). People with MCI often have difficulties with day-to-day memory, but such problems are not bad enough to be classified as dementia. Currently, the FDA has not approved any drug regimen to effectively treat MCI, and those people diagnosed with it are at increased risk of developing dementia. Some patients, however, will stabilize to the point that there are only mild disruptions to their daily lives. The hope of many is that Terrie will be one of those lucky few.

There is an old saying: "What goes around comes around." Usually it has a negative connotation, but in this case it's a good thing. Rocky, the young boy whom Terrie embraced as her own son, now a husband and father, says he will always be her son and she will never have to worry about a roof over her head or enough food to eat. Because she'd opened her heart and home to him, because she'd become a mother even though she would in her words *never ever birth a baby*, because she'd shown kindness and sincere concern for someone who needed a presence—as do all the kids who become the future of this nation— God put someone in place who would make sure she lives out her days with the courage, grace, and dignity that she has shown her entire life. Maya Angelou once said that a hero is "any person really intent on making this a better place for all people." Terrie Williams is a hero to more people than she will ever remember.

LESSON FROM A LIONESS: *Have the courage to recognize and honor your challenges and your strengths.*

Helping others is something Terrie has done effortlessly all her life, but being able to ask for help was not. Even as a trained mental health professional, Terrie was unable to reach out to Rocky or her closest friends until she was in the midst of a crisis. As with any health issue, early intervention is critical. (Links to helpful resources for mental health can be found in the book's companion website, www.power-ofpresence.com.)

In a handout for Terrie's first book, *The Personal Touch*, she laid out her own blueprint for success. The tips she shared were a reflection of her passion to meet life on its own terms. To be able to put her heart into everything so fully takes courage—especially while also being vulnerable to a progressive disease. We can all take her advice on courage, which I think is suited both for the boardroom and for life. I'd like to share some tips—some original by her and some from people she respects.

- Power: The mind needs to think it, the heart needs to feel it, and the soul needs to stomach it. It's what you need to achieve it.
- Face the truth of who you are—the good side and the crazy-as-hell side.
- Know that you don't always have the answer. Ask for help.
- Remember upon whose shoulders you stand.
- Step outside your comfort zone daily and understand that the butterflies inside mean you are taking your game to the next level.

A Mom's Hug Can Last Long After She Lets Go

I learned that courage is not the absence of fear, but the
triumph over it.
—*Nelson Mandela*

My divorce from Nikki's father, Bill, two years after we separated, was contentious over one thing—Nikki. The only thing I asked for was custody, but he contested. At the time, he wasn't giving me any financial support whatsoever, so I walked into the court fully prepared to fight for my daughter. At the eleventh hour, however, Bill had a change of heart and dropped his petition for custody. We ended up with a no-fault divorce, an agreement that he could see her at any time, and a child support order. As it turned out my real fight that day was with the judge who refused to give me back my maiden name. His rationale was that he didn't think it would be right for Nikki and me to have two different last names. I couldn't believe his argument or his audacity, but he was adamant. As I was leaving the courtroom, a clerk tapped me on the shoulder and whispered that if I went to the clerk of a certain judge that afternoon, she was sure that judge would sign the order to change my name. Thank goodness for the court clerk network because, following instructions, by three o'clock I'd become Joy Thomas again. I promised myself I would never give away my name ever again.

On our own, Nikki and I thrived in our new independence. Even though Wes had taken a news job in New York, his parents, sisters, and Rae Carole provided the pride I needed to maintain a real presence for Nikki while advancing at work. I was promoted to public affairs director when he left, and our little department went on to win numerous awards over the next couple of years. Wes and I continued to date on and off, even after he left New York to take a news director's job in Oakland. Whenever he came to town to visit, Nikki beamed in his presence, and her smile became even broader when we told her that her uncle Wes would soon become her daddy.

The three of us lived in Oakland for a year, and it was magical. For me, it meant cooking my very first Thanksgiving turkey all by myself, going to a tree farm to cut down our own Christmas tree, and sitting in the vineyards in Napa, sipping wine and listening under the grape arbors to stars like Carmen McRae. These were times for us as a couple as well as family time I'd never thought Nikki or I would have. I felt like it was my reward for having the courage to end a bad marriage.

But as sweet as it was for me, for Nikki it was even more wonderful. She quickly became the mascot at Wes's station as she frequently went to work with him. Oakland loved its young and energetic news personality and Nikki loved being KDIA's own "Chatty Cathy." She thrived in childcare and loved the Oakland Zoo and walking around Lake Merritt with us, eating the incredibly fresh fruits and vegetables native to California. Wes's cousin Virene, her husband Tray, and their daughter, also named Nikki, only a year older than our Nikki, lived just ten minutes from us, and the girls bonded like sisters.

At six years old the only dad Nikki knew that year was Wes. We invited Bill to visit whenever he wanted and offered to bring her back to visit him if he wanted. Wes was totally supportive of making sure Nikki's relationship with her biological dad remained intact. While Bill never missed a child support payment, aside from a card she received from him on her birthday, Nikki had no communication with Bill the year we lived in Oakland.

Then a call came from WMAL, offering a package deal for Wes to go back east as the evening news anchor and I, as community affairs director. That was a tough decision. We loved our life out west, so our first inclination was to say no. But as we were weighing the offer, we discovered I was pregnant. With a new baby on the way, we both felt the need to be closer to our families on the East Coast, so we accepted.

Once back, Nikki had the benefit of two dads as Bill finally became responsive to our calls. At least twice a month he'd call or pick her up and take her to Chuck E. Cheese or to visit with friends. We made a special effort to reach out to him when Wes and Shani were born so he knew that as our family grew he was not being moved out of his position as Nikki's birth dad and an extended family member.

All that changed on April 16, 1982.

The day Wes died sent our world into a tailspin, taking me into unimaginable territory. The technical arrangements were one thing—the funeral and the aftermath filled with chores like closing accounts, obtaining the necessary copies of the death certificate, or applying for Social Security benefits for the kids. But filling the void the kids felt without their father was the toughest work. Friends and family were great, especially with the younger two—there wasn't a circus or Ice Capades or picnic they weren't invited to. They missed their dad but their tender ages and the activity distractions helped their transitions enormously. But Nikki was now almost ten and her world was shattered. The man she called Daddy had died, and the man she knew as Daddy Bill had once again disappeared.

The last time Nikki had seen or heard from Bill was at Wes's funeral. He was sitting near the back, and we got a glimpse of him when we were leaving the church. For a fleeting moment I found comfort that he cared enough to be there and thought the gesture bode well for his continued relationship with Nikki. But then he dropped out of her life, and the child support checks stopped the month after Wes died. At a time when I thought he'd step up and become more of a father, Bill became a ghost.

I couldn't believe he was doing this to Nikki. So giving him the benefit of the doubt, I called. Then Nikki called. No response, and all the while she was asking me about the father who couldn't be there and the one who could, but wasn't. It was Bill's absence, coupled with the death of the father she loved, that was steadily eating away at her self-esteem. I found myself not only grieving for the father she'd lost but also for the little girl who couldn't understand what she could have done for her life to have changed so drastically, so quickly, so completely. She couldn't verbalize her feelings, and I wasn't skilled enough to convince her it wasn't her fault. We did family therapy for a while, with limited results. I couldn't get her to talk out her feelings there or when we were home. Telling Nikki we were going to move to New York after her sixth-grade graduation really upset her.

"I told you I don't want to move to New York," Nikki said once again the night before our scheduled departure.

"Sweetie, I didn't want to move us before your graduation. Now you can have a fresh start in junior high school in New York, your brother can start fresh in first grade, and it won't matter to Shani. This is the best time for us to go."

"But what about my friends or my room? And what about Daddy Bill?"

Her friends I got, even missing the room she loved, but I was shocked she even mentioned Bill because she hadn't seen her biological dad in more than two years. Her outburst finally made me realize, though, that there was a daddy hunger she hadn't talked about but was clearly feeling.

"We'll let him know where you are and hopefully he'll be able to see you up there." I tried to hide the anger I was feeling because of the anguish he was causing her.

"I love visiting Mama Win and Papa Jim," she conceded, "but I don't want to live with them in New York forever. I don't," she added emphatically.

"Well, this is best for our family at this point. We'll do this for now and see what happens."

Nothing seemed to work for Nikki—not parochial or private school. Finally when she was in eleventh grade I found the Beekman School, a small private school housed in a historic brownstone in New York's Upper East Side. The classes were intimate, with no more than ten kids each, so Nikki couldn't get lost in a crowd. But by then, it didn't matter because she had totally lost interest in learning.

During those tumultuous teen years, I tried everything I could think of to reignite her spark for not only education but also herself and her future. "I hate it here, and I hate you," was a recurring theme at the end of each argument since moving to New York. I was in the crosshairs of her anger and there were many nights I would go to bed wondering what I was doing wrong and what I needed to do to make things right. I kept asking myself over and over, *How can I help her grow into someone I want to be around again?* I loved my daughter and it pained me to admit that oftentimes I wondered if I liked her.

Once a happy and content kid, she was now sullen, unmotivated in school or anything educational. She seemed angry all the time and I couldn't help but wonder if her attitude would have been different if I wasn't the only parent. I didn't want to involve my parents because I knew her angry outbursts would overly upset them at their advancing ages. Instead, I walked a fine line with her most times. Everything was a negotiation, and generally I would give in because it was easier not having to deal with her defiance.

Finally one day she blurted out, "You are working all the time so why don't you let me go and live with Daddy Bill?"

Then it hit me. I had become the trifecta in her sense of abandonment: One parent couldn't be with her. Another parent didn't want to be with her. And I wasn't there for her because I had to work. In her mind, not only wasn't I present for her, but I was standing between her and the only other chance for a normal life.

School was out in another two weeks, so I called Bill. I told him what was going on with her and that it was time for him to get involved in her life.

"So what are you thinking," he asked with what sounded like genuine concern.

"She wants to come and live with you. I know this is a huge risk because I haven't seen or heard from you in years and I don't know where your head is now. But unless you've gone completely over to the dark side or don't have space for her, she needs to reconnect with you. She has too many unanswered questions about you, questions only you can answer."

A pregnant pause was broken by a sheepish "Gee, I don't know."

"Look," I said on the heels of his timidity. "You haven't been there for her for most of her life. You need to step up now." After all these years of non-communication with him, I had no problem finding the courage to speak up for the daughter he had abandoned.

Still not hearing an affirmative answer, I added an ultimatum. "Either do this now or I file for back child support." She wasn't eighteen yet. He knew I'd have a case.

As soon as school let out, I drove Nikki back to Maryland to live with her father for the summer.

Fear once again gripped me. Was I doing the right thing? Was he still into the same bad habits or had he—I so hoped this was the case—moved beyond them? (Surveillance from mutual friends indicated he was doing "okay," so I wasn't afraid for her safety.) As angry as she was with me, would she bond with him and want to stay with him beyond the summer? Would he bad-mouth me to her, further confirming her feelings that I was the worst parent ever? Would I lose my firstborn to someone who had abandoned her when she needed him the most? But unlike our ride in the car for the move to New York, Nikki was really talkative. She was tasting victory, and I guess for the first time in a long time she felt in control. As we rode down I-95, I knew these were risks I had to take and I had to have courage to follow through with my decision.

As we arrived at the house he shared with four other guys we knew from our college years, Bill met us on the front steps. He hadn't changed much—a little gray was peeking through but he was still good-looking and charming. Nikki ran to him as though all those almost seven years of silence didn't exist. I felt a pang of anger. Nikki could dish out so much disrespect to me after all I'd tried to do, and in walked Bill, like the prodigal son, getting all her love! As he took her bag, though, my anger turned to hope that maybe this would

work and that Nikki would finally find contentment and self-worth.
She and I hugged goodbye in a really authentic way for the first time
in a long time. I headed back to the Bronx.

The next day as I sat drinking coffee, I hoped that spending time
with Bill would cure Nikki of her curiosity. I had made it a point
never to put him down so I guess in her mind he was bigger than life
and it was my fault he wasn't present in her life. It was natural, after
all, to wonder about the other part of you, to try to put together all
the pieces of who you are. Maybe he could help her feel better about
herself, find herself—things I was obviously failing to do. Maybe during the summer he could help turn the light back on so that her last
year in high school would be more successful than the other three.
My maybes were interrupted by the ringing phone.

"I want to come home. Can you come and get me?" On the other
end of the line was Nikki.

"What? What are you talking about? You just got there yesterday.
What happened?"

"Nothing happened," she replied. "He's all right I guess but I just
don't like it here. He lives in the basement and it's dark and I just
don't want to be here. I just want to come home."

I was so glad she couldn't see the huge grin on my face.

Sounding as empathetic as I could, I replied, "I'm sorry things didn't
work out but I won't be able to get back down there for a couple of days.
If you really don't want to stay there until the weekend I'll see if you can
go over to Grandma Gwen's until I can come and pick you up."

As I replaced the phone in the cradle, my sigh of relief filled the
morning air. I'd hoped Nikki's time away would suspend the fantasy
that had gripped and paralyzed her over the past few years. I'd hoped
in some small way she'd understand why my marriage to her father
had ended and that he would never fill the void that Wes's death had
created. I'd hoped she'd realize the life she had in New York wasn't
as bad as the script she'd written in her mind. It had been really difficult, and I had been afraid to let her go, but I realized that I needed

to trust my daughter's need to learn for herself whether she was in the right place. As I prepared to make the arrangements for her next couple of days with Wes's mom in DC, I envisioned my new hope— that I could help Nikki use this moment to see her own beauty, brains, and strength.

Though it wasn't immediate or dramatic, Nikki's trip to Maryland did turn out to be a pivotal moment in her life. Her last year in high school went much smoother, and that fall Nikki enrolled in a nearby junior college and did very well. Her grades there helped transition her to a four-year college. Not only did she reach her goal, but her success helped motivate her brother and sister along the way.

Because I had the courage to hug my daughter goodbye, she eventually returned to me and, most important, to herself.

LESSON FROM A LIONESS: *Sometimes you must look back to move forward.*

There is a bit of wisdom that's made it into pop culture. It's called the Tester Pancake Parenting Theory. The Urban Dictionary asserts that the firstborn child is like the first pancake on the griddle on a Sunday morning. "It usually gets temperature neglected, and often undergoes premature flipping." In many ways, Nikki was my first pancake! I didn't know what I was doing, and circumstances in our lives—the divorce, my venturing out as a single mom, my remarriage, and then the sudden death of her beloved daddy—added to a recipe for confusion, anger, guilt, and rebellion in Nikki's formative years. She was suffering from childhood trauma, and until I could recognize that, and understand how important it was to help her heal even if going back to those wounds was scary for both of us, there was no way we could move forward.

Bruce D. Perry, MD, PhD, says in an article for *Scholastic*, "Parents, often coping with the same loss, may underestimate the impact of the

separation, move, or death on a child, thinking 'children are resilient.'
Underestimating the vulnerability of the grieving child actually pro-
longs the child's pain and increases the probability that the effects of
the loss will persist." Some of these persistent symptoms are emotional
numbing, anger, irritability, episodic rage, and regressive behaviors—
all things that I saw in Nikki but failed to respond to earlier.

Inspired by the Dougy Center, the National Center for Grieving
Children & Families, here are some suggestions for helping children
deal with loss:

- **Answer the questions they ask, even the hard ones.** Parents
  need to let kids know it is okay to ask questions; it's parents'
  responsibility to answer as truthfully and age-appropriately
  as possible. Use concrete words like *died* or *killed* instead of
  passed away. If you use vague phrases like *passed away*, the child
  will ask the next logical question: "Passed away where? And
  when is that person coming back?" This so resonated with me
  because this is exactly what Wes had said: "I was still in the
  wind tunnel. I heard that my father had 'passed on' but had
  no idea where he'd gone...when I looked into the casket and
  asked my father, 'Daddy, are you going to come with us?'"
- **Don't be afraid to talk about the person** who died or who no
  longer lives in the house. Bringing up the person's name gives
  the child permission to recall happy memories too.
- **Keep pictures of the person around the house.** Share memories, and if there is a special keepsake that brings fond memories
  to the child, make that a special gift.
- **Respect differences in grieving styles.** Watching and listening to what is said and how a child is reacting will provide you
  with the cues on how best to help him or her cope with the loss.
- **Listen without judgment.** We as parents often choose to say
  things like "I know just how you feel" or, worse, "It is time
  to get over it," or the person is "in a better place," or "We are

better off without so-and-so." The Dougy Center says, "Using such responses negates the child's own experiences and feelings. If a child says, 'I miss my dad who died' simply reflect back what you've heard, using her words so she knows her words are being heard. Use open-ended questions such as 'what's that been like?' or 'How is that?'" Children then feel more comfortable responding without pressure to respond in a certain way.

- **Hold a private memorial service** and allow kids to say goodbye and express their feelings in their own way.
- **Take a break** and do something or go somewhere fun. Having fun or laughing is not disrespectful. It is a necessary part of grieving and moving forward.

Courage Is a Choice: The Allessandra Bradley-Burns Story

It takes courage to grow up and become who you really are.

—*e. e. cummings*

While most of the women profiled in this book I've known and admired for many years, there are some whose stories I heard about and whom I couldn't wait to meet. One recommendation came from my good friend Lisa. Not knowing quite what to expect, I left Baltimore and drove the fifty miles or so to the rolling hills of western Maryland. Seeing horse paths kissing the long driveway leading up to the majestic gray stone English manor house, I felt like I was traveling into a different time. And then walking into the oversize kitchen and seeing two ovens, two refrigerators, and two sinks, my diversity IQ kicked in and I knew I was standing in the midst of a kosher kitchen. I immediately started to make assumptions about who I was about to meet. Boy, was I wrong.

The seeds of Allessandra Bradley-Burns's story were planted long ago by her own single mother, Patricia, who was divorced and living in Boston in the throes of its desegregation plan for public schools. Raised Catholic, Patricia was determined to provide her two daughters, Allessandra, six, and Monique, four, with the best possible education where they didn't have to travel hours away from home, sometimes through hostile neighborhoods, every day.

On her lunch break from her job as a lab technician, Patricia would get on the train and ride twenty minutes in every possible direction to see if she could find someplace to live that was close, affordable, safe, and had great schools. She found a town called Brookline and negotiated her way into living in a building that was built and intended strictly for Orthodox Jews.

So here comes my mom, who is white with two half-black daughters. Even though the community knew Mom wasn't Jewish, seeing her biracial children came as quite a shock. But my mother had agreed that she would be very respectful, learn, understand, and become engaged with their faith, and we did. She never converted but we lived fully in the Way. We truly had an idealistic childhood because we lived in a community with lots of moms around us who were very protective and always kept an eye on us.

Allessandra's mother had assembled her own pride in the midst of Brookline. Her goals were to give her daughters access to the best education she could find, and instill a sense of survival and adventure as well as values of tolerance, compromise, compassion, perseverance, self-esteem, and courage. Armed with these values and aspirations, Allessandra's sister went off to Dartmouth and Allessandra traveled south to Georgetown in DC. There, Allessandra continued to openly practice her adopted faith, though it somewhat isolated her from other students. And because she also self-identified as African American, she was particularly at odds with the black student union leader, who was totally confused by this half-white, half-black practicing Jew.

But Allessandra didn't let anyone's disdain or opinion derail her from her pursuit of international studies, and following her sophomore year she was off to study abroad in Dar es Salaam, Tanzania.

Her planned semester away turned into a life-altering adventure to say the least. She survived a month of linguistic isolation, a six-month university strike, poisonous snakes, fire ants, and panther-like animals roaming freely around the campus.

But she also found love with a State Department diplomat, whom she eventually married. Her one semester abroad turned into three years. This is where her journey into motherhood, and eventually single motherhood, began, thanks to a Muslim woman who became a good friend.

Muslims are required on Fridays to give homage to the poor. So as we were leaving to go to lunch she asked if we could make one stop first. "I'm delivering this firewood to a Mother Teresa orphanage on the outskirts of the city."

We pulled in, and four Sisters of Charity, in their recogniz-able white-with-blue-stripe habits, came out and greeted her, and she introduced me. We unloaded the wood. I said, "What is this place?" They took me on a tour.

We walked into orphanage, a room with fifty beds and cribs. I was just mesmerized.

I told my friend, "I don't want to go."

We went back and forth like this for a few more minutes and I finally said, "I have to stay. I don't know why, but I know that this is where I'm supposed to be."

We finally saw the Mother Superior walking up the road and in Swahili, which I now spoke very well, I told her that I was drawn here and I wanted to do something to help.

She said, "Show up tomorrow at 6 AM."

The next morning they sat me in this teeny, tiny chair and placed into my arms this baby that was maybe two pounds at best, and a little cup of milk and a medicine dropper. Mother Superior said, "If that baby is still alive at the end of the day, you can come back tomorrow."

I held him, fed him, walked around with him while he slept. I did a few things that I don't even know how I knew to do, like at one point I could tell he was cold, even though it was 120 degrees in the shade in Tanzania. I took off his little outfit and I put him down the front of my dress. I must have done something right because he was alive at the end of the day.

I ended up spending eight months there. But that first baby they put in my arms ended up being the baby I adopted before I went back to finish my last year at Georgetown.

With her husband reassigned to another African consulate, Allessandra, still a student and now a mother, ventured back to the United States with their son, Kitu. Because of his critical condition when she'd first held him, she was warned that Kitu might have special needs as he grew up. Allessandra didn't care. Kitu had captured her heart and she had the courage to take on whatever the future held for them.

Her immediate goal was to finish the few semesters standing between her and graduation. Allessandra created a pride of student babysitters around her that helped her go to class confident that her son would be properly taken care of. As she struggled to achieve a state of presence in her new role of student-mother, the constant refrain in her ear was her mother's challenge to determine what it was that she wanted to accomplish and then figure out how she would achieve it.

Anxious to reconnect with her husband, after graduation Allessandra and Kitu flew back to Africa. They were there three weeks before an escalating civil war forced them to leave in a US military plane under cover of night while her husband had to remain. The stress on the relationship would mark the end of their marriage and the beginning of her life as an official single working mother.

Within the next few years, Allessandra co-founded a nonprofit organization in Washington, DC, got a green card for her son, formalized Kitu's adoption, and found love again with Tony. Out of this marriage came a daughter and a set of twins. Tony traveled often for work so even though she was married, Allessandra often felt like a single mom with four kids when he was gone—which was most of the time. Each day was a carbon copy of the day before. A daunting schedule of city buses, multiple caretakers, different schools, and a demanding job, yes, but thanks to her mother's emphasis on time management and multitasking a workable one. For the most part, the family thrived, but her husband's absence for so much of the time began to reveal conflicts within Allessandra. She needed a large amount of courage to not only acknowledge this but also do something about it.

> *It was a confusing time, because I loved Tony very much. We had a great marriage, we had a great family. We were leaders in a community of people. But about six years into our marriage, I said, "I think it's a disservice to you . . . to think that I would be . . . fully satisfied if I lived the rest of my life married to you." I just felt unsettled, and that feeling was likely to grow. It wasn't right for him, it wasn't right for the kids. We very painfully separated and then divorced.*

The late feminist author and founder of NOW Betty Friedan was quoted as saying: "It is not possible to preserve one's identity by adjusting for any length of time to a frame of reference that is in itself destructive to it. It is very hard indeed for a human being to sustain such an 'inner' split—conforming outwardly to one reality, while trying to maintain inwardly the value it denies." Without realizing it, this inner conflict had been Allessandra's companion throughout her two marriages, preventing her from experiencing the true joy of authenticity. So with the end of her marriage to Tony, Allessandra resolved that to be truly present to her children, she had to be true to herself.

Once again in official single-mom status, but now in full aware-ness of her sexual identity, Allessandra became even more deter-mined to be the most present mom possible for her four children. This got easier when she became a consultant, which meant her schedule was more flexible and accommodating to her children's needs. Some years later, she became a candidate to be a transitional head of a nonprofit that was changing direction. As fate would have it, the chairman of the board making the decision was the very same head of the black student union at Georgetown who'd once ques-tioned Allessandra's authenticity!

Melissa and I were like oil and water in college. She thought I wasn't black enough and I thought she was too busy being black and we couldn't quite come to terms around that. She thought I was stuck up and I thought she was bossy. I was convinced this job interview was not going to end well.

Much to her surprise, whatever differences existed in college were inconsequential next to the job that needed to be done, and Alles-sandra was offered the position. As time went on, the onetime adver-saries became allies and eventually partners of the heart. With her temporary position drawing to a close, Alessandra was able to leave the organization, avoiding any conflict-of-interest issues and allow-ing the new romance to fully bloom.

They eventually married fifteen years ago, and using Melissa's eggs, Allessandra gave birth to another set of twins. Now, sur-rounded by love and their parents' unconditional dedication to be present, all six teens and young adults are thriving. It's a family much like the United Colors of Benetton—diverse, colorful, innovative, quirky, and full of love. On the first day of sixth grade, one of the kids came home and said, "I told everyone today that I'm black. I told everybody that I have gay moms. Can I wait until tomorrow to tell them I'm Jewish?" Allessandra proves that being fully present with your children only comes once you are first fully present with your-self. Author and politician Roy T. Bennett says that having courage means being brave enough to "Live the life of your dreams according to your vision and purpose instead of the expectations and opin-ions of others." Throughout her life Allessandra Bradley-Burns has cast off the mask of conformity and lived her best life. Her mother's embrace of all religions, races, and ethnicities provided the frame-work for how Allessandra would orchestrate her own life with the choices she would ultimately make.

Mom always said that being yourself will not always make every-one happy but if you are a good person who has integrity and who is honest and loving, good things will follow. The courage to follow my heart and marry Melissa has made my life bigger. I am able to influence more people because she challenges me to be my best self professionally. I live in my magic and that would not have hap-pened to the same degree had I not acknowledged my authentic self.

LESSON FROM A LIONESS: *Throw off the mask.*

Like Allessandra, we confuse who we are with the labels we give our-selves, or allow others to stick on us. We identify with attributes that really do not define us or deepen our essences. Allessandra was both blessed and cursed with more masks than the typical person. She was black, she was white. She was a student, a wife, the mother of an adopted autistic boy. Running around trying to be the best of all those things brought Allessandra further away from her truth. It wasn't until she got to a place of security and experience that she found the courage to put her confidence to use, hear her mother's words in her ear, and put into practice all the lessons she had learned through her journey.

For Allessandra, a key lesson was that we cannot and should not fight our true nature. We all need to cling to something, but what are we clinging to, and—more important—is it helping or hindering? Do you wear your masks to keep you safe, keep you on a path to what you think you need or want? What would happen if your titles—of race, or singledom, or executive status—were lifted? Then who are you and what do you do to build a life that is meaningful?

We put on masks to protect ourselves from judgment. But we have to come to a point where we just don't care, where we have the courage to just say, "If you love me and you're in my inner pride, you won't care who I am without the label." In fact, the truth and beauty of it all is that those who love you and are in that pride you have built probably see the authentic you before you do. Not only is it critical to do this for ourselves, but it sets an example for our children to pursue their best selves and their best lives.

Start peeking out from the confines of your mask, even the mask of strength, by remembering something author Susan Ann Darley wrote for InnerSelf.com. The next time you are about to cast a quick judgment, ask yourself the following questions: Is it true? Is it useful? Is it necessary? This could work when casting judgment on ourselves. Further, she says that the key to removing labels is to begin by valuing yourself. How do we even begin to find the courage to do that, especially if so many things have gone wrong and so many mistakes have been made? By repeating to ourselves that we are not our experiences and we are not our mistakes.

"That very truth," Darley writes, "when deeply felt, will prevent you from devaluing yourself or others. People you might have walked away from in the past because of hasty judgments might even become wonderful new friends. And never again will you be intimidated or influenced by the judgments of others. What people think of you will become none of your business.

"You will be too busy designing the life you truly want. The power of constructive love will then be yours to build with as you wish."

Presence of Resources:

The ability to recognize and manage resources, financial or otherwise, while teaching children the wisdom and rewards of delayed gratification, innovation, self-regulation, and wise planning.

V

Presence of Resources

Introduction

A big part of financial freedom is having your heart and mind free from worry about the what-ifs of life.

—Su*z*e Orman

When I was growing up, finances were the business of adults. While I certainly had a sense of where my parents stood on the income scale, I never was told how much we had, and I dared not ask. My "job" was to go to school and do well; the job of my parents was to take care of me, and how much money they earned was none of my beeswax.

While the stories within this section from my own experiences, and those of many others, showcase some of the ways we manage to balance finances and come to terms with our financial lives, it is my observation that there are two opposing ways of handling money that can create problems: We either overshare and overburden our children, creating money neurotics who become fearful about their security, regardless of whether they happen to be secure; or we spoil our kids out of guilt, trying to overcompensate for whatever it is we think is a void in their lives, trying to "buy" their love or distract them from their circumstances. The problem here, aside from the ludicrous idea that love can be bought, is we usually don't have the money but charge away anyway, burying ourselves in credit card debt and missing out on the opportunities to give our children what they really are craving: emotional security through presence and connection. As the Reverend Dr. Martin Luther King Jr. said, "Our children need our presence, not our presents."

Therefore, having Presence of Resources becomes less about fiscal security and more about emotional well-being as we rise to the challenge of providing for our families.

Ninety percent of single-parent families are headed by women, and not surprisingly, single mothers whose children still live with them have the highest poverty rate, no matter the demographic. According to a paper by Jacqueline Kirby, MS, at The Ohio State University, mother-only families are more likely to be poor "because of the lower earning capacity of women, inadequate public assistance and childcare subsidies, and lack of enforced child support from nonresidential families." Kirby goes on to write, "The median annual income for female-headed households with children under six years old is roughly one-fourth that of two-parent families. However, the number of children per family unit is generally comparable, approximately two per household."

So why *wouldn't* we be losing sleep?

Finances are so complex because how we deal with and relate to money is dependent on so many emotional and social components. Just as the relationship we might have with food, with phobia, with animals, and so on, is somewhat shaped on our past experiences and personal lens, so is our money personality. I was often worried— no, *panicked*—about how I would make ends meet and sustain the life my husband Wes and I had plotted for our children. The thing that helped me stay focused was asking myself what kind of money personality I wanted my children to have when they grew up. I didn't want them to see me struggling to the point where they would choose careers motivated by salary scales or penny-pinch to the point of annoyance, but I also didn't want to shelter them from the realities of money, or lean away from teaching them how to be responsible with it. Achieving middle ground in this sense offers financial freedom, in my opinion, because you and your children are neither tethered to the evil money nor blind to its bounty.

I have my practical reasons why Presence of Resources remains one of the steadfast values of my life, like being able to buy a home or a car, or being able to send my kids to the schools and colleges best suited to their needs and talents, or not having to worry about where the next meal will come from, but being present in this value also is super critical to ward against mental and emotional distress. According to Kirby, income loss affects the well-being of children indirectly through the negative impact on family relations and parenting. Many studies have reported the link between economic stress and mental health. But as Kirby writes, "Financial strain is one of the strongest predictors of depression in single parents. Higher levels of depression is predictive of more punitive disciplinary practices and decreased parental nurturance, support, and satisfaction with the parenting role. The chronic strains of poverty combined with task overload significantly increases vulnerability to new life stressors. Poor single mothers often experience a cycle of hopelessness and despair, which is detrimental to both themselves and their children."

No doubt you have been there, as have I. And no doubt you are rolling your eyes at the findings of Kirby, thinking, *Yeah, no kidding, I could've told you that,* but I reiterate her study here because being mindful about all of the resources available to you can alleviate the insidious effects that money (too much without a value system or none at all) has on all of us.

I'm no Suze Orman, but I want you empowered, not depressed; fiscally conservative and creative with solving money issues, not ripped off by con artists who want to "loan" you money or provide a can't-miss scheme to some quick pie-in-the-sky money windfall. Presence of

Resources allows you to prioritize basic needs, get ahead even when you think you don't have the means, set monetary goals that you can attain, spend your time being happy instead of depressed, learn to find the resources you are entitled to in order to get ahead, create precious moments with your children, and enjoy a functional relationship with money. Your books will be balanced, so you can cash in on life!

A Blank Canvas

Coming out of your comfort zone is tough in the beginning, chaotic in the middle, and awesome in the end . . . because in the end it shows you a whole new world!

—Manoj Arora

After I left my first marriage to Bill and moved into the basement of the house Rae Carole and her mother, Barbara, shared, I poked out my chest, thinking I had finally shed the cloak of dependency and become my own woman. I had found the courage to leave my unsatisfying marriage in search of happiness and more stability for Nikki and me. And even though I had moved miles away from the childcare conveniently located in the same apartment building we lived in with Bill, my new regular work hours enabled me to keep the woman who had cared for Nikki during the weekdays since she was six weeks old, thus maintaining a sense of continuity for Nikki. My promotion from a news assistant who had to come in at 6 AM to a public affairs researcher not only gave me a nine-to-five shift but also provided a pay increase that was extremely helpful as I set out on my own. My salary allowed me to pay the babysitter, buy groceries, and give rent to Rae Carole, which she had significantly reduced. At the end of the day, I still had a little something left over to keep my hair done and Nikki in clean diapers.

But as comfortable as it was, in the six months I lived there I had to admit to myself that despite physically moving from one location to another, I still hadn't transitioned from the financial comfort zones I had known for years. I grew up in my parents' home, left for college on their dime, moved into a dorm with two other roommates, got married to a business major who took care of all the bills and literally gave me an "allowance" every week. Other than a car payment, which I paid monthly with money orders, I hadn't established a credit history and I didn't have a savings or checking account. Hell, I didn't even know how to balance a checkbook! I'd never had to fend for myself before and now, with a child dependent solely on me, it was time for me to toss the crutches and stand on my own.

The dilemma I faced, like most single mothers, was my willingness to trade my physical and emotional dependence on Rae Carole for the financial independence that I needed in the long term. I had never really tested my own resourcefulness and stamina, and I wasn't sure I had the wherewithal to venture out of the limits I had boxed myself into. Left to my own devices, I didn't know what I was capable of doing on my own. I instinctively knew that if I was to authentically achieve the maturity and presence Nikki would need me to have down the road, moving had to be my next step.

That spring I found a beautiful first-floor, two-bedroom garden apartment in Rockville, Maryland. Rockville's close enough to be considered a suburb of Washington, DC, but far away enough that you could get more space for the money. Fortunately, with the history of my car payments and a steady paycheck in hand, I had enough credit to sign a lease with my own name on the bottom line for the first time in my twenty-five years of life. It was substantially more than the $200 a month I was paying Rae Carole and I wasn't getting child support yet, but I was determined to figure out a way to make my dollars match my needs.

Moving from the basement and out on my own was actually terrifying, even more so than when I left Bill. What was I thinking, taking on this responsibility all by myself? What if I fell behind in the rent and we were kicked out? Where would we go? How embarrassed would I be? Safety was an issue too. I never really worried about that when I lived with someone else, but now I had to be the lone sentinel and protector. I was more than a little leery of being on the first floor, but that was the only unit available. The rental agent assured me that the security bar at the bottom of the patio doors would prevent any burglary, so at this point I had no alternative but to send up a little prayer for reassurance and believe her.

I had left my husband with only a suitcase for me, one for Nikki, a portable crib, and no furniture. During my time at Rae Carole's, I did go back for our clothes and some of Nikki's toys. Once I knew I had the apartment, Nikki and I went shopping together to purchase a queen bed, a bed frame, and a youth bed with bars, which Nikki loved because it made her three-year-old self feel so grown up. That's all we had. The rest was a blank canvas.

That first night, looking around, instead of feeling pathetic because I couldn't afford anything else, I realized that a blank canvas was exactly what I needed. In the words of author Shannon L. Alder, "All great beginnings start in the dark, when the moon greets you to a new day at midnight." A new day was beginning for us and I needed not to fear it, but to embrace it.

In the months that followed, I relied on my ingenuity and worked out a budget based on my new position at WMAL Radio as a public affairs researcher. At work I was a super-sleuth researcher, efficient and effective. At home I was a novice, teaching myself how to balance a budget and a checkbook simultaneously, things I had never done before. I knew you couldn't spend more than you brought in, but determining priorities proved to be my immediate challenge. So I made a list of priorities. Nikki proved to be my partner in this too, weighing in on which piece of furniture we needed to buy first. Kitchen table or living room sofa? Never a shrinking violet, she had definite opinions and actually some solid reasons why! Although she wasn't the deciding factor, I certainly kept her opinions in mind as I started pinning my furniture shopping to all the holiday sales days—Memorial

Day, Fourth of July, Labor Day, Veterans Day, Thanksgiving, and Christmas. By the new year I had all my essential furniture pieces.

I limited my credit cards to two—one had to be paid off monthly, and the other allowed me to extend payments for larger items if I needed that flexibility. I will admit that over the years the number of credit cards ballooned as I had more children and they started needing more and more, but at least in the beginning I was very disciplined—I had to be. If I didn't factor my credit card payments into my monthly budget, I knew I would run the risk of a late or missed payment—and those are the first steps to lowering my credit score. I didn't realize it then, but being a single mother made me more responsible financially.

I was by no means wealthy. It was paycheck-to-paycheck most of the time, but I was able to successfully manage the money I did bring into the household. That gave me the confidence in my ability to make it on my own and stop fearing the unknown. It meant a new-found respect for myself and my ability to grow in a way I could never be sure of before. It meant freedom from the belief that I had to find another man to "rescue me" from single motherhood. It meant that if and when this blossoming relationship with Wes developed into something else, I would be going into it based on our love, our compatibility, our joint aspirations, his love of Nikki, and our desire to spend the rest of our lives together.

I became very grateful for those days of watching every penny, sticking to a budget, planning every major purchase, and embracing deferred gratification as a gift rather than a failure to get what I wanted, when I wanted to get it. By learning these skills, then I was much more prepared, understanding, and hands-on with our finances when Wes and I eventually got married. We even ended up making a ritual around our finances, and in doing so we could find some pleasure in what usually is a stressful, mundane task.

Every payday, after we put the kids to bed, we would pop open a bottle of wine, put all the current bills in front of us, and decide what got paid and maybe what needed to wait until the next pay-day. But one thing we were absolutely committed to was "paying our-selves first," by putting at least $25 each pay period into our savings account. This was an idea that Wes picked up from a story he was working on about stabilizing family finances. Adapting the idea of paying yourself first to what we could afford, we got through paying our bills on time (well, most of the time), and we took turns as to who would update our monthly ledger and who would balance the checkbook. It became a bonding experience that we had fun doing, even as we went about the serious business of controlling the money we brought into our household. I never imagined that within five years this ritual would make it possible for me to pay for Wes's funeral with our accumulated savings, or that I would confidently revert to the role of managing the family finances alone.

I was able to teach my kids the importance of learning these skills sooner rather than later in their lives. Just as Nikki shadowed me on our early apartment decorating schemes, after their dad died I knew I had to be even more diligent with the children about sticking to a budget, especially since I wasn't working full-time and instead relied on Social Security and freelance and part-time writing assignments. I talked to the three of them about budgeting, and made it clear that much of our money was going into their education so other things might have to wait. Did they love the idea? No, but eventually, as they grew out of the typical me, myself, and I stage, they understood. I also tried to get a jump on common financial traps for young people.

Before cell phones became ubiquitous, I delayed getting phones for the kids until they learned to drive with the intent that it would be used only to communicate in case of an emergency. I also gave them a credit card that was linked to mine for them to use, again, in an emergency. That way I could monitor their spending. I could let them know right away that emergencies did not include "starving" on the way home from school, or not being able to pass up an incred-ible deal on a dress, blouse, or basketball sneakers. I found that their earlier introduction to how to use a credit card lessened the lure and novelty of the credit card offers that flood college campuses. It also allowed me to interact with them about interest rates and late fees in real time as opposed to conversations during school breaks and holidays. Today I am thrilled that my now grown children are much more financially savvy than I ever was at their age, and I could not be more pleased that they didn't have to start learning these financial survival skills at the age that I did.

It pleases me even more that my grandkids are starting their financial literacy at an even younger age. When they reached three and five, we gave them a piggy bank that I first discovered on the Money Savvy Generation website years ago when I was working on financial literacy issues with communities around the country through the Annie E. Casey Foundation. It's a sturdy plastic piggy bank with a stopper in each foot, which is connected to four separate compartments that have these words printed on top: SPEND, SAVE, INVEST, and DONATE. Whenever Mia and James get some change, they work with their parents to select which slot to deposit the coins. This allows their mom and dad to talk about what the various words mean and why selecting one over the other makes the most sense at that moment. It's a fun teaching tool that's already beginning to help them understand the value and purpose of money. To find out where to purchase your own bank, please visit this book's website, www .power-ofpresence.com.

LESSON FROM A LIONESS: *Know how to control your money before it controls you.*

Financial freedom should start early, at home, and on a personal level. There are great resources online that won't bog you down in nitty-gritty details, but that share great ideas for simple spending reductions we can make throughout our daily lives. You will find some of these resources at www.power-ofpresence.com. I love asking around and seeing how people like to save money or ways they teach their own children the value of money.

- Talk to other lionesses about the ideas they have implemented or advice they have. There are more and more ways to comparison-shop for both the things we need and the novelties we desire.
- Don't be afraid to say no to your children, even though it completely stinks to have to disappoint them. If it is helpful, and if they are old enough to understand, provide context by showing children some numbers or bank statements so they understand more fully what the family's circumstances are. But at the same time, don't overburden them with the fear that the family is in such dire straits, the only alternative is for them to take matters of bringing money into the household into their own hands.
- I truly believe that even if it is five bucks spared, it is important to have your own personal rainy-day fund first. Having that savings, albeit small, after Wes died, taught me how powerless I am over the unexpected and that preparation, even in small doses, can prevent an onslaught of panic, debt, and self-doubt about being able to handle finances solo.

Champion for the Path to Financial Freedom: The Hilary Pennington Story

You must tell your money how you want to live your life, and not the other way around.

—Manoj Arora

Hilary Pennington spent much of her time as a toddler shuttling back and forth between her father's native South Africa and her mother's hometown of St. Louis, Missouri. As a white child of relative means, she got a glimpse of two worlds thousands of miles apart but eerily similar: South Africa's apartheid and segregated St. Louis. But by four years old, the back and forth stopped for her, her younger brother, and her pregnant mother, Vanessa, when her father was diagnosed with aplastic anemia and they all returned to St. Louis for his extended medical treatments.

While they provided invaluable support to the young family, Hilary says her grandparents didn't know quite what to make of her mom. She was the first woman in her family to go to college; the first to move to the big city, New York; and not until she was thirty-six did she meet and fall in love with a poor, unknown teacher from South Africa. Hilary calls her mom a visionary, a woman ahead of her time, determined to make a mark in the world. But in that moment, she was a caretaker, a pregnant mother of two, and a woman struggling to keep her family together.

And perhaps that's why Vanessa thought it a stroke of luck that on the day she went into labor, her husband was already scheduled for his regular blood transfusions—in the same hospital. Hilary says what happened next changed their family forever.

They put my mom on a gurney and in a room, and literally forgot about her. The doctors gave her something to speed up and intensify the labor but no one stayed around to monitor her. By the time they came back to my mom, the baby was in distress and my sister had already suffered oxygen deprivation and brain damage. It wasn't noticeable at first. She was just this beautiful little baby girl and my dad was there and they rejoiced over the birth. My dad died a few months later, and it wasn't until some months after when Tracy was diagnosed developmentally disabled.

As the family emerged from the impact of this double tragedy, Hilary says her mom made the conscious decision to take control of their lives by moving out of her grandparents' home and into their own space. It was only a few blocks away so they still had the babysitting support all young families need, especially single-parent families with a child with special needs. This was especially important as her mother learned how to raise Tracy without a partner. It was, however, enough to provide the independence her mom needed to really embrace her role as head of household.

As Hilary spoke about this phase of her mother's life, I could so relate to what she was feeling. I remember a moment when I sat in the relatively empty garden apartment that Nikki and I moved into after living with Rae Carole. I had just laid a piece of remnant carpet in my living room, and as I sat in the middle of the floor there was an overwhelming feeling of accomplishment. *I bought this. I brought it home. I laid it. I did it myself and it is mine.* In that simple moment, I knew that armed with my job, my education, and the support I enjoyed from family and friends, I could make it as a single mom. But I knew the advantages I enjoyed for financial stability were not available to everyone. So did Hilary's mom.

In the 1970s my mother started something called Continuing Education for Women. And it was during that amazing decade with the huge upheaval in society, and the idea was to help women who wanted to learn more to go back to school to get either a degree or a certificate. Mom convinced Washington University to let her develop this curriculum, although they would not let her use university property in the daytime, so she had to teach her classes at night. When she didn't have a babysitter she would take all three of us with her. She also got other professors involved by convincing them to help teach the classes. Mom wanted women to develop their minds and develop themselves as leaders. It was one of the first certificate programs at the university, and she became one of the founding members of the board of what became CAEL—Council for Adult and Experiential Learning, where a person could assess prior learning so she may not have to start out as a freshman in college. My mother was indeed remarkable.

But even as Vanessa pioneered in this area, Hilary says she always knew her mom sacrificed what could have been a huge career to be present for her and her siblings. For example, Vanessa negotiated a three-quarter appointment at the university so she could work school hours and be home for them. Rather than go on the speaker's circuit during vacations or holidays, she took that time off to spend what Hilary calls plenty of quality time with them. She fought for every possible opportunity she could for them.

My sister was born before the Americans with Disabilities Act that provides for mainstreaming children with disabilities. My mom sent her to some really good private schools for kids with cognitive disabilities when she was little but there was nothing when she became a high school student. Then she was placed in a special school district in St. Louis, which was basically a dumping ground for the city's poorest children. It was despicable, awful, shameful. My mother finally took her out and worked out some kind of apprenticeship with the children's hospital for Tracy.

But Hilary says her mother was furious about the kids, most of whom were kids of color, left behind because they didn't have that kind of access to opportunities. As much as she could, she advocated for them as well. Looking back Hilary says that this situation and how her mother handled it helped shape many of her later views on education equality.

While she fought hard for all of us, she demanded a lot. In addition to working hard at school, we had chores that had to be done even if it meant missing the big football game! At the time it was hard for me;

being the oldest there were the typical mother-daughter conflicts. I
wanted to differentiate myself and grow up to be different from her.

But the exact opposite happened, at least as far as educational attainment, gender equity, and financial resourcefulness go. Hilary so embraced her mom's values that she went on to Yale, Oxford University, the Yale School of Management, and later the Episcopal Divinity School.

As Hilary continued down her own career path, she also realized how much of her mother's values around economic security she had internalized and how badly she wanted to put them into action. In 1983 Hilary co-founded Jobs for the Future, then a small nonprofit working with a few states to figure out their workforce needs, help them find skilled workers, and help those workers move into higher-wage jobs. Today, Jobs for the Future works in more than 120 communities across forty-two states, dedicated to helping fix what it calls the "leaks" in the education-to-workforce pipeline. As its president and CEO, Hilary helped it become one of the most influential and respected organizations in the country around issues of education, youth transitions, workforce development, access to opportunities, and future work requirements.

When given the opportunity to put the force of even bigger dollars behind her ideas, Hilary became the top higher education official at the Bill and Melinda Gates Foundation. After six years there, she moved across the country to the Ford Foundation as its Vice President of Education, Creativity, and Free Expression. At Ford she is marrying all the parts of her experiences, beliefs, values, and passion for economic security, education, and gender equality globally.

While Vanessa passed away a few years ago, the lessons Hilary learned from her about values, dedication to passions, presence for one's family, and the special place single moms hold in society preparing the next generation will live on forever in her heart and through her work.

LESSON FROM A LIONESS: *No matter how small your wallet, have a big mouth.*

Financial independence isn't about having as much money as a two-parent home; it's about trusting yourself to manage the resources you have and being able to provide for your family's health, safety, and growth. Maintaining presence required Vanessa to take a less prestigious job, but she still turned it into something huge beyond belief! She sacrificed some of her ambition in order to have summers off. She taught her children, by her example, how to work and fight and that education is key to breaking any negative cycle. She spent a lifetime working for economic parity for women, a passion she passed on to her daughter.

Vanessa used her voice to gain access to as many resources as she could for her special-needs daughter, before the benefits of the Americans with Disabilities Act (information about ADA can be found online at www.power-ofpresence.com).

Not everyone finds it natural to fight for themselves or speak their mind, even for the sake of their children. How can you begin to speak up and speak out when it just isn't your nature? How can women defeat the double bind that says a woman who doesn't speak up gets lost in the shuffle and the one who does is a raving bitch? In his TED Talk, "How to Speak Up for Yourself," Adam Galinsky explains that it can be easier to stand up for what you believe when you're doing it on behalf of others. "When [women] advocate for others," says Galinsky, "they discover their own range and expand it in their own mind. They become more assertive. This is sometimes called 'the mama bear effect.' Like a mama bear defending her cubs, when we advocate for others, we can discover our own voice."

Galinsky believes that what we need to do is to be mama bears to ourselves. It makes sense, as we have all heard the common wisdom that people should treat themselves as they would their best friend, yet it is one of the most difficult things to do, no matter how logical it seems. "When I've asked the question around the world when people feel comfortable speaking up, the number one answer is: 'When I have social support in my audience; when I have allies,'" Galinsky explains. "So we want to get allies on our side. How do we do that? Well, one of the ways is be a mama bear. When we advocate for others, we expand our range in our own eyes and the eyes of others, but we also earn strong allies." In other words, advocating for others is a win-win: It increases your stature in your own eyes and others', and it expands your army of allies.

If people understand you are motivated by goodness and genuine need, articulate it with intelligence and humility, notice how your opinion or gesture is perceived by the receiver, ask for help and advice, and advocate for others—so you don't come off as you fighting for numero uno—you won't have to be afraid to speak up and step up for the rights of your family.

Becoming a Single Grandma: The Ona Caldwell Story

From what we get, we can make a living; what we give, however, makes a life.

—Arthur Ashe

Ona Mae Gooch Caldwell's rented two-story house stands in the midst of one of the South Side of Chicago's toughest neighborhoods. At night, the sounds of police sirens rushing past often drown out the sound of gunfire. Ona didn't start her life in these streets but in the rural town of Water Valley, Mississippi, where she picked cotton and produce as a sharecropper, as everyone in her family had always done. She dropped out of school in the fifth grade to work in the fields full-time, though she kept reading everything she could get her hands on and repeated simple math problems daily so she wouldn't forget how. She married at seventeen, and from that union came seven children. She worked the fields every day and learned to drive the trucks and the trailers. She learned the secrets of growing healthy crops and how to get the most out of the soil. But what she learned in the fields was compromised by what was happening at home. Her husband abused her often and after one very severe beating, Ona fled for her life.

Saving money wasn't possible as a sharecropper but she was confident that she could take care of herself and her kids if she could get a fresh start. But that wouldn't happen in Mississippi. Using $35 her father got for selling a cow, Ona took a bus to Memphis and then a train to Chicago to live with her older brother. She left her children with her mother so she could find a job and save some money to send for them. She was twenty-seven years old.

Ona worked several menial jobs at a time, sometimes late into the night. Eventually she saved enough to bring her children, one by one, to live with her. She also brought some of the country life to the city, planting in whatever patches of land she could find in the lots behind her rented homes. This provided the fresh fruits and vegetables they needed to supplement whatever store-bought food she could afford.

The beatings she endured in her married life forever jaded her view of the institution and although she gave birth to six more children, she never remarried. She told me she probably scared everyone off because she would say, "If you ever put your hands on me, you'll be one dead SOB!"

But that made her a single mother of thirteen. An obvious question for her was: How did she do it? Ona had clear and definitive answers. She had faith in God that there would always be enough food to eat and a place to sleep. She also had faith in herself that she could manage her family as long as she enforced strict rules: She simply had to or they would all be lost in chaos. Going to church every Sunday was another part of the family routine. Her grandson Robert says that there were the usual rules about taking out the garbage, doing the dishes, and staying out past curfew, but surprisingly the rules she was most adamant about, at least for him, was that there would be no television until all the homework was done and she saw it. He said she may not have understood what it said because she didn't go past the fifth grade, but she knew what was neat and what wasn't. If she thought the work was sloppy, Robert said she would tear it up and they'd have to start all over again.

She relied on her older children to help the household run smoothly while she worked, as well as to keep the peace. She admitted that sometimes she felt she was running a military operation with harsh consequences and concrete rewards being issued every day. But it worked. As she spoke to me, it was clear that she was proud that all her children had escaped serious trouble with the law, no small feat in the neighborhoods where she could afford to live. The only one she had trouble with was Lucille, who rebelled in her teen years and eventually became a mom at sixteen.

Now eighty-eight years old, five foot two, and 130 pounds, Ona carries herself with a grace and confidence that make her seem younger and taller. She never licked a habit she picked up when she was six years old, chewing tobacco, because she says it calms her. But emotion gripped her nonetheless as she told me about the events of more than twenty years ago, when before the sun made its debut, a loud knock at the front door jolted her from a deep sleep.

Well, it was early in the morning. The doorbell rang and my son Gregory answered the door. I was still in the bed. I slipped on a housecoat and came downstairs. He and the police was sitting there and Gregory said, "You gotta sit down." I said, for what? He said, "Because they're going to tell you some bad news." Then I just told them, I said, go on tell me what is what. So the policeman said, "Your daughter was killed. She was run over by a car." I could say nothing. They said they would take me to the morgue to view her body.

The police said her children were at home, by themselves, and they would take me there. Lucille had seven children. It's been so long. The two youngest were still in diapers.

Ona told me that as she drove in the backseat of the police car to her daughter's house, there was never any doubt in her mind what she was going there to do. It was her moment of unconditional clarity, although she'd never dreamed she would be taking these next steps well into her sixties.

They were still asleep when I got there. The oldest one woke up first. "Grandmomma, what you doing here?" [I said,] I'm looking for some clothes so you can come home with me. Then they were all awake and asking "Why? What happened?" I finally said, Your Momma's been killed and y'all are coming home with me. They started screaming at once and I did my best to comfort them, even though I wanted to scream and holler myself. But I didn't have time for that. I just kept saying to myself I don't know how I'm going do it or what I'm going do, but as long as I'm living they were going to stay together. So that morning Janail, Brandon, Mitchell, Nicky, Corvette, Robert, and Austin came home with me for good.

I prayed all the way and every day and night after that, Lord, let me raise these kids, together, the best I can.

Ona remembered how she had to separate her own children to bring them one by one to Chicago. She was determined that her grandchildren would grow up together.

I was sick in my heart for a long, long time but I knew I had to pull myself together for the kids. For a while, some folks thought I was crazy. They said, "You can't keep these kids." No, they gonna stay here with me. They're not going no place. "Well how you gonna do it?" I said, If I sleep, they sleep with me. If I eat, they can eat. We'll make it some kind of way.

From then on I went to everyplace where they were giving out free food. My church helped and then I worked at the food pantry and stuff like that. I wasn't getting paid but I could bring canned food home and I didn't have to buy it.

Then I did what I did back in Mississippi. I grew food. I had a backyard so I grew tomatoes, peppers, okra, turnips, mustard and collard greens, and sage. I grew it all 'cause I knew how to do it. I even grew some cotton once, to remind me of where I come from.

Nights were hard but everyone had a place to sleep. I had two bedrooms, a living room, and dining room. I turned my dining room into a bedroom. I had a big bed on this side and a half bed on this side. I gave them my room and I slept on the couch. The two in diapers slept with me.

I did get help from the city. I went to the aid office and the lady who was helping me said she was on public aid herself. I think she was getting $700 and something a month. She said she got that much because she was the head of the house. I said, What the hell do you think I am? I bet you think I'm crazy, but when I get angry I have to speak my mind. I said, "I'm the head of the house too." At that time they wasn't giving me but $300 for all the kids. I may not have gotten past fifth grade but I know how to fight for my kids. After I opened my mouth, I finally started getting $500.

That was enough to keep clothes on the kids and a roof over our heads. And if anyone had anything to say about my kids, I said, If the kids can't stay, I can't stay either. And I never been put out. I've never been threatened to be put out or nothing.

I asked Ona what sustained her through her abusive marriage, raising her own children as a single mother, the death of her daughter, and the years after raising her second family of grandkids.

She told me about her aunt Alice, who was also a single mom

making it on her own. Alice was always there to listen to Ona, encouraging her to leave her abusive husband and to stand up for herself and her children. Alice was a role model, showing Ona that it was possible to be independent and keep her household functioning. Ona also turned to her faith regularly.

When times were hardest the only thing I did, I just prayed for the Lord to help me. God helped me out of that marriage and got me here to Chicago. With my kids and later with my grandkids, I never had any real trouble with any of them. Lucille had her issues but didn't none of them steal or take nothing didn't belong to them or nothing like that. Ain't never been in jail or nothing. I did my best, and I know it was only with God's help.

I asked Ona if there was any one moment in her life that made all the sacrifices, all the planning, all the marshaling of resources to make her families, as mother and grandmother, worth it.

When I brought my grandkids home with me that morning, the next to the youngest one, Robert, was only two years old. Now remember, I didn't get past the fifth grade. Well, two years ago I got to see Robert graduate from college. He's the first in our family to do that. I didn't want him to go away at first, but he got scholarships and loans and we made it work. He did real well too. When he walked across the stage and got his degree, he looked to me in the audience and pointed to me while he touched his degree. At that moment I was so proud! It made everything worthwhile.

You know, it seems like just right now I can go to sleep and I'll have a dream about God. And I think back on my life and I'll say, "The Lord helped me. Took me through this and that and brought me to be eighty-eight years old." All through the day and all through the night I say, "Thank you Jesus. I know you won't leave me now."

Never has. Never will.

LESSON FROM A LIONESS: *Embrace your strength and don't settle for less than you deserve.*

Despite her deep grief and advanced age, Ona had enough faith in herself and her God that her strength transcended reason, quelling any doubts that she might not be strong enough or be smart enough or have enough money to take in all her grandchildren. Ona heard her aunt's voice in her ear from decades before that she could take care of herself and her children; just as important, she knew she did not deserve to be abused.

Advocating for the family can be a constant challenge. Ona was able to provide for her family because she got so creative about where she found her resources. She knew that income from her work wasn't the only way to support the family—in fact, it would never be enough. So she expanded her search for resources—she wasn't afraid to tend her garden or seek help from wherever she could find it, be it at church, from family, or from social services. She was determined to do whatever it took to get the help she needed and to fight for the resources she was entitled to. No matter what your circumstances, you must believe that you are smart enough, strong enough, and creative enough to succeed as a head of household, no matter who you are caring for. Like Ona, you must gather as much information as you can and be willing to fight for the resources that you are entitled to. According to the advocacy organization Generations United, there are more than 1.5 million grandmothers responsible for raising their grandchildren. Today there is increasing attention on how to help these "grandfamilies" thrive in the midst of economic hardships and the traumatic incidents that often cause the guardianship by the grandparent in the first place. For more on Generations United and the increasing role of and resources available to grandfamilies, please visit www.power-ofpresence.com.

But before Ona could have the confidence to fight for the well-being of her grandchildren, she had to fight for her own survival. What she learned from the words of her aunt was that you must not settle for an unhealthy home environment out of fear of not being able to be the head of a household. Staying in a dangerous or unhealthy relationship is simply not worth it. There are services and resources out there that can help. Most notable is the National Domestic Violence Hotline, which began operations in September 1994. As of 2006, the hotline had logged more than four million callers. This is a highly confidential and trusted resource for any person who's a victim of physical, mental, emotional, verbal, or sexual abuse. Additional information can be found on www.power-ofpresence.com, but I think it bears repeating here. It is a national resource and will ask you only for your age, gender (yes, men get abused too), race, and location. It will help you start thinking about a plan to leave the abusive situation safely. The number is 1-800-799-SAFE. The website is www.thehotline.org, but if you are still in your home, be sure to delete your browser history. The hotline also has an online chat feature that will not tell you what to do but will help you figure out what your options are and provide the local information to make it happen.

For Every Child There Is a Window

Knowledge rooted in experience shapes what we value and as a consequence how we know what we know as well as how we use what we know.
—*bell hooks*

As much as I wanted to maintain my independence after Wes died, I made the decision to move back home with my parents as a way to stabilize our financial situation and to expand the size of the pride that could help me with the kids on a day-to-day basis. It was a move that gave my budget some breathing room once all three kids were of school age. It also gave my children consistent male interaction that I hoped would be a mirror for what I believed men should be and how girls and women should be treated by men.

Living with my parents on a daily basis allowed the kids to see what a man has to do to keep a marriage going for almost half a century. They saw how a man works and provides for his family, yet can be present for the family's important events. They witnessed little things, like the loving way my parents spoke to each other. They called each other "dear," so the frequent question around the family when wondering where they were was, "Where are the dears?" My mother and father were always laughing with each other, sharing glances, and finishing each other's sentences. Did they have arguments? Of course, but seeing how quickly and how well disagreements were resolved were lessons for a happy marriage in and of themselves. And when it came to keeping the household going, almost everything was done side by side. Chores were shared, like cooking in our tiny kitchen or their daily bed-making ritual: They would start with the sheets, blanket, and bedspread pulled to the bottom of the bed. Mom and Dad, standing at opposite sides, made sure each piece of cloth was hospital-corner-ready at the bottom. They pulled up each piece, one by one, to the top of the bed until each was flat and perfectly horizontal with the headboard. Then they would take the bedspread and fold it back to the size of a pillow plus three inches so that after the pillows were placed, they could tuck those three inches under them, creating the picture-perfect bed. To me, it was routine because I had seen it all my life, but for Wes its message was clear: There is no such thing as "man's work" or "woman's work." Life's a partnership.

A few months after we got to New York, my younger brother Howard and his wife, Pam, moved back to the Bronx and lived in our basement apartment. Life got even sweeter for Wes. Howard was intelligent, with an always ready smile, an air of sincerity, and a sexy swagger that made him an instant magnet in any room he entered. He made friends wherever he went, and people naturally felt comfortable opening up to him. And that's exactly what Wes did. He and my brother spent endless hours exchanging views about sports, music, and the latest designers of men's clothes. Because of Howard, Wes sought to adapt the styles of Hugo Boss, Gucci, Members Only, and Nike's Air Jordan. Of course, he couldn't afford the real things but the style was planted, ready to sprout whenever the opportunity connected with the money.

As Howard's career in the pharmaceutical industry took off and he had to travel more, their time together became less and less. Around the same time, Grace Reformed Church in Brooklyn coaxed my dad out of retirement. As interim pastor, he and my mom began living in the church's parsonage most of the time. As Wes turned eleven, he barely saw these two men who had become so important in his life. Once again, the reality of single motherhood presented its ever-present sobering dilemma: that no matter how hard we try, a mom can't be a dad. We can teach our sons many things, but we can't model the way a man walks through the world, or the way he shaves; we can't participate in father-son events.

Suddenly on his own, without his primary male role models around, Wes took on the persona of the Fresh Prince of the Bronx, a man-child in a household of females. Things like cleaning up his room were beneath him. He would hold court on the phone: As one call with a classmate or neighborhood friend ended, another began. While it wasn't until years later that I found out that he would pick and choose when he attended a full day of school, I could see that his grades were dropping. When I lectured him about a report card dotted with C's, he said with a shrug, "Hey, I passed."

I always told the kids that all they had to do was their best, and I would be okay with that. But I knew this wasn't my son's best, far from it. Plus, there was an anger and a hardness that was seeping into his personality, and that worried me just as much. He was crying out for a course correction, but all the punishments I devised didn't have any effect. I met his defiance over doing homework with pulling the plug of his video games. I tried to limit his time on the phone but that wasn't enforceable because I wasn't at home during those critical afternoon hours. Our arguments were always the same:

"Wes, you need to give yourself a chance to see what you can do."

"I know what I can do and I'm doing fine."

"No one is paying you to be the class clown. You're in school to learn."

"Mom, I am doing the best I can."

"No, you're not."

"I am!"

I worried that I was losing my ability to influence him. The neighborhood around us was changing. I no longer felt comfortable walking the three-quarters of a mile from our house to the subway every day because so many of the shops on our main street were now gated and graffiti-adorned. I knew the kids he was hanging out with when he got home as most of their mothers knew my family, but there seemed to be more going on with them than any of their parents knew.

I thought I could counteract negative influences creeping into the neighborhood by his attending Riverdale Country, one of the most rigorously academic schools in all of New York City. The problem was I placed him in a vortex of perception and reality and forced him to wear a mask. He was learning more about rap at Riverdale than he was on the so-called mean streets of the Bronx! At school he had to play a role, and he was getting a thrill out of trying on the persona of a gangster. In the neighborhood he began to extend that persona, flirting with the gang life, tagging and hanging around the basketball courts with the kinds of older kids who lead the young ones into trouble.

There were also financial implications for the different masks

Wes was wearing. At the time, Riverdale's upper school tuition was about $7,000. There was no discount for multiple kids so I had to find that tuition—for him and Shani—every year, no matter what. I didn't care how many jobs I had to work or how many hours it took, because the most important job I had was to provide the education the kids needed to chart their own course. As long as they were doing their best, I never resented a moment of working. But as Wes was becoming more and more disinterested in school, I began wondering why I was wasting my money on him. As his disinterest grew, so did my resentment.

As a result, our relationship started to decline. We seemed to be fighting all the time. He was never disrespectful to my parents because he knew that would be a line no one in the family would allow him to cross, but he was disrespectful to me. When I asked him to do something, he was deliberately non-responsive. As we edged into seventh grade, and I used my maternal guilt and persistence to get him off the couch, when he stood up I realized something. He was getting bigger than me, and he was physically stronger.

Now, it was drilled into his head that under no circumstances should he hit a girl. So while I never feared that he would consciously hit me, if ever rage took over I knew we were getting to a point where I was no longer a physical match for him. If I didn't get control of him soon with my words and wit, I'd never be able to do so as he grew. I was terrified that he was slipping into a place and an attitude that was so harsh that if he got much deeper in, it would be impossible for me to reach him.

Honestly, I didn't want to send him away, but my mind was increasingly going to military school. I was also fearful of the kind of son I'd get back if he spent high school there. He was always such a fun-loving and playful boy, and most of the military people you see on television don't smile. They seem rigid and aloof, which is something I didn't see in Wes and didn't want him to grow into. That was one fear, but the fear that I would lose him to the streets and that because of that he'd never fulfill his true potential was much greater. I would miss Wes terribly if I lost him to a boarding school, but I realized it would be a lot tougher to lose him completely. I saw the words of Frederick Douglass before me: "It is easier to raise strong children than to repair broken men."

I started researching other schools. I talked to friends, relatives, and educators who knew Wes and who might know a school that would better fit his needs. About two weeks into my investigation, Doris Atkins, a longtime friend of my parents, suggested Valley Forge Military Academy, a school in Pennsylvania that had had a powerful and positive impact on her son, whom she'd also had to raise alone when her husband died. She suggested that VFMA's summer camp could provide a simulated dry run for what school would be like for Wes. In two weeks I packed him up and his soccer ball and drove him to spend the next four weeks there.

Summer camp went great. When Wes got home, there was something about him that was decidedly different. He had filled out significantly, a testament to the daily calisthenics and sports. Beyond the physical there was a maturity of spirit that I saw. He no longer wore his defiance like armor. He was to begin Riverdale in a few weeks but if he failed to straighten up, Valley Forge would be there next year. I felt good that my threat of a future in military school now had a name.

The future, however, came one week later.

"Mrs. Moore, I'm Colonel Bowe, in the admissions office at Valley Forge," the deep voice on the other end of the phone said. "While your son was here for summer camp, he took one of our assessment tests and he did very, very well. We have an opening in our incoming class of cadets and we were wondering if you would be interested in enrolling him in Valley Forge for this school year?"

While one part of my brain was pleased that Wes had scored well enough to be admitted, the practical side said that there was no way

I could afford to send him there so soon. Just about every penny I made working, combined with the annuity I received after Wes's death, went to educating all three kids. Over the seven years Wes and Shani attended Riverdale, the financial aid office was my best friend, allowing me the flexibility to pay as my freelance money came in. I knew there was no way I could finish paying my current Riverdale balance and add on an even bigger bill from Valley Forge.

Even though I was almost positive what my answer would have to be, I thanked Colonel Bowe and told him I would have to get back to him.

For the next week I scrambled to see if there was any way I could pull together the money I needed to send him to Valley Forge. Then my mom, the consummate teacher, interrupted me from my calls to friends and my neighborhood bank and told me that in every child there is a window, a little opening when you can reach the child and change the way he or she sees the world and interacts with it. If you act at that moment, you can reel that child back in, but if you let your self-doubt control you—or even financial challenges—you're sunk. That moment, that open window, is unlikely to come again. She told me I had to trust that little voice inside me, the disturbance that told me this window for Wes was open now and likely just for a moment or two. If I didn't act, both of us might be lost to one another for years to come. She and my dad offered to get a second mortgage on their house to cover the first year. The second year, well, we'd have to face that when and if this was a fit for Wes.

With tears in my eyes I gave my parents one of the longest hugs I can remember. Then I called Colonel Bowe. "Yes," I told him, I was sending Wes to Valley Forge.

The next conversation was to tell Wes that he was going away to school. I hadn't told him about the possibility before because I really didn't think it would happen. But with the finances worked out, I braced myself. I knew he would be unhappy, but I wasn't prepared for the intensity of his reaction, which rapidly turned from disbelief to outrage when I first sat down with him at the kitchen counter to tell him.

"Are you kidding me? Camp was cool but I'm not going to that school," he said as though his was the last word on the matter.

"Wes, the last thing I want to do is to send you away, but right now I think this is the best place for you to see what you are really capable of doing."

"I said I'm not going," he said as he stiffened his twelve-year-old shoulders and stood up to storm out of the room.

Over the next few days, I filled out all the forms that were required and used my credit cards to shop for the items from a very long required supplies list. One evening, as I was sewing his name on practically everything he owned, he came into my room with a determined, almost military, stride.

"Mommy, we need to talk about this," he said loudly.

For the next hour he went through his own particular stages of grief: First, defiance. "I'm not going anywhere, Mommy. You know you can't get along without me here. You can't make me go." Then came the pleading. "I promise I'll do better. You know I can and I will. I promise!"

I wouldn't budge.

On the two-hour ride to Valley Forge that late August with his aunt Pam at the wheel, Wes just looked out the window from the backseat. As we approached the driveway where scores of families were saying goodbye to their sons, he looked pleadingly at me, and then at his aunt Pam, to see if he would be granted a last-minute reprieve. Receiving none, he unloaded his bags and boxes. He gave Pam and me goodbye hugs, but my hug noticeably lacked warmth.

As we walked to the parent orientation, he walked to the red doors of H Company, the residence hall for the youngest of the newly arrived, feeling, as he recalled later, abandoned. I tried to picture him in the bunk beds that night instead of his full-size bed in his room at home, and I felt tears begin to well up again. How could I bear not overhearing him talk to friends about a game-winning basketball shot or the newest rap song? I would no longer get his spontaneous bear hugs or the sloppy kisses he loved to plant on my neck. He could be so frustrating at times, but he touched every soft spot of my heart.

As the six-foot wrought-iron gates got smaller and smaller in the rearview mirror, I was grateful Pam was driving. She kept the car moving forward when every molecule in my body wanted me to turn around and take him home.

Less than a week later the phone rang at one o'clock in the morning. No call coming at that time of night is good news. My heart started racing. It was Wes, who had just failed at his fourth attempt at running away from Valley Forge. Rather than an immediate expulsion, the night tactical officer let him call me at home.

"Mommy, I don't like it here," he began. "I want to come home, and I promise I'll do better in school and I won't mess up in school or at home. I'll do anything you say..."

"Wes, you know I love you and I'd do anything for you," I interrupted, "but you've got to give the school a chance... you've got to give yourself a chance to see what you can do. Too many people sacrificed to get you there. You're staying." I never told him specifics about my parents getting a second mortgage or how I had to scrape together every dime left after paying his sisters' tuitions, denying them things that they wanted. That there were sacrifices made by others was enough information for him to know now that it was his turn to ante up.

Then I offered him a deal.

"After this year, I'll give you the choice," I said. "Do well and you can either stay there or come back to New York to attend school here. Just give it a try for one year."

My hope was to put the power of "choice" back in his hands. If he really wanted to come home, he had to buckle down and do his best first. After that, the decision would be his. If he did poorly, though, he'd have no choice. I'd find a way to keep him in Valley Forge whether he wanted to be there or not.

I was praying that he could look beyond himself in that moment to see the bigger picture of family, of expectations, of compromise, and of sacrifice. These were the traits of the man his father and I and all who loved him wanted to see in him. I was counting on him to show me through his actions that he understood.

Now, Wes will be the first to tell you that his turnaround was by no means immediate. He still got his share of demerits those first few weeks. But slowly, as his grades improved, he started being recognized for the good he was doing. He started feeling better about himself and he began feeling more like a leader, instead of a follower. About a month later, when I received a "Cadet-a-Gram" postcard saying that Wes had excelled in his math class, I knew his metamorphosis had begun.

Six weeks later, I went up for parents' weekend, the first time we were allowed to visit our sons. My first glimpse of Wes was in the staging area by Eisenhower Hall. Out of the sea of hundreds of cadets ranging in age from twelve to twenty-three, I spotted him as he lined up with the rest of H Company for their first official parade. I immediately noticed Wes's glistening brass cap shield, the sign that he had passed all the requirements for him to graduate from plebe to full-fledged cadet. I thought about his dad and what a huge grin he'd have on his face seeing Wes on the parade field. I closed my eyes and pictured him sitting next to me and whispering that I'd done the right thing. As each company advanced to its designated position on the field and the marching band started playing the Stars and Stripes marching song, I watched Wes, head erect with his cap shield glistening from the sun, his shoulders pushed back and in perfect rhythm with the rest of the youngest cadets of H Company. What I saw with each determined step was that he seemed to have found self-esteem and purpose, key elements in the arsenal he would need in his own march to manhood.

Wes got through that first year with vastly improved grades and stellar reviews about his behavior. Keeping to our agreement, I asked him that May what he wanted to do the following year.

"Mom, if it's okay with you, I'd like to come back here," he replied. I was delighted. He had found his stride in a place where he could become a leader and not get ridiculed or teased. He no longer felt compelled to be the class clown, or just to do his work, which he'd finally realized he could do and do well. He did so well that I was able to get substantial financial aid for him the following year and increasingly more aid every year after that. As he took responsibility for himself and his future, he actually helped ease the financial responsibility for his journey. The dollars I had spent on his education made sense, and I could not have been happier or more grateful that I had swallowed my pride and sought that initial help. Being able to take advantage of that open window made all the difference in Wes's life and helped me and our family eventually take one step closer to financial freedom.

LESSON FROM A LIONESS: *Parenting means making decisions that may not be popular.*

Sending Wes to military school was one of the hardest decisions I have ever had to make as a mother. It was a considered risk taking on such a financial burden, especially given all the other demands on my resources. I really wrestled with whether I was copping out of my responsibilities as a parent by taking money from my parents, and whether the whole thing wouldn't be easier if we'd just kept doing what we'd been doing with Wes at home. But thinking of that time as an open window—that small moment of time when

Wes was really vulnerable, at a major crossroad in his life—helped me see that the sacrifice was one that I could not afford to avoid. I was able to make an informed decision about what was right for my son at that point in his life. Military school is not for everyone, but for Wes it was the right decision and well worth the investment. Don't be afraid to consider extreme measures, whatever the circumstances.

If you're at a crossroads, think about what kind of decision you would make if money was no object. Would you sign up for that class, make that move, hire that help, send your kid to that school? If money is the only thing standing between you and an important parenting decision, trust your gut. It may not be easy but there are ways to get financing for a life-changing move for your child. That window will not be open forever.

From Cookies to Cosby: The Pam Warner Story

When you focus on problems, you'll have more problems. When you focus on possibilities, you'll have more opportunities.
—Author unknown

The year was 1984, and a new series had me and millions more glued to NBC on Thursday nights. It was *The Cosby Show*, a groundbreaking comedy sitcom that thrust Bill Cosby, Phylicia Rashad, and their television children into the ratings stratosphere. Sharing the everyday lives of an upper-middle-class African American family, it became the number one rated television series for five of its eight years on the air, becoming only one of two sitcoms in the history of the Nielsen ratings to accomplish this.

Current-day revelations notwithstanding, it was revolutionary for its time. With the exception of the 1968 series *Julia*, which featured Diahann Carroll as a widowed nurse raising her son, no other series dared a storyline featuring middle-class African Americans. And *Cosby* pushed the envelope even further by featuring an intact, two-parent professional family. The daughters were smart, beautiful, and talented and the one son, Theo, struggled academically but prevailed and excelled in the end.

While Theo Huxtable was the lone son in this idyllic two-parent family, Malcolm-Jamal Warner, who played Theo, was actually the only child of single mom Pam Warner.

Pam and Malcolm's dad, Robert, had been childhood buddies, a friendship that blossomed into love and then marriage when they were both attending colleges in Illinois. Following his graduation they moved to New Jersey, where Robert was offered a job. In time, their family grew to include Malcolm. For a while, things were wonderful, but they grew apart and divorce followed when Malcolm was five. Now officially a single parent, Pam moved with her son to Los Angeles. Their first address was with her father, in a one-bedroom apartment over his garage. Malcolm slept in the bedroom and she slept on the floor in the living room.

I'm a little reluctant to say I was a single mom because once we got our act together, his father was very, very much involved in his life. I had help. Robert would send for him every summer so I had a three- or four-month break from parenting. I didn't have the day in and day out, so that was my respite during the summer for years. When he came back from his father, Malcolm came back with suitcases full of new clothes, so all I had to do was fill in clothes during the year. But more important than the material things, we both missed each other so much, there was an emotional rebonding that would take place every end of summer and it was wonderful for our relationship as mother and son. In retrospect and even then, I never felt the burden of, "Oh, I'm a single mother, I'm by myself." I just never felt that. I'm a single mother technically, but when you look at the big picture, I was not.

Because Pam and Robert made the choices they did, Malcolm grew up in an emotionally stable environment. However, the financial situation for Pam and Malcolm was anything but. Robert did what he could but he was in graduate school and had remarried. Pam did not have a college degree so her choices for work were limited. She would go to work in an office, for example, and work hard but could never advance.

> *I did a revolving-door thing for years. I would work and then I knew that I was not going to get a raise or a promotion, I didn't have a degree, so I'd get tired of that and I'd quit that and I'd go back to school. Then I would get tired of really not having any money, then I'd go back to work, so I did that until I made a commitment that we're going to have to eat beans and rice every day because I'm not going back to work until I get my degree. Malcolm was getting closer to going into junior high school and I knew that there were things that he would need because kids need things and they want to be able to fit in.*

While she went to school, she received public assistance, calling it a means to an end, her "Forty Acres and a Mule." She was determined that public assistance would never become her lifestyle once she earned her degree. But when she graduated, she couldn't find a job. Depressed, she needed a jolt from a close friend to bring her back into a more positive mind space.

> *"Well, girl, just do something, anything," she said. "You know, go sell sodas at the beach, do something." I used to make cookies because I couldn't afford gifts so I took her advice and I started selling cookies on the corner of Vermont and Martin Luther King Jr. Boulevard.*
>
> *There was a bus stop right there and the welfare office was right down the street so I got all that foot traffic. That corner was great*

for me, I would sell out, go back to my Pinto station wagon where I was keeping the hot pots and boxes with more food, fill up my straw baskets, and go back to my corner and sell out again. I was on that corner, I would say, a couple of months. But eventually I knew I could go to the Crenshaw Boulevard area and get even more foot traffic.

Crenshaw was very different then. It used to have a lot of mom-and-pop stores along there. There were no Burger Kings, no McDonald's, none of that. So I would stand out in front of the telephone company at the corner of Stocker and what used to be Angeles Vista, on the first and the fifteenth because I would make a lot of money. Those were the days people got their welfare checks and where they went to pay their bills. The security guards would make me move from in front of the telephone company so I would just shift to the shopping center parking lot, which was adjacent to the telephone company building. No problem. I just about sold out there too. If there was anything left over, I would go to some of those mom-and-pop stores and sell what was left to the store owners there.

One day a woman from one of those stores said to Pam that she loved her cakes and cookies but what she wanted was some meat. So Pam went out and bought two chickens. She fried one, and the other she barbecued. She cut them up and made sandwiches. They sold out immediately; soon, she went from two chickens to five, then ten, and finally twenty chickens a day. Soon what she calls her street-corner catering business included cakes, cookies, chicken sandwiches, collard greens quiche, hot links, and salad. She started cooking at the crack of dawn, stacking up the straw baskets, pots, and boxes on her small apartment kitchen table so that everything would be ready for her to sell by lunchtime.

Eventually, Pam found a rewarding office job with a chemical company that she likely would not have gotten without her degree, so she does believe that her education paid off. But until then, the income from her kitchen ensured they had a place to live, enough to eat, and enough extra to provide Malcolm with different opportunities to keep him busy, out of trouble, and on his way to following his passion, which turned out to be a theater group.

So that's how we made it in those early years. While I worked I put him in the children's theater group because I was looking for extracurricular activities for him. My philosophy was that you don't learn how to manage your time when you're twenty-five years old. It starts as a child, learning how to manage your time and having responsibilities. So I told him, "You're going to do something else besides go to school, come home, and do homework." He loved it. I would make it more difficult for him to go. I would increase his chores or have him help me more, just to see how badly he wanted it. His homework had to be completed, his chores done, and I told him that he couldn't go unless everything was done. He would accomplish everything because he really wanted to act. This was my first indication of things to come.

Pam's work in the chemical company was going so well she considered going to graduate school for engineering. Malcolm was doing well with his acting so that by the time he was twelve he had an agent who was always on the lookout for acting jobs for him. As fate would have it, one Good Friday the agent heard about an open call for this new Bill Cosby series and they were auditioning that day. The problem was that Pam had taken the day off and she and Malcolm were spending the day exploring Los Angeles together. They got home around four thirty to a slew of messages from the agent on the answering machine. The messages said that Malcolm needed to get to the audition before 5 PM. Pam and Malcolm broke all kinds of speed records to get to the other part of town, and fortunately the agent convinced the casting agents to stay until they could get there.

Malcolm auditioned and got a call back for that following Monday. When Pam got home from work that day, there was only one message on the machine this time. It simply said, "Mom, I got it."

So off they went to New York. Pam sublet their apartment, just in case.

My thing was, well, I can always come back and get a job typing somewhere. There weren't computers at the time but my typing was pretty good so I knew I could get another job if I needed to. I also wanted Malcolm to go into this with a realistic view of what could happen. I told him that he had to keep in the back of his mind the question, "What are you going to do if the show is over tomorrow?"

Fortunately, with the show's success, he didn't have to answer that question for eight seasons. But today he credits Pam publicly for keeping him grounded and open to new experiences and opportunities like playing music and directing. Pam has had a constant presence in his journey as not only his mother but also his manager, a role she still fulfills to this day. She started out letting other people play those advisory roles to Malcolm because she thought that they knew better. But she began seeing things done to and around Malcolm that didn't seem right to her. She says that while she was naive to the mechanisms of show business, she was not naive to what she was seeing, thinking, and feeling as a mom. Juggling her roles as a college student and single mother provided the foundation she needed for her new role as his manager. At first, Malcolm was dead set against it, but Pam was determined.

Once I cut those questionable business ties and once he settled into the fact that I was going to manage him, he was okay. The other thing that was going on was that he was now a thirteen-year-old hormonal teenager and the whole world's thinking he's wonderful. But I told him that The Cosby Show was just a job and it didn't

*absolve him from any of the responsibilities he had before. I said,
"When you come home, you've still got to clean your room, clean
the kitchen, and take the garbage out." So that wasn't well received,
you know what I'm saying?*

*I had to be very firm but I also had to allow him certain free-
doms. But most of the time, I was right there with him whenever he wasn't on the set. I would talk to him about what's really
important in life, that this is not permanent because there's always
someone who's as cute, or maybe even a better actor than he was
coming right behind him. I would say, "Don't get it twisted. This
is not about you. Yes, they're all over you now and saying you're
the best, but they will turn around and do the same with the next
person."*

In addition to keeping Malcolm grounded, Pam says that she was
determined to make sure that he was involved in every aspect of the
business so he'd have a broader perspective of show business, behind
as well as in front of the camera.

*One of the things I did immediately was to get a business man-
ager and an attorney. When I got the business manager, we'd have
meetings to close out [our fiscal year] in June. We'd start preparing
taxes and compute whatever estimated taxes we'd need for the following year. At fourteen he was going to these meetings. He didn't
want to go. He went kicking and screaming, but I was like, "Okay,
if anything happens, you are not going to say my mama took my
money because you were sitting right there with me, whether you
understood what was going on or not."*

*I insisted that he learn how to handle his finances and under-
stand the business of show business. He would need to know how
to take care of his own business affairs and to know what was going
on with his own money. He takes charge now and is very much in
control of those meetings. I'm there, but he runs them.*

Pam has started giving seminars for parents who are thinking of managing their own children. First and foremost, she says the foundation for raising grounded, secure young people is teaching them responsibility and that choices have consequences.

> *I always said, "You can do whatever you want to do or you can do what I've asked you to do. Your choice, but there's a consequence for either one." So I think if nothing else, if a parent can impart that to their children—a sense of responsibility for themselves, and others—I think that may not take care of everything, but it is a great foundation for life.*

LESSON FROM A LIONESS: *Motherhood is a time to parent. It's no time to be a friend.*

Children can take advantage of your need to make them happy, especially when they become tweens and teens and you are seeking to ease their pain, rid your guilt, or otherwise let them know they are loved. But as Pam did with her son, even when he had every reason to feel like and act like Hollywood royalty, we must remind children of the family values and what really matters in life.

Clearly, one of the most important of these family values in the Warner home was to keep Malcolm grounded. The other was fiscal responsibility, which led to their financial freedom. Laura Shin, senior editor for *Forbes* magazine, interviewed Beth Kobliner, author of the bestselling book *Get a Financial Life*, who offers money lessons that are good to teach children at any age:

- **You may have to wait to buy something you want.** Kids need to learn delayed gratification as early as possible. The next time they ask for a relatively big-ticket item, for example, say, "Sure. Let's go home and figure out how long it will take you to save for it."

- **You need to make choices about how to spend money.** Even if money is not an issue in your household, kids need to know that money is not infinite and they need to make wise choices about how each dollar is spent. Elsewhere in this book I introduced you to the Money Savvy Generation piggy banks, which are divided into four compartments—Save, Spend, Invest, and Donate. Kobliner suggests a cheaper way of accomplishing the same thing: Put these four labels on four jars. Then, whenever kids get extra coins (from grandparents like me) or their allowance, work with them to make decisions about how they should divide the money. She also suggests taking young children to the store and giving them $2. Tell them they can spend it any way they'd like, but they should ask themselves first, *Do I really need this, or is it just that I want it?*

- **The sooner you save, the faster your money can grow from compound interest.** Obviously for tweens and teens, this lesson gets them to start thinking long-term. Among other tips (including teaching the concept of compound interest!), Kobliner suggests setting a longer-term goal for something that is more expensive. She calls these "opportunity costs"—a way to discuss the wisdom of giving up smaller, perhaps spur-of-the-moment acquisitions to save for a more enduring item or opportunity.

- **College students should only use credit cards if they are going to pay the balance in full every month.** It's too easy to fall into the credit card trap that banks are notorious for setting as soon as students arrive on campus. If they do get one for true emergencies (not an emergency haircut or dress for the fall fling), only get one with a low interest rate and no annual fee.

A link to these and other helpful tips can be found on www .power-ofpresence.com.

Just a Book of Stamps

It's not hard to make decisions when you know what your values are.

—Roy Disney

On a Sunday morning early in January, at the end of the holiday break, the house was buzzing with activity as the kids prepared to start back to school. Nikki was finishing up a paper, Shani had an assignment due her first day back, and Wes was in his room packing to return to Valley Forge. We'd all had such a nice holiday that year, but at a cost. I was sitting on my bed listening to the automated voice at my bank giving me the scary news about my balance. I had just enough to get us through to Thursday when I got paid. As long as I had no surprises, everything should work out okay. I thought back to the last time I'd looked at the gas gauge in my car. I needed three-quarters of a tank to get Wes to school then return home, so I should just make it.

Wes entered my room.

"Hey, Ma, can I have some stamps please?"

I reached into the side compartment of my purse where I kept a book of stamps and handed them to Wes. He took a quick look inside. "Mommy, there's nothing inside." Still on the phone, I fumbled for my wallet to give him a $5 bill so he could buy a book of stamps when he got to school. I opened my wallet to find there wasn't one there.

I hung up the phone.

Is this what it's come to? I can't even afford to buy my son a book of stamps?

I felt like an idiot. Even with all the support I had and my two degrees and several freelance jobs, my family's day-to-day economic security was completely dependent on what I could earn and bring home every other week. I was the head writer for *Essence: The Television Program* and picked up other writing or field production jobs when I could. I even began working part-time in a fur salon. But it still wasn't enough. It was one of those moments when you realize the fragility of the way you live, when you're only a paycheck or misstep or two away from financial collapse.

The actual size of my bank account, however, was more a symptom than the actual disease I was afraid of. My fear was that I was on the verge of jeopardizing my kids' sense of security—their feeling that I could adequately provide for them. If not me, who? I think that may have been the first time in my adult life that I truly "got" what happens in many low-income single-parent homes when kids, sensing this insecurity, assume responsibility for the family's finances. Most kids don't fall into street crime because they're bad. They are trying to fill a need that no kid should have to. I became more determined than ever that this was not going to happen in my home.

Politicians' favorite sport is dumping on single moms, saying what a terrible environment we create for our children, how we hamper their chances for success. That's why they don't want to give us any help; to do so, they say, is to subsidize dysfunction. The only thing dysfunctional about my family was our finances. We loved each other deeply and were very involved in the community and in each other's lives. But the cost of living in this country is high, and my life plan had been on a trajectory that involved two incomes. With the sudden loss of my husband, I found myself alone on that path with no way to recoup what Wes had been providing. What we need and deserve is the opportunity to earn enough money to have Christmas, good educations for our children, safe streets, and good places for them to play—and enough left over to afford a damn book of stamps.

That book of stamps set me on the path of doing a better job of providing for my family. I never, ever wanted to have that feeling in the pit of my stomach again. I knew I couldn't work harder but I had to work smarter. I needed a family-supporting full-time job, with benefits. I began sending out résumés to production companies, and just when I was beginning to wonder if anything would come through one of my girlfriends from college, Mary, once again called, as if by radar, to tell me about a position at the Annie E. Casey Foundation in Connecticut. It would become my work home for the next fifteen years.

Which is not to say that this was the end of our financial challenges. Far from it. College was next, with three kids overlapping one way or another for the next seven years, but at least we had access to student and parent loans, scholarships and grants, and the security of a regular paycheck and benefits from a full-time job. Most important, because of the foundation's mission to help strengthen children and families, there was heightened sensitivity to the family lives of its employees. Luckily, my boss, Bill Rust, a single dad raising sons, provided a flexible and compassionate environment that allowed me to maintain my presence with my kids, without guilt, when they needed me.

And oh yes, I always keep some stamps in my wallet, as a reminder of where I was that day, and how fragile finances can become. And just in case anyone needs one.

LESSON FROM A LIONESS: *Channeling Shonda Rhimes!— Come from a place of yes.*

We all have our personal book-of-stamps moments. I hope you won't let them frazzle you, but let them help *you* find *you*! Sometimes we have to sacrifice one thing we love doing or toss out our best-laid plans for something practical. Based on my experience, I now try to look at these instances as blessings yet to be born. I had to pursue financial stability over the flexibility of freelancing, but doing so put me on a career course I never would have found otherwise and for which I am hugely grateful. I was able to create an environment that allowed me to open up to a world I never knew existed and that had actually felt like a calling never before answered. When we make a pragmatic decision based on our family's needs, we don't have to sacrifice personal satisfaction and fulfillment. Believe that it is possible to find new things you love to do, or at the very least embrace and accept them as necessary steps toward the money and opportunities you need to thrive.

Presence of
Connectedness:

The ability to physically and/or emotionally experience spark and magic with our children, even in our absence, while nurturing self-care and the comfort and ease we feel with those around us so we may mutually help and support one another.

VI

Presence of Connectedness

Introduction

One of the greatest barriers to connection is the cultural importance we place on "going it alone." Somehow we've come to equate success with not needing anyone. Many of us are willing to extend a helping hand, but we're very reluctant to reach out for help when we need it ourselves. It's as if we've divided the world into "those who offer help" and "those who need help." The truth is that we are both.

—Brené Brown

Being a parent, especially a single parent, can be a lonely job. It's hard to know for sure when you're making the right decision, setting the right example, fighting the right battles. It can also be hard to know when you're getting through, especially as your kids get older. This is when it really helps to have a pride of trusted friends and advisers to turn to. By helping your child find mentors, by curating the group of adults in your child's life, by surrounding yourself with people who help you stay on track, you create a network of support that you can rely on in moments of doubt, need, or indecision.

Of course, being a parent means that you will always be the first line of defense, and looking for ways to strengthen your connection to your children is an incredibly important part of your role. My years of freelancing were critical to my staying physically and emotionally connected, but as our needs evolved I knew I had to adjust.

Connectedness come in many shapes and forms. Connecting with a reliable pride is one. Another is that all-important connection to ourselves.

As single mothers, how often do we deny our bodies in the service of raising our children? We don't get enough sleep, we rarely get the time to exercise, and sometimes we reach too often for a glass of wine or something stronger to soothe the tension that all the responsibilities and insecurities visit upon us every day. Health and appearance become just another area of life in which we berate ourselves for not doing more, or doing better.

I doubt if there's a parent who hasn't experienced some or all of these emotions at one point or another. True, a family's strength is directly related to the level of support around it—support that can provide a moment of respite when you are overwhelmed by everything a single mom needs to keep in her head on a daily basis. But it's equally true that if you have a partner in the house—someone who intimately knows what makes you tick, your moods, idiosyncrasies, and vulnerabilities—that person can become your early warning system, the yellow canary in the mine, when something is off kilter, when things just aren't right. The partner can also be the safety valve helping you let off steam from the pressures of the day. But if no partner exists, you'll have to either take out your frustration on the kids or keep them bottled up inside. Before this happens, I've learned the first and best course of action is self-care: You can't be present for your family if you can't connect with your own needs and yourself. As holistic health practitioner Laurie Buchanan, PhD, says,

"Self-care is a deliberate choice to gift yourself with people, places, things, events and opportunities that recharge our personal battery and promote whole health—body, mind and spirit."

And finally, there is the job we have to teach our children about connectedness—the different ways to relate to different types of people, why manners matter, and how to connect even with those we have little in common with. And as I learned, being able to accomplish a seemingly impossible task is a connection with an inner source of strength that can reap huge dividends not only with our children but in building our own self-esteem.

Connectedness is taught like most other things, by illustrating our own involvement and respect for the different connections we come in contact with every day—from our inner circle and pride to our churches and schools to charities and causes within our communities. Connectedness provides lessons for compassionate involvement with others, passionate connections with causes, meaningfully connecting to ourselves as well as creating the memories and lifelines that establish and maintain lifelong presence with our children.

Two Games, One Day

Nothing is impossible to a willing heart.
—*John Heywood*

When my husband Wes and I moved into a brick duplex in Takoma Park, Maryland, we began what felt like a whirlwind of family activities. Only about twenty minutes from work, Takoma Park was straight out of a Norman Rockwell painting, complete with a gazebo in the middle of town and a Fourth of July parade every year. It was the first city in the United States to extend voting rights in municipal elections to sixteen-year-olds, in keeping with its commitment to the idea of family activities and full community participation.

Things-to-do with the kids became a priority. We already had a plan for drop-offs and pickups to the bilingual Montessori school in nearby Silver Spring, Maryland, which all our children attended. Since we selected Spanish as their language, cultural activities like Día de los Muertos (Day of the Dead) or Cinco de Mayo were stamped on our calendars. Swimming classes were next on the list. Wes and I took the littlest ones to classes at the YMCA together. Since he was a much better swimmer than I was, he handled little Wes, and I helped six-month-old Shani. For Nikki there were also music and dance lessons. She took to dancing like a duck takes to water. She even performed at one Fourth of July celebration in the town's gazebo. With some extra tutorial help from my girlfriend Pam Higgins-Harris, an amazing dancer in her own right, Nikki dazzled, stepped, twirled, and strutted her stuff around the gazebo and later at a school talent show to everyone's delight, especially Wes and me. It was an idyllic time. Although our schedules were packed, Wes and I tag-teamed the kids to ensure that one of us would be there as any of the children enjoyed the enrichment we worked hard to provide. We wanted to give our presence to our kids. Together as a unit, with heartfelt love, we shared (or shared in) our parental responsibilities.

It wasn't just around fun activities that we were able to be a parental relay team. When Nikki was seven we noticed a growth in her leg that the doctor thought best to remove. The day before her surgery, I checked her into the hospital and got her settled. Wes was a newborn, so as soon as Nikki fell asleep I picked him up from my in-laws and took him home. When Wes finished his last newscast, he went to the hospital and spent the night with Nikki. To this day, Nikki still talks about the calm she felt waking up in the middle of the night and seeing her dad asleep in the recliner.

That was our wonderful life for almost five years. We were partners. But in an instant that life was gone. It wasn't just my best friend who died. It was my parenting partner, someone to look to for guidance, to co-sign or suggest a better way, to play good cop to my bad cop, to show a united front when necessary. The baton toss had become a solo sprint, and that seemed lonely and very tiring.

While Wes's mom, dad, and three sisters were close by, as were my dear friends from college, my partner of the heart was gone. There was a hollowness in the pit of my stomach and a gaping hole in my heart that I thought might never heal. But I was determined to continue supporting my kids in their extracurriculars, financially and physically, as much as I could. Single mom or not, I had to find a way that I could do this.

I've always listened to my head by making lists, being pragmatic, planning, and prioritizing. That certainly came in handy, but this time I had to do some deep reflection on my ability to keep up with my kids while tending to myself. Going on with things as if Wes were still here wasn't possible; I needed to knock some things off the list. I had to really consider my priorities so that I could keep as much as I could and make choices based on what I wanted for the family and not just what might be easiest.

I narrowed the list to the most important activities: taking the kids to and from their schools, going to the required teacher-parent meetings, and attending family gatherings with the Moores. Once we moved to New York in 1984, the limitations on activities eased, as I had in-house support from the rest of my family. I started working for *Essence: The Television Program* and other freelance and part-time assignments; if I had to work during an activity, my pride was there as backup for school drop-offs or pickups, baseball games, dance classes, theater rehearsals, gymnastics, and basketball tournaments. I once again started to feel like I was providing the activities, presence, and support the kids needed, even if I had to give some things up or if at times, a surrogate had to pitch in.

It's said that New Yorkers don't need cars because of the extensive transit system. That's probably true—if you don't go outside the five-borough bubble. But the kids' activities took me upstate, out-of-state, and to all points in between. As such, the car became not only necessary but a treasured resource. When there were conflicts with the kids' schedules, I called on my pride to help me be in two places at once. The presence of family and close friends at any child's events seemed to be enough for us all—I think the kids knew it was my way of making sure they felt loved and supported, and also that they could feel my presence even if I could not be physically with them.

In 1994 Shani and I moved back to Maryland because the Casey Foundation relocated its headquarters from Greenwich, Connecticut, to Baltimore. Shani was just starting high school and Wes was well into the academic, tactical, and athletic life of Valley Forge. I was back on a one-man mission to juggle schedules. Fortunately, it worked out okay 95 percent of the time primarily because I had a great boss, Bill Rust, who related to my parental challenges because he was a single dad himself. As long as I finished my work, he gave me all the flexibility I needed to remain present for my kids. But one day, the inevitable happened. Shani and Wes had basketball games on the same day with just two hours between the end of one and the start of the next. It wouldn't have been a problem if their schools were across town from each other. But their games were in two different states!

I told Wes and Shani my dilemma and each graciously told me not to worry about it. But I could sense disappointment. Rather than decide to go to neither one, I decided to figure out a way to do both.

Like an athlete in preparation mode, I planned and prepped for the big day. Having learned from past promises gone awry, I didn't tell Shani or Wes my plans ahead of time so that they didn't get disappointed if things didn't work out. The night before the games, I worked extra late, and I went in to work the next morning early. By noon I left Maryland and headed up to Valley Forge, Pennsylvania, for the start of Wes's game. I hit a little traffic in Delaware but got to campus right before the game started. As the team came out of the locker room to start warm-up drills, Wes ran past me and I caught his eye. The look on his face was priceless: surprise and happiness rolled up together in his signature Kool-Aid smile. The team was playing extremely well, with Wes leading in scoring and rebounds at halftime. I would have loved to stay to see a win, but Shani's game was starting in another hour and a half. As soon as the halftime buzzer sounded, I made an about-face to Maryland. The universe was on my side that day because I didn't get caught in one single traffic slowdown—a pure miracle given I was on an interstate approaching rush hour.

I got to her high school gym right after the third quarter started, and I can still remember the look on Shani's face when she saw me walking in. She didn't expect me to be there, but in her heart, she told me later, she was feeling disappointed after not seeing me for the first two quarters. When she saw me there to close out the game, though, all was well. I could feel the effects of the seven hours of total driving time on my knees, and I was starving since I hadn't stopped anywhere to eat. But with all of that, watching Wes's face earlier in the day and now Shani's, I wouldn't have done one thing differently.

None of us can remember which teams won that day. But Wes and Shani say they both felt like winners. What they do remember is the effort I made to support them both and that they were grateful I even tried. I had let my Presence of Connectedness guide me to following the priorities I had set for myself, and I felt like I had won big.

After I arrived home that evening, I kicked off my shoes, and—realizing there was way too much adrenaline pumping through my body to go straight to bed—I made a sandwich, poured a glass of wine, and reflected on the day. Presence of Connectedness had provided the fuel for me to make both games. Most important, the "I love you" I sent from the stands to my children on the hardwood had the most enduring impact. Those are the connections that will survive beyond my lifetime.

LESSON FROM A LIONESS: *Sometimes the effort is just as valuable as your actual presence. But if it's at all possible, be there.*

Kids will forgive if you try and fail. The feat I had accomplished that one day went farther than the distance I had driven. However, it wasn't the actual presence at the two games I was going for, it was the message I was trying to convey by making the effort.

Let's face it, parents have to miss some of the milestones in a kid's life. There's not enough time in the day, gas in the car, or energy in our bodies. And having our children know this reality is not a bad thing. It could be a valuable and bonding moment as we teach this lesson and share its burden as you discuss the events of the week with your children; my kids understood that when I took a time-out, it was because I was human and needed to take a break before I could be their mom the way we all wanted me to be. But ultimately, we know what is most important to a child. I daresay it's not only that our smiling faces are in the third row of every ballet recital; it's whether the child believes we wanted to and tried to be there.

When people make an effort or acknowledge an event, it goes just as far as when they are physically present. At least this has been true for me. When my husband was suddenly taken from us, there were many people who couldn't physically be at his memorial. But a few weeks later when Wes's uncle Bobby came to take little Wes fishing, or his cousin Camille sent me flowers on the day of our wedding anniversary, those acts of kindness stuck with me and made me realize how special we were to so many people. Little things mean a lot, and that especially goes for children. Their hearts are so big that they require so little.

Obviously, there will be times when no matter how you plan or scheme or plead or beg, you won't be able to switch a shift or shift a meeting to attend an event. In those cases, we can let technology be our friend. Consider FaceTiming a fellow mom while she attends the Cub Scouts award ceremony and then having your son see you on the screen afterward, surprising him by telling him you saw the whole thing. I've known mothers who couldn't be at the science fair, but were able to FaceTime teachers during the workday and say hello to their child. Many schools live-stream their events. You could plan a private viewing in your living room after work, and order in and make a big deal about watching the repeat together. It's all about acknowledging your pride in your child, and that can happen anywhere and anytime, if you make the effort. Just because an event is over doesn't mean it has to be over.

Make it known that one of your family's core values is to be with each other whenever possible. Make scheduling a family affair— communicate. Your children will understand that it stinks when they can't have you at functions (and that you think it stinks too), but a roof over your head and medical insurance are pretty darn good too. Let them know if you're sad that you're going to miss something, but also let them know you are doing that for them, which goes a longer way than the holiday sing-along. Try to look at the school and sports calendar and prioritize together which games will be critical, and find out which school events are non-negotiable. The effort of taking into consideration how your responsibilities affect your children will let them know that when it comes to priorities, they are at the top of the list!

Blogger Desiree Campbell reminds us that children's lives are made up of little moments; moments that may seem small, like nightly reading of their favorite books, are almost insignificant to adults but are huge in the lives of kids. The school assemblies, the softball or basketball games, the parent-teacher conferences—all things we may feel we can miss sometimes, because there's always another game, conference, or concert around the bend. But for our kids, each event is unique and important, and not attempting to be there is something they'll remember. This is especially true for kids of single parents, because they may already feel cheated by not having enough parental time. But when they see their single mom, regardless of the obstacle, doing whatever you can to be present, either in person, virtually, or through a surrogate in those special moments, they see your true heart and desire to be connected.

A Surrogate's Love: The Gina Davis Story

We live in a world in which we need to share responsibility.
It's easy to say "It's not my child, not my community, not my
problem." Then there are those who see the need and respond.
I consider those people my heroes.
                                                    —*Fred Rogers*

One of the reasons I cherished working at the Annie E. Casey Foundation is that I fell in love with the story of its founder, Jim Casey. More than a century ago, Annie, his widowed single mother, was doing her best to provide for her four children in an impoverished section of Seattle, Washington. Jim decided that as the "man of the family" he had to financially assist his mother, so he started doing package deliveries for local companies on his bike. At nineteen years old he decided to go into business for himself; borrowing $100 from a friend, he officially established the American Messenger Company. From those two wheels grew the United Parcel Service, UPS, today the world's largest package delivery company. In 1948, Jim decided that making money wasn't enough—it had to have a purpose and meet a need. He founded the Annie E. Casey Foundation, named for his beloved mother, to help children who, like him and his siblings, had desperate needs and few options for help. He was especially drawn to children in the foster care system, who through no fault of their own couldn't live with or be cared for by their mother or father.

The Casey Foundation became my home base for fifteen years,

and I worked alongside some enormously talented and dedicated people. One of them was my colleague Gina Davis. She was not a single mom, but she found herself in a position where she realized she could offer help, guidance, and relief to family members who needed a lifeline. Her story is an example of what can happen when you're willing to accept help from those in your pride.

Gina is the daughter of an immigrant mother from Mexico and a Texan dad, who died when Gina was very young. Her mother remarried twice more, the family moving throughout the country, to wherever the new husband needed to live. Gina is the eldest of three children, five years older than her brother Bidal and seventeen years older than her sister Linda. Gina was heading off to college when Linda was born so they never really knew each other as siblings. Gina excelled in college and went straight from graduation to a training program for young journalists of color in New York City, sponsored by *Newsday*. During her occasional visits home, time was always too short for Gina and Linda to bridge the gulf between them so they never established a strong relationship.

Gina says Linda was challenging throughout her childhood and teenage years—from truancy to engaging in high-risk behaviors, dropping out of high school, and finally getting pregnant when she was eighteen. Linda named her daughter Eliza and they both moved in with her mother. Two years later a son, Shawn, was born.

By then, Gina was married and an established education reporter in Baltimore. Not having children of her own (her husband had three daughters that Gina helped raise), she tried to respect the mother-child relationships of her sister but with each visit to her mother's house, Gina became more alarmed by Linda's constant yelling, especially at three-year-old Eliza.

I said, "How would you appreciate going to work every day and all your boss did was yell at you from the moment you walked in until the moment you left and just nothing you did was ever good

*enough, and everything you did would set that person off." I said,
"We both know by lunchtime you can be ready to run for the hills.
Put yourself in that space, and what that feels like, and how degrad-
ing it is, and how demoralizing it is, and just how bad it makes you
feel."*

Gina appreciated that part of her sister's frustration came from the
fact that she really didn't have any career goals. She finally received
her GED but she was without a job, without a direction. Then Linda
came up with the idea that she wanted to become a nurse, and Gina
saw this as her opportunity to help her sister achieve her dream.
With her husband's support, Gina offered to take Eliza back to Baltimore to stay with them while her sister went to nursing school.
Shawn, who was just turning two, would stay with his mother and
grandmother. Gina went to Eliza's fourth birthday party and brought
her back to Baltimore with her that night.

After about two and a half years, Gina brought Eliza back to Virginia, to a sister now holding a nursing degree. Gina continued to
maintain a regular presence in the lives of her niece and nephew.
When Eliza was about twelve years old, Gina found out that she had
fallen two grades behind in both reading and math. She was in a
public school that had diagnosed her with ADD and put her in a
special education class. The school devised an Independent Educational Plan (IEP) for her and promised Linda that it would provide
Eliza the very best resources available to address her ADD. This is
when Gina's background as an education reporter and communication strategist paid off big time. She and her sister demanded a meeting, and the principal and special education team said they would
grant them twenty minutes.

Instead the meeting lasted ninety unsatisfying minutes, with the
last straw being the school's decision to promote her to middle school
despite her lack of progress. Gina left the meeting and spent her summer visiting Eliza, who finally admitted she was being bullied, saying,

"I don't want to go back to that school." Gina sprang into action, researching private schools in the area that could better serve Eliza's needs. She found a faith-based academy, located not far from their house. Gina called and explained the situation, and in Gina's words, "God's plan was at work that day." The school had a contract with a cognitive education specialist who also did tutoring on the side. Her approach to tutoring was rooted in neuroscience, aiming to rewire the brain in the areas she knew needed to be engaged. The decision was made that day to not only enroll Eliza in the school but also hire the tutor to bring her up to grade level. They also decided she would repeat the fifth grade since she was so far behind. Gina offered to pay for everything and says what has happened in the past few years has made it worth every penny.

In the first few months, Eliza was late for school forty-eight times because her mom and her mom's husband didn't get her there on time. What they didn't realize was that state law stipulates that three latenesses equals one absence. So Eliza was starting the school year with sixteen absences through no fault of her own. Because state law also stipulates that anything over sixteen absences means a student can't advance to the next grade, no matter what the grades are, Gina met with the principal, and the principal made some unique fixes.

We worked out a transportation arrangement whereby a different person at school picks her up and brings her back home every day. The janitor would rotate with the principal, or tutor, or math teacher, and that even included coverage when she had to stay after school for band rehearsals or other after-school activities. Eliza began getting the whole school experience because so many people cared.

Gina said that she really began to appreciate how for single mothers and those who are surrogates, it sometimes takes a pride of caring strangers to make the biggest difference in the life of a child.

Getting her into the proper school addressed one challenge. To help Eliza confront her learning challenges, Gina turned to another stranger.

Even though I'm not a physician and all of that, I knew she didn't have attention deficit disorder. What we learned was that she has what's called auditory processing deficit. It simply means that as she was listening to someone convey information, her brain was processing the information in a less efficient way so kids in the classroom were moving along faster than she was and the teacher was certainly moving along faster than Eliza could comprehend.

For all of fifth grade we had her working with the tutor after school three days a week.

The next summer Gina brought both of the children to live with her in Baltimore. For her not to lose the ground she had gained with the tutor, Eliza continued her tutoring sessions over Skype. For the first ten minutes she would be so grouchy, Gina made her apologize to her tutor. Eventually, with some discipline, Eliza got into it. The next school year she not only closed the gap in reading and math, but made honor roll four straight semesters.

Gina's surrogate status deepened even further as both her sister and her sister's husband were arrested, convicted, and sentenced to prison. Gina's mom was designated the official guardian, and since then Gina has assumed responsibility for both the financial and emotional well-being of her niece and nephew.

Gina is helping to create a new reality for Eliza and Shawn, much like Jim Casey was determined to do for foster children. Auntie, as she is called affectionately by the other kids in their neighborhood, is making sure they have the opportunities all kids should have. During holidays and vacations Gina exposes her niece and nephew to museums, festivals, amusement parks, just like any mom who is present for her children would do. And they are thriving. She knows there will be challenges when their parents get out of prison, but she's ready to remain their advocate and surrogate whenever that time comes.

LESSON FROM A LIONESS: *Allow your heart to lead you to resourcefulness.*

Talking to the women I've met along my journey, I have discovered that most of us at some point question our resourcefulness. Whether it is on behalf of our own children or, in the case of Gina, for those children we advocate for, we forget our own power, our own influence, our own perspectives. But these are the building blocks of the presence that's required to assist them.

According to blogger Jennifer Young, in an article in *Psychology Today* online, being resourceful means that you are able to meet the needs of a situation and can develop the process you need to accomplish a task. If ever you doubt your resourcefulness, think about times in the past when you have been able to achieve a goal, and what it took to make that happen. Think about times when:

- **Someone called on you for help.** You are obviously wise and have experience and are trusted.
- **You accomplished a superhuman feat.** Look back on the deadline that was impossible to meet, the kid who just wouldn't sleep, the virus that wouldn't go away. You still made it through and lived to tell about it. Call upon those instances. You are able to do things others might have found impossible—and then do them all over again.
- **You found resources where there seemed to be none.** Gina looked beyond the confines of her niece's public school to find what her niece needed. She didn't take no for an answer. Let this serve as a reminder that where there is a will, there is a way; we just need to find it.

- **You got help when others were turned down.** Did you ever feel like a fool because you didn't fight the cable bill spike but your neighbor did and won? We don't want to feel like that when advocating for our kids. Relying on our inner resources will lead to our winning while others don't—not because they're losers, but because they don't even try. Where there is a mom, there is a sneak attack, a better way. That Gina got help when others were being turned down is exactly why her niece and nephew are thriving.
- **You rallied others to a cause.** Gina's pride is evident through her story. From her husband who first agreed to take in Eliza to the staff at the private school, Gina helped people see through the outer circumstances to nurture the inner spirit and gifts that lay within the children.

We have a host of inner and outer resources. Our heart space holds inner resources that include creativity, intelligence, confidence, courage, and passion. Using those inner resources, we can gather our outer resources—people, money, or technology. When combined to create connectedness, we can accomplish anything!

From the West Side to Washington: The Rosie Castro Story

There is no better example for our children than the one we set before them every day.
—Davin Whitehurst

San Antonio's West Side is a community of historical contrasts. It's a story of a slaughterhouse, where daily runoff turned the streets a crimson red near a regal Catholic basilica, one of only sixty in the

United States, where the faithful made daily pilgrimages; a story of boundaries encircling one of the nation's first public housing communities as well as three Roman Catholic colleges; and one where day laborers, factory workers, and military personnel shared space with some of the city's most vocal and successful community activists and government officials. And out of this eclectic environment emerged a single mother whose life, legacy, and progeny have and will continue to shape the future of San Antonio as well as the rest of the country for decades to come.

Maria del Rosario Castro is simply known as Rosie. She is a longtime community activist and matriarch of an emerging and dynamic political dynasty. Nothing in her history would have predicted the life she now proudly claims.

Her mom, Victoria, was a six-year-old orphaned Mexican immigrant who, along with her sister, came to the United States. Victoria quit school in the third grade, but she continued to teach herself to read and write in both Spanish and English. Rosie told me that her mother's lifelong quest for literacy became the gift she passed on to her only daughter when Victoria became a single parent in her early thirties.

I grew up in a house of two women, my guardian Maria Garcia and my mother, both of whom worked. I think that's why even though my mother drilled in me the need to get my education, I've always worked. It's the only example I really saw, mainly that women worked outside the home. My mother continued to clean homes and do babysitting and things like that. I went to Catholic school. My guardian worked for the Carmelite priests that ran the parish. She paid my tuition so I was able to go to the Little Flower School for twelve years.

She was an excellent student so she had no problem getting scholarships to attend Our Lady of the Lake College. But she soon rejected her strict upbringing to become, for the first time in her life, a free spirit.

While I was at the Lake, I was chomping at the bit to be on my own. But that's not the way our traditional families work. You don't get out on your own unless you're married. I was kind of stuck, but I was very rebellious. I had been twelve years in Catholic school. Now I'm in Catholic college, so I really was doing stuff like I was involved with the Young Democrats. That was not seen as a good thing at home because men did the politics, not women. My mother was afraid that I would get involved with other things too. This is the '60s. At one point, I went off and stayed with a friend and basically I had called home to say, "I'm going to stay over here." She said, "If you don't come home now, you're not coming home." I never came back home.

I was studying to become a teacher and what happened was that a friend of mine, Dr. Jose Cardenas, was working a project in Austin called the Southwest Migrant Project. The basis was that we would travel to where the migrants went, Michigan, Ohio, all those places. You were really supposed to get your master's at the end of the project. The project didn't quite make it, but by this time, I'd left home and was fending for myself. I hadn't finished college, but I wound up sharing a house with another friend that had gone to Our Lady of the Lake, and I was teaching, but uncertified. That year, my salary was $4,600. I was very active in the Democratic Party and then later helped establish the Raza Unida Party.

Smitten by the political bug, in 1971 Rosie ran for the San Antonio City Council. She lost. But a few years later, she was smitten with something else, love, but it came with multiple complications.

I met Jesse Guzman. He, however, was still married. We didn't live together yet, but when I got pregnant I was twenty-seven years old and on my own. My faith and desire to start a family dictated that I keep the baby, not knowing there were going to be two of them. As my stomach grew so did my need for support so my mom came to live with me after the twins were born. I was still living on the West Side, in the Edgewood School District. That's where I was teaching. After Jesse got a divorce we started living together.

This became Rosie's first real grown-up example of her ever-so-Catholic mother providing unconditional support. Even though Rosie was pregnant by a man who was not her husband, her mother stood by her, despite the strained relationship the two had had in Rosie's youth.

On September 16, 1974, the twins were born, identical boys Julián and Joaquín Castro. They came early and were jaundiced but otherwise healthy. For several years, they functioned like a picture book nuclear family, mom, dad, children, and grandmother, there to lend a hand.

Initially, it was scary because I wasn't married, even though he was there. I needed to make sure that I could provide for the kids, so I always had a job during that intervening period. My mother was there and she really helped raise them because I couldn't have worked without her being there to help take care of them.

There was never a whole lot of money. I didn't have a car. He had the car. After he left it became difficult in terms of groceries and we now had to use the bus all the time. It was a change. What I worried about most was how it would be for them to be without their dad. But I was determined to keep moving forward, for me but especially for them.

Eventually the pressures of finances, family, and work life, as well as the political action activities of both Rosie and Jesse, took their toll. Jesse moved out for good when the twins were eight years old.

At some point, I had gone back to school for my master's. I had fin-
ished the BA through a program at Edgewood when I was teaching.
Then I had the opportunity to apply for funds that had been put
out for a master's degree in urban studies at University of Texas,
San Antonio. I got it. Then to complete the master's, you had to do
an internship. I applied for one with the city and I got selected for
human resources through personnel. They kept me after I gradu-
ated and it provided the stability I needed to take care of the boys.
It wasn't a great salary but at least we got insurance. Eventually I
found a house for us to rent right across the street from my cousin
Teri, who had four kids. Now Julián and Joaquín could have con-
stant contact with their cousins, connecting to them so they could
do homework together and just plain have fun under watchful eyes.
It also provided me with additional backup while I continued my
education and community work.

I could really relate to the sense of security Rosie felt when she
found that house close to family. When my parents and Dad's siblings immigrated to the United States from Jamaica, they all either
lived together or found housing close to each other. As cousins, we
loved it. We had a ball together and always felt secure and connected
with each other, and knew if our own parents weren't around, we
could always turn to our aunts and uncles. When I became a single
mom, like Rosie, I could always rely on my mom or Wes's mother to
help out with the kids. But Rosie's work with the broader community sensitized her to the need to get the boys engaged with community sooner rather than later, instead of always relying on relatives
to keep them. There is enormous value in exposing our children to
our work and our passions. Julián and Joaquín shared Rosie's world,
and as Julián would say years later, "My mother is probably the biggest reason that my brother and I are in public service. Growing up,
she would take us to a lot of rallies and organizational meetings and
other things that are very boring for eight-, nine-, ten-year-olds."

When you're a single parent, as you well know, you have to take them everywhere if you want to stay connected. Before they were born, I was an active community organizer with the Young Democrats and then Raza Unida. As they grew up, I would take them to meetings. During elections, I would always take them with me both into the booth to see me vote, but also we worked outside the poll giving out flyers. We worked several different campaigns. If you're going to maintain both work and then outside work, volunteerism, or any of the organizing, you'd never see them. They were always with me. But I made sure it wasn't a one-way street. I also had to find time to make sure that I could get them to sports stuff and their own activities so that it's not all about, "Hey, you got to be doing what I'm doing." I would take them on the bus to karate, or basketball, or any number of things they were involved with.

But then her mother was diagnosed with diabetes and Rosie became part of what is known as the "Sandwich Generation." Her mom had been such a big help when the kids were growing up but now she needed Rosie to get her to the doctor, try to keep her on a diet, and make sure she took her medication. On the other hand, her boys were growing up and had their own special needs.

I never felt burdened by what we did because the boys were very focused and self-motivated. I tried to instill that in them from when they were very young. I'd say, "Look, every single one of us has a job. My job is to go to work and make sure that we have income for you to eat, enough clothes, and all that. Your grandma's job is to help take care of you. Your job is to go to school and get good grades." I always reinforced that so they really felt that was their only job. They wouldn't clean their room but as long as they were doing well, and connected to their purpose, I cut them a little slack.

Another thing that I think helped them focus on college from when they were very little was when one of their godparents was

*traveling and they'd ask what to give [the boys] for Christmas. I
responded to give them a sweatshirt or something with a college name on it. And I said this to everyone who asked what they
needed. So from a very young age college was always in their sights,
and I kept them connected to the value of education. And they
were very fortunate that education was how they were recognized
in high school, at Stanford and later at Harvard Law School.*

Following graduation both Julián and Joaquín began working at
law firms, but it didn't take long before Rosie's tutelage in community action and public service connected them to their own passions
to make life better for others. Joaquín began his public service in the
Texas House of Representatives. A decade later he was elected to the
newly drawn 35th Congressional District from Texas, where he still
serves today. Julián served in the San Antonio City Council. He was
twenty-six when he was elected, making him the youngest city council member ever elected. He represented District 7, a precinct in his
mother's beloved West Side. He lost his first bid for mayor but won
the second time around in 2009. He easily won reelection his next
two terms. In 2014 Julián accepted President Obama's invitation to
join his cabinet as Secretary of Housing and Urban Development.

There is no debate between Julián and Joaquín about the influence their grandmother and mother have had on them. In delivering
the keynote address at the Democratic National Convention in 2012
(where he was introduced by his brother), Julián delivered one of the
most memorable tributes ever given a grandmother and mother on
such a public stage:

"In the end, the American Dream is not a sprint, or even a marathon, but a relay. Our families don't always cross the finish line in
the span of one generation. But each generation passes on to the
next the fruits of their labor...My grandmother never owned a
house. She cleaned other people's houses so she could afford to rent
her own. But she saw her daughter become the first in her family to

graduate from college. And my mother fought hard for civil rights so that instead of a mop, I could hold this microphone."

LESSON FROM A LIONESS: *Show, don't just tell.*

Rosie's passion for public service meant long hours away from home, but instead of just telling her son's where she was going and why, she brought them with her to show them. Even when it may seem like they're not paying attention, they can see what it takes to be committed; they can sense your excitement and can see how change happens. Being present in connectedness means showing up every day in your kids' lives and inviting them to see you in action as a person—not just a parent. We can be very passionate about our children, and some of us, if we're lucky like Rosie, are passionate as well about our careers or other dedications in our lives. Channel that passion by learning ways to communicate it to your children, to have them connect with what you connect with. They don't need to follow in your footsteps, like Julián and Joaquín; however, this type of connection ensures a family tie that will transcend the confines of your home and send waves into the future.

Connecting to a New Life: The Calynn Moore Story

I define connection as the energy that exists between people when they feel seen, heard, and valued; when they can give and receive without judgment; and when they derive sustenance and strength from the relationship.

—Brené Brown

It is the oldest international fellowship and considered the most prestigious, bringing together young people from around the world to connect with each other, to study together, and to dream big on how they will contribute to a better world. Being named a Rhodes Scholar is a recognition of a sincere and ongoing commitment to education, to community and public service, to demonstrated leadership, and to physical and mental agility. For the thirty-two American scholars chosen each November, it is the beginning of a new worldview: excited by the international experiences they will soon have; informed by the life journeys of their Rhodes contemporaries; and buoyed by the stories and successes of those scholars who came before them, like journalist Rachel Maddow, President Bill Clinton, Senator Cory Booker, athletes like football great Myron Rolle and basketball's Bill Bradley, and diplomats like Susan Rice. And, I am proud to say, my own son, Wes.

I had the pleasure of catching up with Calynn J. Moore (whom I'll refer to going forward as CJ), the mother of Caylin Moore, an extraordinary young man who guided by his mom's strength, presence, and resiliency joined this enviable club of the world's next visionaries in 2017.

Caylin, with his older sister Mi-Calynn, and younger brother Chase, grew up in a middle-class suburb of Los Angeles. Their father, Louis, and CJ provided them with all the trappings of middle-class life—big house, multiple cars, great schools. Louis worked, CJ worked, and to the outside world, they led an ideal life. Until Louis quit his job and all the responsibility of keeping up with the kids, the house, and the expenses fell on CJ. She said at first, wanting to be supportive of him, she handled everything without complaint. But as a darker side of his personality emerged, she found herself changing to adjust to his psychological abuse.

It got to the point where the only opinion that he wanted to hear was his own and the only opinion that he wanted from me was the one that he gave me. So I started giving him back exactly what he wanted so we wouldn't argue. I learned how to walk in silence, to quiet myself, but that started bringing on some different forms of anxiety.

Feeling totally disconnected from her husband but not wanting her kids to grow up in a single-parent home or disappoint relatives, who didn't believe in divorce, CJ stayed—until the psychological abuse became increasingly physical, particularly toward their children. Having already started law school with an eye toward possibly having to support herself and her children in the future, CJ decided to make her move to independence. She moved to her mother's house in Carson, which neighbors Compton, Los Angeles, some sixty miles away.

Space was tight, with the four of them sharing a room, and food was a daily challenge. Caylin remembers that there were times that his mother didn't have enough money to feed all three of the kids so she would say that each could get one item from the Dollar Menu at the fast-food restaurant. This is when he started doing push-ups to transfer the pain from his stomach to his arms. While it did wonders for his upper-body strength, sometimes he did push-ups until he passed out in a pool of sweat.

CJ was determined that their financial situation would define neither their lives nor their futures. So she set out on a course of actions that would allow her and her children to take advantage of any opportunity that might come along. Her first decision: Despite the distance, the kids would remain in the school that offered them the greatest advantages. Her next step: She would continue her law school education so she'd have more options to support the family.

I'd get up at four in the morning, get them dressed and in the car, and I would drive the seventy-two miles to Marino Valley where their school was located, and then I'd take Chase to childcare. Then I would drive the forty-five miles back for law school, where I was attending classes from nine until twelve a couple days a week.

The school didn't know what I was going through. The only thing they knew was that I was the best-dressed student on campus because you know we sisters know how to put it together, and I would always

have on my suit. I believe in "dress the way you want to be addressed,"
so I was always dressed decent and in order and they'd be, "God, it's
finals. Can't you put on a sweatshirt and some jeans." I'm like, Uh,
no. I'm dressed for the job that I'm looking for, not the job that I have.

After I'd get out of school, I'd go back to pick the kids up, and
I would take them to the park and we would do homework at the
park and then we would go for tae kwon do classes. We would get
out of there maybe eight o'clock at night, then we'd drive back home
and then start all over again.

Most families with kids will agree that connecting around activities is the ultimate bonding experience. But the Moore family bonding didn't stop with tae kwon do. There were dance classes and community improvement projects that they did together. There was also involvement with the Snoop Dogg and Pop Warner football leagues, which not only provided her sons with skills that would carry them into the future but also connected CJ with coaching roles that would ultimately help her gain financial freedom. But before that would happen, a tumor in one of the chambers of her heart landed her in the hospital—and following a successful surgery, a male nurse sexually assaulted her. The aftermath put all the progress she was making as a single mom in jeopardy.

I didn't tell the hospital what happened because I knew I still had
several more days to be there. I feared that they could put an air
bubble in my IV or something. But I did tell everybody who came
to visit me. I told them what had happened while it was fresh, and
we all kind of agreed it was best to get out of the hospital as soon as
possible. I didn't report it until the hospital sent a follow-up ques-
tionnaire once I got home.

After that, I was in a deep depression. I mean, I was probably
about thirty days lying on the couch, not moving, and I don't know
how I was taken care of.

I really don't remember that time. What I do remember now is that after this thirty-day period of time Caylin picked me up and brought me to the bathroom. He had a dining room chair and a plastic bag over it and it was sitting inside of the tub and he was like, "Come on, Mom. You need to take a bath. You need to feel better. You need to wash your hair." He took my clothes off me and I sat there and I'm thinking now I probably cried. I realized how low of a point I was to have my fourth-grade son standing here to bathe me. I realized, I've got kids I've got to live for. I've got to keep pushing. I'd checked out on them. I don't know how my babies got to school. I don't know how my babies ate. I couldn't keep doing this to them because they deserved better. I've got to check back in, in a hurry, so I can take care of my kids. I knew I had to live for them. To myself I declared, then and there, "My pity party is over!"

CJ slowly worked her way back to the state of presence her children needed. She had gone through a stunning reversal of roles where her children became her pride, her circle of support. It took the recognition that she had experienced PTSD and needed professional therapy to help her the rest of the way. But even though she went through all this, CJ feels that because the kids were such integral players in her recovery, they learned a valuable life lesson about resilience: that no matter what happens, they can return from it.

CJ went on to receive her law degree and started working in a midsize boutique law firm. At the time, Caylin was in middle school and was playing for the Snoop Youth Football League.

I would drop the kids off with the sitter and she would give them breakfast, make them lunch, pick them up, give them dinner, and then I would come pick up my kids. I was paying about $1,800 a month in childcare and I realized that was as much as a salary.

I didn't want the kids to grow up without me. I was concerned about what high school they were going to be going to and how I was going to be able to manage if the boys were going to continue playing football, and I had to sit back one day and say I missed it all. It was a tough decision. I did the math and said, I'm paying so much for childcare right now. If I scaled back and took on one or two clients on my own, just one or two clients, I'd be probably clearing the same amount, so I decided to leave the firm.

We suffered financially at first, but life has been so much more enriching. I got it in my head that when you work for yourself, you can wake up and decide how many zeros before the decimal you need, and I liked that. You wake up in the morning and say, "I have a bill due. How much do I need to make today? Okay, let me call some clients and generate some income," or if your kid calls you and the school says, "He's sick. Can you come pick him up?" Yeah, here I come.

I sacrificed my professional life, in some aspects, but God had a way of leading me into a different profession that I may not necessarily have been able to go into. Once I stopped working for the firm, I was able to participate in community improvement activities with the kids. I was also able to go to all the boys' football games and since I was always there, knew the game, and could motivate the team, I became the first female hired by Snoop to coach in his league. I'm the first female to be a head football coach in Pop Warner, and I'm one of the first, I believe, females to coach at a high school level. And now I'm breaking the glass ceiling with a coaching position at the college level here in Los Angeles.

CJ became adept at spotting players with potential, so coaches around Los Angeles began relying on her to point out players who would fit into their programs. Soon she was recruiting for football programs around the country, and now as one of the first female college coaches in the nation, CJ hopes she can continue her now successful ten-year-old football player recruiting enterprise. As football has helped her achieve her own family financial freedom, her efforts in recruiting have assisted more than two hundred students get into college and generated just over $45 million in scholarships for kids from underserved areas.

CJ's daughter is now a California-licensed registered nurse and a mother to her own little girl. Chase is a student at the University of Texas–Austin and an emerging football and academic star. He is also spearheading the effort to begin a chapter of SPARK, which stands for Strong Players Are Reaching Kids, a testimonial outreach program for underserved elementary and middle school students that was co-founded at Texas Christian University by his brother Caylin. As for Caylin, his journey as a Rhodes Scholar continues to fulfill a dream of academic and personal excellence that was fueled and nurtured by the inspiration, expectations, presence, and true grit of his mother.

LESSON FROM A LIONESS: *Connect with community, connect through community.*

We can gain so much by keeping busy with members of clubs and organizations that have members who are like-minded. And as we saw with CJ and her kids, through community involvement and shared experiences, they tightened the bonds of their own family while meeting honorary extended-family members who ultimately changed the direction of all their lives. The football community turned into a career for CJ that she could never have anticipated or sought out; her presence on the field and at the games brought out a talent she didn't know she had while also strengthening the bonds that held the family together.

National Geographic provides an extensive list of ideas to get you or your children (if they're the right age) involved with friends, neighbors, and civic organizations. Keeping your kids busy with connections like these can lead them to connect with their inner purpose, raise their self-esteem, and teach them to be responsible. Some ideas on its list include:

- **Raise money.** Start a drive to help members of your community or another community. For example, start a book or coat drive, a disaster-relief drive, a fund-raising drive, or a canned goods drive.
- **Help a neighbor (great for your tweens and teens).** Adopt a neighbor who could use some extra help. Lend a hand with shoveling snow, scraping ice from a car, yard work, taking out trash and recycling, walking a dog, grocery shopping, or other tasks.
- **Join a group.** Participate in a community organization such as the YMCA.
- **Community heritage.** Research the cultural heritage of your community. Find out why different groups settled there. Did they move to be near family? Were they displaced due to war, poverty, or persecution?
- **Community jobs.** Find out what different people in your community do. With a family member, go talk to a firefighter, a librarian, a construction worker, and people in other professions that interest you.
- **Improve your neighborhood.** Make your neighborhood a better place. Volunteer with your class to do things like pick up trash or other community improvement projects.
- **Find your parks.** Use the internet or Google Maps and zoom in to find your community, taking note of all the public parks, big and small. Then visit a new park each weekend. Take pictures and make your own guidebook of parks in your community. Don't forget about dog parks, which are great places to meet other people with pets, and perhaps begin volunteering with animal shelters.

The complete list of suggestions can be found on the book's companion website, www.power-ofpresence.com.

Making Time to Connect with Ourselves

Self-care isn't selfish. You cannot serve from an empty vessel.
—Eleanor Brownn

Lifestyle author Eleanor Brownn says self-care is a simple formula but essential. "Self-care can be getting more rest, eating healthier food, spending more time in thoughtful reflection, being kinder to yourself, smiling more, playing, or engaging in any activity that renews you," she says. "By making time for self-care, you prepare yourself to be your best so you can share your gifts with the world." But this simple formula becomes complex when you add in the ingredient single motherhood.

Three months after my husband died, I was talking to my mother, and as she said later, what she heard in my voice was sheer exhaustion. By the next morning, after all my early-morning chores were complete, she called. She found an ad for a spa that promised "rest, revitalization, and renewal" and thought I should invite some of my girlfriends to go with me for a week away. She and my dad would come down to stay with the kids so all I had to do was decide who I wanted to go with me, make the reservation, book my travel, and go. At first I thought the idea was preposterous. After the death of their dad, how could I possibly go away for a week, for pampering, no less? How could I justify spending that money on myself when there were so many other needs and unexpected expenses? Besides, who in the world would be able to take off a week to do something as frivolous and self-indulgent as go to a spa? My mom convinced me that investing in myself for something like this was not frivolous. Besides, credit cards should be reserved for the unexpected, and there was nothing more unexpected than Wes's death. Still not convinced anyone else would or could join me, I made some calls anyway and surprisingly both Mary and Gail thought it was a great idea. So off the three of us went to Rancho La Puerto in Baja California.

Its pastoral setting was exactly what I needed, especially since I was sharing it with my girlfriends from college. We woke up to beautiful sunrises and welcomed each day with yoga or meditation on a bench, perched among desert grasses and flowering succulents. At the end of the day, we talked about everything: Wes's death; my new life as his thirty-two-year-old widow; how helpless they'd felt the night Wes died; and how much our connections meant to each of us. I've always said that a therapist is like a friend that you have to pay to listen. With a great set of girlfriends, you don't have to pay!

Each of our daily schedules was individualized with exercise classes and/or spa treatments. And even though the food was a little healthier than the comfort food I might have wanted, it was delicious and exactly what I needed. At the end of the week I really did feel renewed. I had lost a few pounds, I had reestablished a healthier sleeping pattern, and I was able to shelve, at least for that week, the responsibilities of single motherhood. But most important, I think, was that by my prioritizing myself, I was able to come up with a more realistic plan as to how to proceed as a single parent without sacrificing the presence my children needed.

After I got back I put into practice some of the relaxation techniques I learned in Baja. I finally gave myself permission to grieve, to employ all my senses to look deep within and imagine the direction our family should go. I decided to pick and choose my battles. Would the world explode if the whites mixed with the colors or didn't make it to the wash at all? Would it really be a bad thing if I forgot to RSVP to that party? Would the food police come if I did takeout a few nights more a week, or allowed my children to worship Tony the Tiger for breakfast? I learned to forgive myself for all the messes—those of my doing and the ones that landed in my lap—and got a little more logical with each breath I took. That logic told me I could worry about bigger things, if I really felt the need, and then when I began to do just that, I found myself not wanting to waste the energy.

I will always appreciate my mother for her compassion toward me, knowing exactly what I needed when I didn't. Obviously, I didn't have the time or resources to run back to the spa whenever I needed to recharge my battery. My challenge was figuring out how to re-create that space to be contemplative and introspective without having to go three thousand miles away. I came up with my answer after a particularly exhausting three weeks at the Casey Foundation.

I call it my Triangle Day. And I celebrate it to this day, as a homage to self-care!

Triangle Day is my day of going from my bed, to the bathroom, to the kitchen, and back to bed. Period. On Triangle Day, I don't check email, pick up the mail, surf the internet, or catch up with friends. I watch TV, read, sleep, or do my own nails, and the catch is that everything must be accomplished within and between those three rooms. On most days, I don't even get out of my pajamas. This is my day to do absolutely nothing I don't want to do, in a setting I alone have access to. I usually get calls from the kids the next morning, wondering how my day went. My Triangle Days are usually limited to two or three times a year, and I understand that not everyone has the kind of job that allows them to go off the grid like this. Still, a variation of this can be accomplished on a weekend by just about everyone as long as you are connected to a pride—neighbors, a group of girlfriends, family members—trusted adults who can provide respite when you are at your wit's end and on the verge of mental and/or physical exhaustion. It doesn't have to be a week in the desert, just a few hours to connect with your inner you again.

LESSON FROM A LIONESS: *Make and take time for you!*

We don't have to kill ourselves to provide a presence to our children that is precious and enduring. It's critically important to take time to restore your own sanity—you won't be the parent you want raising your kids if you're completely strung out. Inspired by author Mariana Lin and others, here are some practical tips for preventing single-mom burnout.

- **Know your limits.** Remembering you are not a machine is a good place to start. We treat our cars better than we do ourselves, scheduling tune-ups every three thousand miles! Think about that! Pace yourself. Your capacity is not limitless, so if there's a period when you are overwhelmed with too much to do and too little time to do it, step back and give yourself a Triangle Day.
- **Get help.** As much as I preach it, I'm still not great at asking for help, but as Lin, a single mom herself says, if you wait around for someone to offer help, "you may be waiting a long time (and get angry in the process)." And if you feel that you are imposing on other people and can afford it, hire help. When you're clear on your priorities, you will be clearer on what's feasible for you to do on your own and when you need others to help pick up the slack.
- **Forget what everyone else is doing or thinking.** Folks will always have something to say about your parenting—you cater to your kid, you don't do enough; you spend too much time with your kid, you don't spend enough; the clothes you buy are too expensive, your kids look like street kids. If you spend all your time worrying about what other people are saying about you, you won't have time to do what is really important, providing presence to your child. Forget what other folks are saying and figure out a plan that allows you space to decompress while also providing for the myriad needs and demands of your children—and go for it.
- **Strike a power pose.** Psychologist Amy Cuddy popularized the practice of helping your physicality empower your mentality, simply by standing upright and in a powerful position. In documenting the relationship between posture and power,

she showed that in standing like a superhero, you can actually unleash hormonal changes in your body chemistry that will cause you to be more confident and in command. Cuddy says, "Before you go into the next stressful evaluative situation, for two minutes try doing this in the elevator, in a bathroom stall, at your desk, and behind closed doors." Being in control at work is important, yes, but it's equally important as head of your household—so strike a pose at home now and then too.

- **Don't neglect your health.** Single moms encourage their kids to eat healthy, get plenty of sleep, and exercise; they're quick to bring their kids to the doctor at the first sign of illness. Why aren't we as diligent about our own health? Why do we feel we have to be Wonder Woman? Or feel that we can wish away a nagging cough, or that if we take a couple of aspirin a low-grade fever will go away? We skip Pap smears, mammograms, blood work, and even neglect our feet (yuck) in the name of busyness. If we go down for the count because we've waited too long to go to the doctor, who takes care of our kids? Your health matters (as do your feet!). Take care of it.

- **Be as proactive about your joy as you are about your child's happiness.** We love to make our kids happy, to see their huge smiles and hear their genuine sounds of joy. But how often do we share what makes us happy with our kids? Lin makes this suggestion: "Do one thing each day that gives you joy—and tell your kids why you do it, and why it makes you happy. Children pick up on their caretaker's emotions more than we realize—and your happiness will do double duty for your child."

- **Hold on to your dreams.** Without question, our kids are the center of our universe. But that doesn't mean our personal dreams and aspirations have to disappear. When moms feel fulfilled emotionally, physically, and professionally, we are much more capable of giving our children the presence they need to flourish. We need to dream and to devise a plan to achieve that dream! That's all part of the puzzle of single parenthood. But while you are figuring out the pieces of the puzzle of meeting your kids' needs and yours, remember one of my favorite quotes by Eleanor Brownn: "God, grant me the serenity to stop beating myself up for not doing things perfectly, the courage to forgive myself because I'm working on doing things better, and the wisdom to know that You already love me just the way I am."

Do Your Work and Stay Connected: The Loida Lewis Story

Values are our inheritance, what makes us who we are as a people.
—*President Barack Obama*

Six weeks wasn't nearly enough to say goodbye. That was the time span between the diagnosis of brain cancer in 1992 and the death of Reginald F. Lewis, one of the richest men in America. He had gained international fame in 1987 by becoming the first American to secure the largest-ever leveraged buyout of an international company, Beatrice International Foods. He then went on to build it into a billion-dollar company, the first African American to do so. At its peak, TLC Beatrice International was 512th on *Fortune* magazine's list of the 1,000 largest companies. But wealth couldn't stop death's march, and at age fifty he died, leaving his wife of almost twenty-five years, Loida Nicolas Lewis, and their two daughters: Leslie, nineteen, and Christina, age twelve.

His death stunned the business world while his loss devastated his family, especially Loida, who in an instant was thrust into single motherhood as well as keeper of the flame of her husband's legacy. Deeply spiritual, she said she never lost her faith but for four months following his death she couldn't say the Lord's Prayer with the words "thy will be done" because she couldn't accept that God's will had taken the man who to this day she calls "my beloved."

With one daughter in college and the other still attending school in New York City, Loida knew that to fulfill her duty of ensuring the continued growth of TLC Beatrice International, she would have to take the helm herself. A celebrated attorney, infinitely qualified and well situated because of the close partnership she shared with her husband, she wasn't scared by the work. What presented the greater challenge was that if she was to assume stewardship of TLC Beatrice International, headquartered in Paris, she would have to build her support system—her pride—around her daughters at home.

She always had a wonderful relationship with Reginald's mother, Carolyn Fugett, so Loida says that whenever she had to go out of town or had a heavy meetings schedule at home, Ms. Fugett would come up from Baltimore to maintain the core physical presence needed for the girls. But Loida made sure she was only a phone call away. Her absolutely inflexible rule for her staff was that if her daughters or Ms. Fugett called, there was no person, no meeting, no event more important than her talking to them.

When in New York, she exercised the ultimate CEO's privilege of unconditional control over her time.

I would adjust my schedule to be home by dinnertime so we could have dinner together. Any activity that Christina had or Leslie had I would go to. On Leslie's birthday, I'd bring her fried chicken all the way to Harvard. For Christina, any activity she had at school I was there because that's what my husband and I would have done together. I would always be there because being present is the best way to support your children.

Loida says being on the inside of the corporate world for her ten years as CEO has led her to better appreciate the flexibility parents, especially single parents, need so they can be present for their children. Her hope is that more and more corporations will embrace and respond to that need.

From the beginning, Loida was determined not to let her added responsibilities or heightened business focus derail the example she and her husband had tried to set for their children. One of the most important values had always been what Loida described as "Do your work."

> You can do whatever you want but if you're a student, do your work, study, finish your homework, and do the best you can. If your room is dirty so be it. If you want to color your head green, so be it. But you must do well in school because that's your duty. They both embraced these values around education and both graduated from Harvard cum laude. I don't claim that I am the sole source of instilling that value system. But both my husband and I believed in doing hard work and doing the job before us as our responsibility for the moment. I kept it going after he was gone.

Loida is well aware that she is not the typical single mother. Living paycheck to paycheck was never an issue for her. What makes her story one to savor is that Loida took her role of raising successful, responsible, and socially conscious daughters as seriously as she took running a multimillion-dollar corporation. She found a way to successfully connect her profession with her passion to do good, and it became a family value.

"To whom much is given, much is required," is the family mantra. Before their dad died, their parents established the Reginald F. Lewis Foundation, and at ages nineteen and twelve, each daughter was named to the foundation's board of directors. Now grown women and mothers themselves, they have become two of their generation's most thoughtful philanthropists. In 2013 Christina founded AllStarCode, an organization that identifies and supports the entry of more men of color into the technology field. You can find more about AllStarCode by visiting www.power-ofpresence.com.

As for Reginald F. Lewis, Loida flashed a huge smile when she thought what he might say about the lives she and their daughters have built for themselves.

I know he'd say, "Go on with your bad self, Loida." My beloved would be very pleased.

LESSON FROM A LIONESS: *Make your presence a rule to everyone around you.*

Your goal is to be present for your children. When it comes to achieving your goals—whatever they are—research has shown that those people who write down their goals, share them with others, and update others on their goals are more likely to succeed. When people only *thought* about their goals and how to reach them, they succeeded less than 50 percent of the time, while people who wrote goals down, and found the support of a pride through work, relatives, and friends to help them, succeeded closer to 75 percent of the time. Just saying she would stop everything for her children was not enough; Loida Lewis made her priorities a rule and was vocal about it, and she succeeded without fail.

To ensure the goal of presence is achieved in your absence, try these suggestions for your daily interactions with your kids!

- **Be specific.** Big ambiguous goals are likely to get us motivated and seem doable, until their lofty nature intimidates us and we give up. Loida's goal was not simply to be present. Hers was specific: "No matter what, I will take the calls from my daughters." I completely resonated with this because I did exactly the same thing. Because I had the specific conversation with my bosses, they knew that if I ever left a meeting it was because one of my kids called. That's specific and leaves no question in the mind of those you enlist to help meet your goal. We like flexibility, but some recent research from consumer psychology suggests that being more specific and less flexible may be more effective in goal achievement. The premise is simple but not easily accepted: Specific directives, done in strict order, seem harder to do at first, but ultimately lead to greater goal achievement than an ambiguous plan.

- **Make presence a shared responsibility.** Like Loida, I made it clear to my children (and their caretakers when they were young) that I would always take their calls when I was working, but to use good judgment as to when to call. As they grew older, they trusted my promise to take their calls, but they also respected the fact that while I was at work, they should only call in an emergency or in a "something really exciting happened and I couldn't wait to tell you" moment.

- **Be aware of your limits.** Wanting to stay present for your children, especially while taking on other lofty responsibilities, will be stressful, and if we don't manage that overwhelm, setbacks can rear their ugly heads. Psychologists call this train of thought an "action crisis." This is the critical point at which you experience an internal conflict about whether you should keep going or give up. Research has shown that experiencing an action crisis increases production of the stress hormone cortisol, which is your brain's way of sending out smoke signals at the sight of an internal conflict. Awareness is a key tool to diverting this train. When it becomes difficult to see a way through your circumstances, take a step back. Go back to your core values, your specific goal plan, and your positive self-talk.

Presence of Values:

The ability to pass down traditions, character traits, expectations, standards, life lessons, and aspirations that empower children to hold themselves accountable when no one else is around.

VII

Presence of Values

Introduction

Your beliefs become your thoughts,
Your thoughts become your words,
Your words become your actions,
Your actions become your habits,
Your habits become your values,
Your values become your destiny.
—Mahatma Gandhi

What do you believe in? What helps you thrive as a human being? What do you honor in others, and how do you want to live? Your values are determined by the experiences, beliefs, and worldview that you carry with you, in both what you say and what you do. Passing down values isn't as easy as telling our children what's good and what's bad, because they are constantly watching us to see what behavior we actually model. Do we practice what we preach? Do the people in our children's lives uphold the values we tell them they should have as members of our family, community, and society? This can be even more difficult to communicate when we aren't able to clearly articulate the values that we want to pass on.

It took me a long time to get myself out from under dirty diapers, financial issues, and a bad marriage to be able to articulate what it is I wanted to stand for and commit to. It was a process. I read somewhere that values are not what we decide we want to embrace; they are what is already inside of us that we are compelled to push out into the world. Isn't that our main job as parents? To nurture what is inside of our children and let those qualities shine in a collected glow of good people?

Executive coach Scott Jeffrey says he sees people from all walks of life struggle with finding a value system. He explains that there are some ways to begin the thought process around discovering what you value most.

Consider a meaningful moment, what he calls a "peak" experience, that stands out. What was happening to you? What was going on? What values were you honoring then?

Then let your mind go in the opposite direction; consider a time when you got angry, frustrated, or upset. He then says to ask yourself, What was going on? What were you feeling? Now flip those feelings around. What value was being suppressed?

Third, reflect on what's most important in your life. "Beyond your basic human needs," Jeffrey says, "what *must* you have in your life to experience fulfillment? Creative self-expression? A strong level of health and vitality? A sense of excitement and adventure? Surrounded by beauty? Always learning?"

Dr. Dan Peters of the Summit Center coined the term *Parent Footprint*, which describes the legacy of values we learned from our parents and the values we want to pass on to our children and, by extension, our future grandchildren. He says, "Whether you are parenting with intention and purpose and whether you are acting in a way that is consistent with what you want for your child...the real question is—what footprint do you want to leave?"

I was lucky. My values footprint mirrored the one my parents created for my brothers and me. Even with their busy schedules in church or at school, I don't ever remember an important event where one or both weren't there to cheer us on. There wasn't a topic we couldn't talk to one or both about. There wasn't a crisis or challenge we couldn't share with one or the other. Nor was there a triumph that we didn't run home to tell one or both about. And herein lies the difference between a single- and a two-parent home: If one parent wasn't available, we could always find the other. As a single mom, my children never had that choice. The values and beliefs they saw and learned were primarily mine or those of people I allowed into their lives.

With that kind of responsibility, I needed to make sure the character-building blocks I relied on to help me raise them were available to me at a moment's notice. So early on I made up my own aspirational acronym, **I AM CHHIPPER** (yes, there's an extra *H*) to fill in as my reminder when I started going in the wrong direction:

I—Intuition: Every parent has to learn to trust that little voice whispering about what needs to happen next. Oftentimes, that little voice springs from the words in your head from years ago. So take heed.

A—Awareness: Most times, to be fully aware simply means listening, first and foremost. And it isn't just when they are talking to you, but also when they are talking to friends on the phone or to other children or adults in situations like church or at a practice, performance, or games. It also means watching for changing wardrobes, attitudes, and even friends. Heightening your senses to become aware of changes in your kids' attitudes or habits, no matter how subtle, is critical in keeping up with what was going on in their lives.

M—Motivation: Motivation is essential for meeting changing needs and fulfilling dreams. There is a lot of friction that can make achieving a goal feel impossible. But I lived by and instilled in my own children the words of Roy T. Bennett: "Believe in yourself. You are braver than you think, more talented than you know, and capable of more you can imagine." Teaching your children to focus on big goals and work hard to achieve them is a way of showing them that it is always possible to change their circumstances.

C—Culture: Believe in multiculturalism. With so many distractions in their world, it is important that they familiarize and hinge themselves to traditions and customs bigger than themselves or what they see and hear around them every day. It is important to help build an armor against hate if this nation is, in fact, to become a more perfect union.

H—Humility: Being humble and grateful for what they have is one of the most important values to instill in our children. Learning to appreciate what they have and the people who remembered or helped them in any way is essential to raising well-rounded adults. That's why writing thank-you notes the day after Christmas or birthdays, for example, was so important in our family. By infusing humility as a family value, my hope was that it would become an ingrained value in their own lives, no matter what their level of achievement.

H—Humor: The ability to laugh at situations you find yourself in as part of a single-parent family is essential to keeping your sanity and your family functioning in tense moments. Multiple jobs in families can sometimes be a source of frustration, but joking about it can sometimes make it easier to understand why they are necessary. Humor can help you get to the heart of what matters. That's why I shoved an extra *H* in *CHHIPPER*—to make sure I never forgot humor's role in family dynamics.

I—Imagination: Lewis Carroll wrote, "Imagination is the only weapon in the war against reality." In the world of single-parent families, sometimes reality can be very cruel. Reality can be limiting. Reality can separate a single mom from her child for hours at a time—and sometimes during important events in that child's life. But with imagination we can sometimes bridge that gap through technology. With imagination we can make limited dollars stretch for meals until payday. With imagination and creativity, we can

make holiday and birthday gifts as meaningful with only a few dollars as with many. With imagination we can make a way out of
no way.

P—Patience: A teaching of Buddha says, "The greatest prayer is
patience." Patience is one of the hardest skills to master because you
first have to have patience with yourself and all your shortcomings
before you can become patient with your kids. The key is understanding that anything to be accomplished has to happen on their
timetable, not necessarily yours. Patience opens the door to the presence that's needed to be fully there for your kids when they need you
the most.

P—Persistence: Putting one foot in front of the other, day after
day, is sometimes grueling. But you have to keep moving forward,
for yourself—professionally and socially—and for your kids. And it
isn't all about teaching a work ethic, although modeling one is critical. Just as important is demonstrating resilience and goal setting.
For me, probably one of the most comical examples was my trying
to climb up the Dunns River waterfall in Jamaica during a family
reunion. As the waters crashed mercilessly against my body, pushing
and pulling me down on the slippery rocks, I wanted to quit midway.
But I knew my kids were watching so their eyes provided me the lift
and motivation I needed to reach the top. It was inch by inch, but I
was victorious.

E—Expectations: Expectations can sometimes be a two-edged
sword. Most parents have high expectations for their kids. But your
expectations have to be tempered so that the individual expectations
of your children can surface as well. All you should ask is that they
do the best they can do. Our job is to provide the environment for
them to develop to their fullest potential and thrive. I reinforced that
notion with a Martin Luther King Jr. poster I hung on the wall outside
their rooms: "If a man is called to be a street sweeper, he should sweep
streets even as a Michelangelo painted, or Beethoven composed

music or Shakespeare wrote poetry. He should sweep streets so well that all the hosts of heaven and earth will pause to say, 'Here lived a great street sweeper who did his job well.'" Regardless of what I hoped my children would accomplish, I made it clear that I expected them to put their hearts, souls, and goodness toward their goals.

R—Respect: Building respect should be a two-pronged process. For me, insisting that my kids respect their elders, each other, and themselves was obvious. But as important was that the kids knew I respected them—no matter how challenging that was at times—because that signaled to them that I cared, unconditionally. To borrow liberally and make a quote from Theodore Roosevelt my own, "Kids need to know that you care before they care what you think."

I AM CHHIPPER has become my partner in parenting. Remembering these values helped me achieve clarity and consistency in parenting. I AM CHHIPPER became my North Star, my compass that helped me become the parent I needed to be for my children. Write down your values and create your own acronym. Mine has kept me centered, focused, and present. Creating your own can hopefully do the same for you.

The Lock Box

Few delights can equal the presence of one whom we trust utterly.
—George MacDonald

You never know what you're good at until you try something for the first time. Nothing teaches us this lesson like motherhood. I never knew I was as hilarious as Eddie Murphy until six-month-old Nikki belly-laughed at the sound of my raspberries on her tummy. I also didn't know I had the diplomacy skills that equaled Eleanor Roosevelt's until I had to negotiate the use of the television between Wes and Shani.

I became a pancake chef after a lifetime spent avoiding the kitchen, a seamstress when a hem fell right before the fall concert, and an insightful therapist à la Dr. Phil when boys became all the rage. There were also plenty of times I just kept my mouth shut, my head low, and maybe let a shoelace go untied, especially when I knew it was time for my children to start relying on their own devices.

As I matured as a single mom and found myself evolving into a jack-of-all-trades for my children, I seemed to find a decent balance between meddling and laying low. I think this came from the belief that above all things, our family must communicate, and part of that communication relied on reading each other's cues. Some times were times for sharing and others were times for glaring. More often than not communication came in the forms of gripes, whining, and telling each other to butt out. But it was still a line of communication that remained open, even if we didn't like what the other had to say. *Keep talking, even when it's hard*, became an even more critical value after Wes died. I knew I couldn't be there in all ways for them, and that no amount of talking was going to release my children, especially Nikki, who was nine when he died, from the grief that comes with the sudden loss of a parent. But I was desperate to keep us a unit, despite our five-unit being cut to four.

This "you can talk to me" mentality is easier said than done. I was no Clair Huxtable. There were so many moments of slammed doors, back talk, threats to pull the car over or to tear up homework, it was hard to believe I could still glue us together. As the kids grew, it became imperative that I figure out ways to foster, nourish, and maintain a relationship with each child—and each child with the others. How could I ensure that my voice in their ear would not be drowned out by the distractions and temptations that would invade their world? Being a single parent, I feared, could make our unit vulnerable. I wouldn't let that happen, not on my watch.

As the kids grew older their lives became more independent of one another's, especially during the summer. With Wes returning to Valley Forge early for leadership training, Nikki spending much of the season at Stagedoor Manor, and Shani engaged in gymnastics or summer law camp, it wasn't enough for me to simply tell the kids to keep me in the loop on what was going on in their lives and in their hearts and heads. I needed them to trust me and to trust I wouldn't judge them. I needed to show them that I had their backs, and that they could have mine. Would I promise not to get mad? No way in the world! But they would understand that the only way around their feelings is through them, and to be accountable for their mistakes—things I had to learn myself when navigating my own challenges, as a kid and as an adult. I innately felt that if I could keep them talking to me, keeping that core value of communication front and center, we as a family would always be akin to a beautiful braid—individual sections neatly and securely intertwined.

While parenting "experts," psychologists, educators, and researchers agree that the secret to children's success is to help them be unafraid to talk to their parents, that communication comes with responsibility. It was my mother who demonstrated this truth to me, and in turn showed me the art of trust and its infinite rewards.

The date was November 9, 1965. I was in tenth grade, and two months into the most liberating experience of my fifteen-year-old life. I had begun my first year at the High School of Music and Art, whose graduates included legendary musicians like Peter Yarrow, artists, dancers, lyricists like Carole Bayer Sager, future producers like Steven Bochco, and actors like Billy Dee Williams, Ben Vereen, and Diahann Carroll. By then we lived in the East Bronx so each morning I would walk three-quarters of a mile to the subway, take the #2 train and ride forty minutes to 135th Street in Manhattan, and walk up the winding stone steps of Morningside Park to the beautiful gothic stone edifice at the top, built in the 1920s, which everyone affectionately called "the Castle on the Hill." I was feeling very grown-up and very full of myself for actually being accepted into what would in the future be called "the Fame School," the inspiration for the early-1980s television series *Fame*.

On the second week of my trek back to the Bronx, I decided to exercise my new freedom without letting my parents know. Rather than heading straight home after school, which would have gotten me home around four thirty, I got off the train one stop early at Allerton Avenue to hang out at the apartment of my best friend, Beverly Henry. She went to high school in the Bronx so when I started going into Manhattan, I missed her very much—until we realized that with both her parents working, she had the run of the place until six thirty or so. I told my parents that we had practice sessions at school and various rehearsals after class so they didn't question the late arrival time. This gave me the space to hang out with Beverly. Our plan worked out great for a good two months, until the Great Northeast Blackout.

It was a little after 5 PM, and Beverly and I had just finished eating some Jamaican beef patties I had picked up for us on the way to her house. At first the lights flickered and the TV sputtered; then came a pop, then nothing. We tried all the light switches. Nothing. After fifteen minutes passed and dusk was beginning to descend on the projects where she lived, we looked out the living room window and saw people congregating on the street. Beverly found a station on her battery-powered radio through which the disc jockey was frantically describing a massive blackout stretching from Canada all the way to New Jersey.

I immediately thought of my mom and knew she would be frantic. How was I going to get home without exposing my lie, and the way I had been lying for months? The best way, Beverly and I concluded, was to act as if nothing had happened out of the ordinary. I had been getting home by six forty-five since I started my little scheme so I waited until five thirty. I was so confident that Beverly and I had this situation completely under control that I convinced myself that my mother probably wasn't even worried yet. I realized how absurd that was as soon as I called her and heard her voice.

"Where are you?" she asked in a voice thickened by her fear.

"I'm fine," I said. "I'm at a phone booth at Third Avenue."

This was the major subway stop between Manhattan and the Bronx, the halfway point on my way home. "The train got as far as here so one of my friends called her father and he's coming to pick us up. Don't worry. See you soon."

I quickly hung up before she could ask any more questions.

Keep in mind that this was before Caller ID and cell phones. My mom had no way of knowing where I was calling from or how to get back in touch with me. I hung out at Beverly's house for forty-five minutes longer and then walked the usual route home. There was a full moon that night and lots of people on the streets so I don't remember feeling anxious at all. In fact, it seemed like a delightful, though eerie adventure. That is, until I walked in the door and saw my mom alone at the dining room table with candlelight highlighting the redness in her wet eyes.

"Where were you?"

"I told you I was getting a ride home," I said dismissively with mock confidence. I thought my mother would be so happy to see me that pesky little specifics wouldn't matter to her.

"After you called I asked our neighbor, Mr. Bonner, to drive me to Third Avenue to find you. You weren't there," she said. "Who gave you a ride? Where do they live? Let me have a number so I can thank them."

I guess if I had been a better liar I would have said I didn't get a phone number or asked her how she'd expected to find me without knowing exactly what corner I was standing on. Instead I pictured Mr. Bonner and Mom driving up and down the streets, with no stoplights, in and around Third Avenue, with her getting more and more upset, and then back home thinking someone had snatched me into a dark place. I thought about her anxiety trying to explain to my dad, who was out of the country on business, that something had happened to me. I couldn't have felt worse at that moment.

Obviously I was busted. It all came tumbling out. Through my tears I told her about my afternoon stops at Beverly's and how sorry I was for worrying her. Instead of yelling at me and giving me my punishment on the spot, she said softly, "I knew where your brothers were and that they were safe, but not you. I had no idea where my daughter was in a dark city of eight million people."

My brothers. I had forgotten how they would take this until that moment.

"Please don't tell them, Mom, especially Ralph."

Being thirteen months my elder, my brother Ralph had a way of lording my indiscretions over me. I felt terrible about the worry I had caused my mom and I didn't want to go through the humiliation of him telling me how dumb my excuses had been. If she told Ralph, I'd never hear the end of this.

"No, it's between us." After that my mom didn't speak to me for the rest of the evening. The hurt that I saw in her eyes was its own punishment.

A monthlong grounding did eventually come. But the two big lessons I learned were much more enduring. First, if I ever thought I could outsmart my parents, forget it. But second, despite the heartache I had caused that night, I knew that what had happened between us was locked away in a box. I took my punishment without complaint, trusting that my brothers would never know what I'd done. That confidence in her word made me beholden to my mom, who was watching me much more closely after that, as she had every right to. The fact that she never told them what I had done, and never opened me up to their unrelenting ridicule, made me so grateful to her that I did straighten up and never (*rarely* is closer to the truth) lied to her about my whereabouts again.

As a mom, I decided to remain conscious of opportunities when I could emulate my mother's grace. I told my children that if they confessed something to me I would keep it in a place where no one, not their brother or sister or anyone else, could enter without their permission. This was the place my children affectionately called the Lock Box.

Most of the secrets I kept were on the scale of school crushes or greatest ambitions, or the clever little thing one wanted to give the other for an upcoming birthday. However small that bit of information might seem to me, it burned bright within that child. Having a place to release what was important to them and knowing it would stay secret meant that, at least within the four walls of our house, trust lived.

And it didn't hurt that while keeping our communication value alive in the house I simultaneously kept tabs on their friends, their feelings, and their foes. I was in the know!

I don't think kids need to be shamed into doing the right thing. I've never seen any empirical evidence that having to wear a scarlet letter did any good! By turning a secret embarrassing moment into a teaching tool, we can seize opportunities to connect more with our children, become closer, and deepen existing bonds.

My mom didn't give my siblings the chance to call me a liar and a sneak, or worse, play that against me in favor of my siblings. If I had had to endure years of taunts about that deception, might it have pushed me further into defiance and more poor choices? If I was seen as the bad girl, would I become one, like a self-fulfilling prophecy? My mother had trusted the good in me and focused her energies on that, just as I decided to do with my kids.

I have a Lock Box secret with each of my children and over the years each has expressed their appreciation of my commitment to our secret. Not too long ago, I came across a "just because" card Shani sent me more than a decade ago. It was titled "How to Be a Best Friend." Next to a drawing of a very stylish woman is a list of seven *you know you're a best friend when* statements, each of which she completed and personalized. Number two is "Keep secrets," after

which she added, "(no matter how many years go by...)." Seeing
that again caused a spontaneous smile.

If a parent shares a child's secret, a bond is broken and the relationship can be compromised forever. Mom taught me trust and how
to be the best at keeping a secret. I also learned that you will share
more if that trust is cemented. Now I'm able to pass that value on,
one secret at a time.

LESSON FROM A LIONESS: *Create a safe place for the truth.*

Being a confidant should also be part of our job description. Our
children will not confide in us if we don't exhibit the traits of a fan-
tastic listener—nonjudgmental, tight-lipped, supportive. After all,
do you tell just anyone your deepest regrets, darkest secrets, or secret
desires? To be a confidant, we have to create safe places for truth. For
my children and me, keeping things private was a core value, and
our Lock Box became that proverbial sacred ground. According to
Amy McCready, founder of Positive Parenting Solutions and author
of *The "Me, Me, Me" Epidemic*, parents can create a safe place for
truth—their own personal Lock Boxes—by implementing the following seven conditions.

1. **Be aware of how you respond to misbehavior in general.**
   Why do people lie? To avoid punishment, shame, or judgment
   are just some of the reasons. Consider whether your usual
   responses to your children's confessions include any or all of
   these reactions. Practice listening with empathy and focusing on solutions instead of pointing the finger. What's done
   is done, but what is to be done in the future depends on your
   response to your child.
2. **Allow your child to save face.** Nobody likes to walk into a
   trap. If you ask your child a question you already know the

answer to, you are inviting her to tell a lie. McCready suggests instead of asking, "Did you finish your homework?" try, "What are your plans for finishing your homework?" If your child hasn't completed his homework, he can create an out for himself by making a plan rather than telling a fib.

3. **Focus on the feeling.** When your child has something to tell you, try to understand why he or she might not be comfortable telling the truth in the first place. McCready suggests, "Instead of calling him out about the lie, try, 'That sounds like a bit of a story to me. You must have felt afraid to tell me the truth. Let's talk about that.' You'll get the honesty you're looking for, as well as information that may help you foster the truth in the future."

4. **Acknowledge and appreciate honesty.** Offer praise and encouragement when your children share. "I really appreciate you having the courage to tell me that. I know it's hard; I've been there."

5. **Acknowledge mistakes.** Mistakes are opportunities to teach lessons. Ask children: If you could do it all over, what would you do that is different? Tell them about a time when you made a similar mistake and how you made it right—and most important, how your child can grow and benefit from hers.

6. **Reinforce unconditional love.** There isn't anything a child can do that could take our love away, but many times kids don't know that. Tell them you might not be happy with her choices, but you are happy that she is your child. That will never change. And I would add, punctuate your words with a hug!

7. **Watch your white lies.** Those little eyes and ears are always watching and listening...Your actions set the example for model behavior. So next time you make up a fake excuse for not returning a call or not showing up to a party that you said you would attend, consider what signals you are sending that aren't in line with the core values you are trying to instill in your child.

The Talk

Every choice comes with a consequence. Once you make a
choice, you must accept responsibility. You cannot escape the
consequences of your choices, whether you like them or not.
                                                    —Roy T. Bennett

While being a confidant is an incredibly important role to play, as a parent it's also our job to make sure our children understand that their behaviors have real consequences. We have to teach them to take responsibility for themselves and their actions, because one wrong prank or one bad judgment can have enormous repercussions. I think one of the reasons my son's book *The Other Wes Moore* reso-nates with so many is that it shows that choice cuts a narrow path between a life that falls short of its promise and a life of purpose. The other Wes went down one road and is now spending the rest of his life in prison for his role in the murder of an off-duty policeman. My Wes, despite a rocky start, went down a different path and today enjoys a life where he can help countless others.

In his book, Wes revealed an incident when he was twelve years old and he and a friend were caught tagging a building not far from our house in the Bronx. The whizzing sound of the police siren stopped him and his buddy in their tracks as they were caught red-handed with spray cans in midair. For the first time Wes felt the cold sensation of steel on his wrists as he was shoved into a patrol car, tears flowing from his fear that he was going to be arrested. That fear intensified when the officer asked for my number. As it turned out, I was never called and Wes was never arrested because thankfully he remembered our "Talk" about interactions with police and he was respectful and apolo-getic. The officer then compassionately explained to Wes that tagging may seem like a small thing but it is against the law and is destruction of private property. He told him that he would be jeopardizing what he suspected could be a bright future if he did it again. Then he released Wes, who in retrospect realized how very lucky he was because this officer was more interested in helping kids make better choices than scarring them for life for foolish ones.

To me, this interaction between my son and the officer symbolizes the intersection that must happen between the community and the police if we are to get past the fear, the targeting, the mistrust, and, most important, the amazingly unacceptable hostility and waste of human lives on both sides. Most experts agree that the first step must be to bridge the gaps between those sworn to serve and protect and a public that feels disrespected and targeted. I don't know a parent who doesn't worry about their child's safety when they are out in the world without them. This fear is heightened when a single parent has to confront it alone.

Tanya Carr, a New York City detective and single mom of a teenage girl, says much of the problem stems from the fact that there is too little attention paid to the value of communication, so neither side really knows the other.

Look, you have a force full of people who don't live in New York City, didn't grow up in New York, and who don't associate with anyone who lives in the city. Then you have a public that only has contact with police when there is an altercation or investigation. Tensions are high, tactics may be suspect, and responses may be guarded. That's no time to build relationships.

Police are required to reside within the five boroughs of New York City or surrounding counties, but they don't have to live within the borough in which they work. Because housing is so expensive and the cost of living so high, larger cities like New York, Los Angeles, or Philadelphia can't realistically require police to reside in the areas they serve. What some departments around the country have put into place, however, is to mandate that police officers start out on foot patrol. It's a lot harder for police or community members to be hostile to each other in a time of conflict if just yesterday they were talking about Johnny's graduation or the best place in the neighborhood to get a good roast beef sandwich.

Philip Banks III began his career in the New York City Police Department straight out of college on foot patrol. He rose through the ranks and had every conceivable assignment throughout the city during his twenty-eight years on the force. In 2013 Phil was promoted to chief of department, the third-highest ranking position in the force. He retired shortly after, and he's now chief operating officer of a private investigation and consulting firm. He's married with two sons and a daughter so he, like Tanya Carr, looks at this dilemma between police and community through two lenses and one heart, from the vantage point of law enforcement and as a parent. Through the police officer's lens, he saw and commanded outstanding officers who would lay down their lives for each other and the community they serve every day. The force is a band of brothers and sisters, and when they use phrases like "bleed blue," or "wall of blue," that's very real to them. But as in every profession, there are people who shouldn't be there, and their fellow officers know that. The difficulty, Phil says, is that unfortunately what the community perceives is true—officers are loath to turn each other in if there's even the slight possibility that an officer who behaved questionably really feared for his or her life. Police connect to that fear from a very deep and almost impenetrable place in their souls. Ironically, he says, they will and do turn each other in for corruption or domestic violence. But fearing for their lives is a visceral reaction that they all relate to. A situation has to be extraordinarily blatant before officers will turn on their peers.

The NYPD and other departments across the country are trying to train their officers to have as deep an understanding of and empathy for the community as they have for their fellow officers. One training technique that they already have in place is after officers have graduated from the academy, and before they hit the streets, they go through sessions with actual community members to hear their genuine concerns and fears, and the community gets a chance to hear from the police. Phil says both police and community have to get creative and committed to addressing the mistrust that exists.

The job of police is policing, and to do that effectively is for the community to know who you are as a person and what you're about. You have to remove that middleman filter, be it the media or other community members who have had bad interactions with the police, and let them know exactly who you are, then the community can make an informed decision whether to trust you or not. And here's the thing, if you are doing your job right and you have your moral compass pointing in the right direction, the community can draw the following conclusion: You are on my side and we are in this together.

Departments have to look at the community as its customers and treat them with respect. That's step one on the police side. On the community side, we have to treat that officer with respect, and start with simple things like saying "good morning." The culture of respect is what's missing on both sides. Getting police out of their cruisers and on their feet is something else that has to happen more. There also has to be more cultural awareness on the part of police and relating to community on a day-to-day basis, and having a real presence is the best way to do that. A kid who shows this kind of false bravado that screams with attitude, "I ain't afraid of you," is displaying the kind of armor needed to stay alive in the street. There are techniques to de-escalate tense situations and to encourage the kid to believe the cop and [they] can deal with each other with respect and understanding.

That reminded me of my favorite quote that you've seen in this book in several places in various forms: *Kids need to think that you care before they care what you think.*

So that's part of the long-game strategy, one that will take years to become part of a new culture. What mothers want to know is what can we do *now* to protect our children. That's what The Talk is all about. It is just another way we can have presence when we are not around. Embrace it! The Talk is a little different in every family and with every kid, but it is a very necessary and honest conversation about how to stay safe around authority figures, aggressors, or other unpredictable influences. And while The Talk is usually associated with police-community relations, increasingly it includes how we handle difficult situations, for both men and women, with dates, supervisors, bosses, and anyone in a position of power over our lives and livelihood. Improving the relationships between those striving to make a way for themselves in the world and those empowered to either assist or assault is critical if this nation is to achieve its true promise. But until then, The Talk, in all its variations, is a necessity for all parents, particularly single ones.

LESSON FROM A LIONESS: *We can't be with our kids 24/7. Have The Talk!*

FOR ALL YOUNG CHILDREN

The Talk for kids ages three to six is essential to warn them, without scaring them, about stranger danger and those I call "friendemies"—family members or friends of the family who are bad influences. Writer Kathleen F. Miller offers some tips to keep our kids safe when we are not around.

- When they are old enough to answer the phone, they should be taught to call 911 in an emergency. They should be taught their first and last name, home address, the best telephone number of the parent(s), and the first and last name of the caregiver(s). If they are tall and old enough to answer the front door, teach them never to open it to someone they don't know.

- Teach them to never go anywhere with anyone without your permission. Teach them to be aware of anyone who is following them or paying special attention to them. If they feel uncomfortable, they should learn to run and immediately tell you or whoever is in charge of them.
- Develop a code word. If someone other than the parent needs to pick them up unexpectedly, teach your child a word that the person must know before your child will go with them.
- Teach them common tricks of predators. Teach them not to accept candy; come to a car to look at puppies; come to a car to give anyone directions; or violate a family rule, like giving a code word before going with someone other than you.
- Make sure school or caregivers know to never let anyone pick up your child without your written permission.
- Teach your child that not all people who might harm them will be strangers. They should be alert to *anyone* who makes them feel uncomfortable, or who touches them inappropriately or who tries to lure them into a room or area of the house that's isolated. Teach them to yell "*No*" and run to a trusted adult if they ever find themselves in an uncomfortable situation.

For Our Boys

For the sake of your son's safety, banish the notion that The Talk is a male rite of passage and solely in the domain of the father. If he's not around and there's no male mentor or relative whom your son trusts and can take on that conversation, it's on you, and that's okay. This is what I said to my kids, and I am positive that variations of this are said in homes all over America, and I suspect around the world:

- Don't talk back.
- Be respectful.
- Say "yes sir," "yes ma'am" (Phil suggests you say "yes Officer").

- Be careful of the colors you are wearing if there are gangs in that area.
- Save the bravado for when you are hanging with your friends.
- Saggy pants without belts and sneakers without shoelaces come from a place no kid should aspire to go—prison.
- If you are in or driving a car and you are stopped by police, Phil suggests these potentially lifesaving actions:
  - Roll down all the windows—front and back—so the officer can see your hands at all times.
  - Stay calm.
  - As the officer approaches the window, say, "I am unarmed and I have nothing on me or around me that will hurt you."
  - If you're the driver, keep your hands on the steering wheel at all times, unless the officer instructs you to do otherwise.
  - Never make a sudden move to the glove compartment.
  - The driver and passengers should ask permission before making any moves within the car. Say "May I reach inside my pocket or my purse to get my license?" or the like.

There is a commercial product called the Pullover Pal document holder. It's a waterproof holder with clear pockets that are designed to fold over a window so that you can keep your hands on the wheel. It holds your driver's license, insurance card, and any special medical alert cards (indicating hard of hearing, autistic, Parkinson's disease, and so on). This way you have all the documents you need in one place to easily display in the event of a traffic stop. Ordering information as well as additional information about the above disabilities can be found on the book's companion website, www.power-ofpresence.com.

For Our Girls

The Talk about community-police interaction is just as essential for our daughters. Just ask Sandra Bland. But statistically, daughters are more likely to be affected by interpersonal situations where their personal space and bodies are violated. Daughters should have already learned all the childhood cautions; as they grow older The Talk has to shift to topics like date rape and physical and psychological abuse among dating teens. As *New York Times* contributing op-ed writer Jill Filipovic warned, we need to alter the way we teach our daughters to protect themselves. When they are young we tell them to tell us if anyone touches them or makes them feel icky. As they grow up, we arm them with pepper spray and rape whistles, make sure they always carry cab fare (or have an Uber or Lyft account), and instruct them not to leave drinks unattended at parties or, if they are old enough, at clubs. We are also vigilant for any signs of our daughters being physically abused. Filipovic says that girls are "taught to be emotionally competent and to be responsive to the needs of others." This, she says can lead to a girl feeling subservient to boys and can eventually carry over to the workplace. Girls don't learn to be "solo aviators" of their own bodies, and instead are positioned to have to accept or reject men's advances. "Nor are we allowed full expressions of rage or other unfeminine emotions when we are mistreated," she continues. "No wonder we try to politely excuse ourselves from predatory men instead of responding with the ire that predation merits." Heroically, the "Me Too" campaign pulled away the scab from this horrific reality for too many girls and women.

I hope that one day the need to talk about all these dos and don'ts will be banished to a box of relics that holds all the symbols of the misguided country we used to be. But for now, these values-inspired conversations are essential at the age-appropriate times in our children's lives. It's sometimes hard to do, especially for a single mom with no physical backups and who has so many other pressures confronting her on a daily basis. But to be truly mindful in our role as stewards of our children's future, we must stop, dig deep within ourselves, and prepare for and have The Talk at times in our kids' lives when they are needed the most.

The Butt Stops Here

You leave old habits behind by starting out with the thought, "I
release the need for this in my life."
                                                        —*Wayne Dyer*

My goal has always been to be a good mother—a role model of discipline, good judgment, and healthy habits, passing on to my kids the
values that I want to see in the next generation and beyond. Mostly
I've succeeded at that, I think, except in one major area. I smoked.

I smoked a lot, sometimes a pack and a half a day, which meant
that to be the perfect role model, I had to hide this habit from the
kids. So I smoked on the back porch before they woke up and after
they went to bed, I smoked when they got out of the car for school,
I smoked at work and with friends over drinks. I seized any opportunity to smoke whenever I was out of their line of sight.

I remember one spring evening driving back to the Bronx along
the New England Thruway after a visit to Rye Playland. I'd spent
almost eight hours alone with the three children in the sun, on the
rides, and eating ridiculous carnival food and sugary soft drinks. By
the time we got back to the car, I was dying for a cigarette.

I kept looking in the rearview mirror trying to ensure that the
kids were all asleep so I could open the window and sneak one. They
were exhausted from the day's activities, but of course they wouldn't
all nod off at the same time. Just as Nikki and Wes fell to sleep, Shani
decided she wanted to chat. Then when she started to close her eyes,
Nikki perked up, eager to describe some trouble she was having with
her teacher. And I'm ashamed to say that while she was pouring her
heart out, I was barely listening, mostly praying that she'd go back to
sleep so I could satisfy the nicotine craving that was driving me to
the edge of my nerves.

For years I was dishonest with my children about my continued smoking. I didn't want them to start what was obviously a disgusting and deadly habit, but I couldn't or wouldn't stop. It had me in its grip. Ironically, with all my efforts to mask the fact that I was smoking, they knew from the smell on my clothes, my hair, my breath. I was fooling no one but myself.

As the kids got older and anti-smoking ads more prolific, all eyes were on me in my house.

My internal battle was hearing what they were saying but not being able to do anything about it. With each "Mommy, you need to stop smoking," or "Do you know what you're doing to your lungs?" or "Do you know what you're doing to our lungs?" I cringed because I knew they were right. Every year, on the Great American Smokeout, I took the pledge, and I did stop, at least while the kids were awake. I could be pure for a few days, maybe even a week. But before a second week began, I was standing outside after they'd gone to sleep to have a smoke. The more I sneaked, the worse I felt about lying to them. At the same time I needed my treat, my one little thing that was just for me in this world of relentless responsibilities.

My indulgence in my shameful pleasure was a rebellion as much as it was an addiction. I was overwhelmed with all the things I had to do every day; it seemed that everyone in the world was telling me what to do and how much I needed to do more. In every way I could, I was being extremely responsible about all these demands. Was it selfish of me to want just one pleasure, one bit of the day that was completely mine, separate from all of the other demands? Something completely under my control?

Well, yeah. That stuff could kill me!

Of my three children, it was my youngest, Shani, who was the most persistent about my quitting smoking. Usually when she found my cigarettes, she'd throw them away, but she was not devious enough to bury them in the trash. The pack sat right on top, easy to put back into use. One day she surprised me. She soaked the cigarette pack under the kitchen faucet for a few seconds before crushing it in her fist. When I saw that soggy pack on at the top of the trash bin, I exploded.

"Who are you to dictate to me what I can or cannot do," I yelled.

"I don't want to be an orphan," Shani yelled back in an almost pleading voice.

Her words, the words of a terrified ten-year-old, jolted me.

How could I possibly become so angry at her when all she wanted was for me to live? Her mind was forecasting a future without the only parent she had left. I think that's the real difference between a one- and a two-parent household. No child wants their parent to die, but when there is only one parent, that fear of potential loss intensifies. But it also spoke to the values I was transmitting to my children. Was my habit more important than their feelings and fears? My words were saying I valued them more than anyone or anything else, but my actions in regard to my smoking said otherwise.

I realized that my main problem was not my habit, it was my hypocrisy. I demanded a lot from my kids and held them to a high standard. They had very little control over how they spent their time because I scheduled them and watched them closely. Hell, I had sent my only son away to military school to reinforce discipline and adherence to standards and values. I encouraged their participation in sports so they'd learn to value their bodies—so much so that they wouldn't engage in any activity, like smoking, that might impair their performance or damage their health. So here I was, abusing my body and jeopardizing my health. It was a double standard. I knew it and they knew it.

I'd be lying if I said I never bought a pack of cigarettes after that soggy mess landed in the trash. But from that day on every time I bought a pack of cigarettes, I told myself that I was not going to start the new year smoking. I smoked all the way to 11:59 PM on New Year's Eve. When the ball dropped, I stopped smoking and I've not bought a pack of cigarettes since. That was twenty-eight years ago.

It took the kids a while to say anything about me not smoking. I think at first they might have thought that I was hiding my smoking again. But when Wes came home for spring break, I overheard the three of them talking about not smelling smoke in a long time and wondering if I had really stopped smoking? I never told them I overheard that conversation. It just made me more determined to show them that I had really stopped, for myself and my health but just as much for them, for their sense of security, and for the love they had shown in wanting me to do better.

LESSON FROM A LIONESS: *Avoid maternal hypocrisy.*

The relationship between children and parents has certainly morphed. Gone are the days of "children should be seen and not heard" or "do as I say, and not as I do." Hypocrisy is to family values as kryptonite is to Superman. You can work a lifetime to define them, build them, and sustain them, but the one time your children see you violate a rule or family value, your credibility slips away like quicksand.

As moms, we are often called upon to do things we might not have done without the urging of our children. Regardless of the habit, be it smoking, drugs, alcohol, or even being a shopaholic, our children can provide a powerful compass away from vice. If we are smart enough to follow, they can help lead us to do the right thing. Of course, we will screw up from time to time. But I've learned not to expend energy on getting down on myself; these times can be the most powerful teachable moments we have. They're times that urgently call for open communication and your willingness to apologize and admit your mistakes. Amy McCready of Positive Parenting Solutions says that saying we are sorry to our kids when we violate our core values, as hard as it can be, puts our children in position to recognize their own flaws—and helps them learn to apologize too.

"It also shows them it's okay to make mistakes," says McCready. "Kids that don't experience much failure have trouble knowing what to do when problems do arise—they don't have the confidence to take risks, they won't courageously face their problems head-on or roll with the punches."

So next time you have a not-so-shining moment, remember you *are* human. Ultimately, making such mistakes—coupled with discussing with your kids what you have learned from them—helps foster resiliency in children. Believe it or not, being an effective role model is not about living in perfect accordance with our values all the time—it's about trying hard and showing a willingness to take responsibility for our mistakes.

If we want to be role models, the times when we are not our optimal selves could be our most precious opportunities to act in the way we would want our children to act. It is through our faults that we can foster true strength.

Reclaiming History/Discovering Presence: The Candace RedShirt Story

Teach your children that we have taught our children that the earth is our mother . . . Whatever befalls the earth befalls the sons of the earth.

—Chief Seattle

Candace RedShirt is originally from the Pine Ridge Reservation in South Dakota. She was born of the Oglala Lakota tribe, the great-great-granddaughter of Chief Red Shirt, whom history recognizes as the most photographed American Indian in the eighteenth century. He became known as a conciliator between the Indian tribes and the white settlers, promoting cooperation with the US Army and even opposing Chief Crazy Horse during the Great Sioux War of 1876–1877. For these and other efforts to promote cooperation and education for all tribes in the newly forming Indian nation,

Chief Red Shirt was posthumously selected for induction into the Nebraska Hall of Fame, and the US Postal Service honored him with a 10-cent Great Americans series postage stamp.

His bravery, integrity, and perseverance, among other attributes, were clearly instilled by the teachings of his tribe, known as the Twelve Lakota Virtues: humility, perseverance, respect, honor, love, sacrifice, truth, compassion, bravery, fortitude, generosity, and wisdom. Living by such a code gave a common language to the tribe and kept its members connected to their values and life purpose. The problem, says Candace, was that growing up she knew next to nothing about her family history or these family-bonding values, because Indian culture was systematically stripped from the day-to-day lives of Indian families. The vehicle for the erasure of the culture was the Native American boarding schools. In their absence, the presence between mothers and their children was lost.

Native American boarding schools were founded in 1882 with the expressed goal of dismantling families and wiping out Indian culture. Attendance was mandatory, and hundreds of thousands of children were removed from their homes to go to these more than one hundred schools located all across the country. Some families were never reunited.

Candace was taken from her home and forced to attend an Episcopal Indian girls boarding school in Springfield, South Dakota, for seventh and eighth grades. Then the government moved her almost 150 miles farther north to attend a coed Indian boarding school in Flandreau, South Dakota. She was then five hours away from home and stripped of her Indian name and clothes.

Beyond the prevalent physical abuse, Candace says it was the systematic dehumanization of the spirit in these schools that has had the most lasting impact. For some, like Candace's mom, alcohol dependency became the salve for the pain of reservation life and then the inevitable family separation. There wasn't even an echo of the Lakota virtues in Candace's family by the time she became a teenager. In fact, because of her mother and father's addiction to alcohol, Candace says there was a lot of family violence. She was placed in foster care several times and, reacting to the dysfunction, rebelled and engaged in risky teenage behavior. The result was an estrangement from her mother in later years that continues to this day.

Candace became pregnant when she was eighteen, and when Candace's son, Brandon, was two months old her mother kicked them both out.

She told me to get my screaming crying baby and get the hell out of there because she had to go to work.

This was quite a far cry from the Lakota virtues of love, compassion, and wisdom, and from a culture that believed in the sacred nature of marriage and family.

When I think back, I felt like we were thrown out like trash. I went to the Denver Indian Family and Health Services and this woman took me under her wing and referred us to a domestic violence shelter for women with children. Brandon and I stayed there for a couple months until I could get into the social service program, and get a little check. Then I had to go walking all around the town, which I didn't know at the time. I got to see the bigger picture of the world of what was going on, where people wouldn't rent to people with children but they would accept pets!

After landing a tiny studio apartment, Candace was let into a program sponsored by the Denver Housing Authority. Using funds from HUD, the housing authority created special campuses of learning where residents could get a case manager who would help them get a job or go back to school. They also created an escrow account for each family to put away a portion of any money earned while they lived there.

> *When Brandon was old enough, he started Head Start, and that's when I learned something about myself. I loved being around the energy of children, the innocence, the things they say. To me, you're always in a state of happiness and joy when you're with children. I started volunteering to go on field trips, and eventually the director asked if I could volunteer every day.*

Candace used these days with Brandon and the other children to help instill in them a sense of history about who they were, regardless of their race, and—most important—to always provide words of affirmation. She says she learned from the staff at Head Start that positive words could give the strength needed to cope with bullying, for example, or the compassion to keep from becoming a bully. Contact with them also helped her make a personal vow to never say anything that would hurt someone's feelings or tear them down. Little by little, Candace was reclaiming the traditional Indian values that she believed underscored who she was and wanted to be. "Always look for the positive or don't say anything at all" became her mantra. These were values she yearned to learn as a child while she was being incrementally stripped of any self-worth or self-awareness. Candace began to recognize the strength in her heritage and turned to history—back to the lost Lakota values—to learn as much as she could about where she came from. That kind of identity was integral to Candace determining the next steps in her life.

Candace passionately believes that a modern-day Native American mom's job is helping her children reach a productive adulthood through the traditional routes to education and career guidance—and possibly most important, through helping them regain the stolen culture and value system of their ancestors. For Candace that journey started within herself.

I wanted to be able to learn the Lakota language at least well enough to speak it and sing ceremony songs. Losing language, religion, and the values held by our ancestors was the result of ethnic cleansing, and there was an impact on how we grew up and what we thought of ourselves. It was like a virus in a computer program.

Getting rid of that virus and allowing herself to take pride in being a Lakota woman, in being a woman of color, in living in poverty and surviving, in experiencing the struggles but still having a beautiful heart that can be loving, kind, and giving—that was Candace's journey to becoming a mother who could be present for her children.

She went on to have two more children, a son, Cody, and later a daughter, Candace Rose. When she had Cody, she was overwhelmed financially and made a hasty decision to allow a couple, whom her sister knew, to raise him. Thinking it would be done in the traditional Indian way, where a family member would take the baby to raise until the mother was able to resume her parental role, Candace agreed to letting them take him home. Shortly after, she regretted her decision and wanted him back. The couple refused, and the case went all the way to the Colorado Supreme Court. Ultimately, the court ruled that even though there were no formal adoption papers, it was in the best interest of Cody to stay with the couple, who were in a better financial position to provide for his needs. The fact is that being a single mother worked against her too. She was up against a two-parent family, and the judges made note of that. Candace recalls one question from the guardian ad litem that haunted her for years: "You don't have a driver's license or a car. If Cody gets sick, how will he get to the hospital?" She became convinced that the car could have swayed the decision in her favor. Eleven years later, by now thirty-four, when she, Brandon, and Candace Rose moved on from the special housing program, she was presented a check from her escrow account for $10,000. The first thing she did was buy her first car.

Candace feels her biggest achievement as a parent is that both Brandon and Candace Rose are caring, responsible, hardworking, culturally aware, and generous adults. Recently, Candace Rose began a charitable effort to work with college sororities in Denver to donate unwanted items like microwaves, bedding, or irons—anything that would otherwise be discarded at the end of the school year—to charitable organizations. And Brandon, after having honorably served in the military and receiving training on Apache helicopters, came home after tours of duty in both Iraq and Afghanistan and started working at Denver International Airport. He began as a mechanic with a small commuter airline and is now working as an inspector at the airport. Although Candace never had a chance to be physically present for her son Cody, she says that several years ago the three siblings found each other through social media and helped the birth family reunite. A recent visit by him revealed, in her words, "a strong, healthy, happy adult man with a good heart, who gives the biggest hugs!"

Candace says other than losing Cody as a baby, she has few regrets in her life, including not finishing college.

To me, there's something much deeper as far as humanity. I don't know if that's part of my Native American way of thinking, but I've gone to college and to me, I don't think it really was the answer to my heart because it didn't answer the question about how it was going to make me a better person or change how I interact with the world. Instinctively, I'm a helper. I'm a learner with peers, with teams. I like discussion and I like thinking about big and small stuff. My degree is in life, humanity, and people. When I die, it will be my children and others who say how I mattered to this world, not my credentials. Passing on a value system that made my children good and caring human beings is the legacy I want to leave.

LESSON FROM A LIONESS: *Establish a value system in your home, one that is culturally relevant and rich in family history.*

In the 1990s, researchers at Emory University conducted a series of studies comparing how much children knew about their families and culture and how they fared emotionally. They found that the children who "knew the most about their family histories showed higher self-esteem, a stronger sense of control over their lives and believed that their families were healthier and more successful." This is great intelligence for all families but for single-mother families, it takes on even greater importance because children may have limited access to information from both sides of their family. Casey Call, PhD, from the Karyn Purvis Institute of Child Development at Texas Christian University, says that whoever passes on this cultural information must do it in a way that engages the children. "I think you have to make it authentic, and it has to address what they're currently going through. Sitting down and giving a history lesson to the family isn't probably going to be as well received as finding authentic, natural times within conversations to tell stories."

Suggestions on how to do this include:

- Relate family stories to what is going on in the moment. For example, during a discussion of a problem at school, talk about an uncle who experienced that issue. Or when a story about a country that's part of the child's background comes on TV, tell the tale of a relative who came from there and what life was like.
- Display photos of grandparents and great-grandparents around the house and tell stories about their lives as you pass by them, in an organic way.

- Turn it into a game. Deanna Mason from Plano, Texas, created something called "ancestor cards" with a relative's picture on one side and simple facts about that person on the back. She then played them with her children like flash cards.
- Create an ancestor scrapbook that relatives can contribute to and can be shared, with the stories behind the photos, at family gatherings.

It wasn't until Candace connected with her heritage and its value system that she could set a course for her life and those of her children. By looking back, she gained the strength to confidently move forward.

Conclusion

The Lakota Prayer

Wakan Tanka, Great Mystery,
teach me how to trust
my heart,
my mind,
my intuition,
my inner knowing,
the senses of my body,
the blessings of my spirit.
Teach me to trust these things
so that I may enter my Sacred Space
and love beyond my fear,
and thus Walk in Balance
with the passing of each glorious Sun.

This prayer of the ancestors of the Lakota Native American tribe was introduced to me by Candace RedShirt, one of the many magnificent women profiled in this book. Her exposing me to something new illustrates how much we can learn from one another, particularly the gifts many single mothers have to offer, if only we are open and eager to receive them.

According to the Native People, the Sacred Space is the space between exhalation and inhalation. It is that pause where nothing is happening, where inaction exists. Too often in life, that pause when we feel neither here nor there is scary, but the Lakota Prayer says that space of the in-between should be our destination. It is where peace lives.

Further, to walk in balance is to have heaven (spirituality) and earth (physicality) in harmony. When this beautiful wisdom sank in, it dawned on me that presence is really all about creating harmony in our lives and especially in the lives of our children. After all, isn't harmony the endgame for all parents, single or not?

I am so grateful for the single mothers, grandmothers, aunts, and mentors who entrusted me with their stories, providing intimate glimpses into their private spaces—their challenges and, equally important, their triumphs. Their examples can become touchstones and teaching tools for anyone who holds a relationship with a child or young person. They and millions of single mothers who have conquered adversity and emerged victorious have powerful lessons to share, if we include them in the conversation, and if we, as a nation, just listen.

A new outlook can change the prevailing narrative about the worthiness of single mothers to one that sees them as teachers of resiliency, experts in resourcefulness, vessels of values, keepers of culture, and masters of mindfulness. Single mothers have produced literary giants, even though they themselves might not have been able to read. Single mothers have produced great statesmen, even if they didn't have enough money to travel outside their home state. Single mothers have produced giants of business, even though they might at one time have been homeless.

Parents in general, and single mothers in particular, hold the keys to many of the solutions needed to help us form a more perfect union. That in-between space the Lakota talk about is the window of opportunity parents need to form more perfect families, which will result in stronger communities.

So simple yet so profound, the Lakota Prayer has gifted me with a deeper understanding of what I had been trying to do all along with my pillars: create harmony in heart, mind, resources, courage, faith, connectedness, and values. The prayer says the way to accomplish this is through being aware of and present in my mind, my body, my spirit, and my intuition, and to trust the sacred space of the in-between. It is my best hope now and for the future that we can create harmony among all families, a space lionesses have perfected in the wild, so we can truly be a pride that offers the very best collective and shared wisdom to the next generation. Only then can our prayer for presence become the ever-present voice in our children's ear.

Bibliography

Bevere, Lisa. *Lioness Arising: Wake Up and Change Your World*. New York: Crown Publishing Group, 2010.

Bologna, Caroline. "Many Kids Feel 'Unimportant' When Parents Are Distracted by Smartphones." *Huffington Post*, July 13, 2015. https://www.huffingtonpost.com/entry/kids-notice-parents-screen-addiction_us_55a3e15ae4b0ecec71bc74e4.

Bonior, Andrea. *The Friendship Fix: The Complete Guide to Choosing, Losing, and Keeping Up with Your Friends*. New York: St. Martin's Press, 2011.

Darley, Susan Ann. "Dropping the Labels: Stop Devaluing Yourself and Others, Inner Self." Accessed February 3, 2018. https://innerself.com/content/personal/spirituality-mindfulness/mindfulness/4810-dropping-the-labels.html.

Davidson Institute for Talent Development. *Mentoring Guidebooks*. Reno: Davidson Institute for Talent Development, 2006. http://www.davidsongifted.org/Search-Database/entry/R14780.

Dougy Center for Grieving Children. *35 Ways to Help a Grieving Child*. Portland, OR: Dougy Center for Grieving Children, 2010. https://www.dougy.org/grief-resources/how-to-help-a-grieving-child.

Dyer, Wayne. "Restore Your Faith." Accessed February 3, 2018. http://www.oprah.com/spirit/restore-your-faith/all.

Faber, Adele, and Elaine Mazlish. *Siblings Without Rivalry: How to Help Your Children Live Together So You Can Live Too*. New York: W. W. Norton, 2012.

Gallup. "Religion." Accessed February 3, 2018. http://news.gallup.com/poll/1690/religion.aspx.

Kamen, Randy. "A Compelling Argument About Why Women Need Friendships." *Huffington Post*, November 29, 2012. https://www.huffington
post.com/randy-kamen-gredinger-edd/female-friendship_b_2193062
.html.

Koreyva, Wendy. "Learn to Meditate in 6 Easy Steps." Accessed February
3, 2018. https://chopra.com/articles/learn-to-meditate-in-6-easy-steps.

McGonigal, Kelly. "Walking Meditation: The Perfect Ten Minute Will-
power Boost." *Psychology Today*, September 21, 2010. https://www
.psychologytoday.com/blog/the-science-willpower/201009/walking
-meditation-the-perfect-ten-minute-willpower-boost.

Moore, Wes. *The Other Wes Moore: One Name, Two Fates*. New York:
Spiegel & Grau, 2010.

National CARES Mentoring Movement. "Mission and Vision." Accessed
February 3, 2018. http://www.caresmentoring.org/index.php/mission
-and-vision.

Neff, Kristen. "Self-Compassion." Accessed February 3, 2018. http://self
-compassion.org/the-three-elements-of-self-compassion-2.

Pargament, Kenneth I. "What Role Do Religion and Spirituality Play in
Mental Health?" March 22, 2013. http://www.apa.org/news/press
/releases/2013/03/religion-spirituality.aspx.

Perry, Bruce. "Death and Loss: Helping Children Manage Their Grief."
Early Childhood Today, April 2006. http://www.scholastic.com/browse
/article.jsp?id=4044.

Robbins, Tony. "Stop Letting Painful Memories Control Your Present—
and Future." Accessed February 3, 2018. https://www.tonyrobbins
.com/mind-meaning/let-go-past.

Stenvinkel, Maria. "A Surprising Way to Let Go of Painful Feelings
and the Past." Accessed February 3, 2018. https://tinybuddha.com
/blog/surprising-way-let-go-painful-feelings-the-past.

Stevens, Eric C. "The True Meaning of Having Heart." Accessed February 3, 2018. https://breakingmuscle.com/fitness/the-true-meaning-of
-having-heart.

Tsabary, Dr. Shefali. *The Conscious Parent: Transforming Ourselves,
Empowering Our Children*. Vancouver: Namaste Publishing, 2010.

Wilkins, Alasdair. "Mothers and Babies Can Instantly Synchronize Their
Hearts Just by Smiling at Each Other." Accessed February 3, 2018.

https://io9.gizmodo.com/5865557/mothers-and-babies-can-instantly
-synchronize-their-hearts-just-by-smiling-at-each-other.

Williams, Terrie. *Black Pain: It Just Looks Like We're Not Hurting.* New York: Scribner, 2008.

Williams, Terrie, and Joe Cooney. *The Personal Touch: What You Really Need to Succeed in Today's Fast-Paced Business World.* New York: Mysterious Press, 1994.

Acknowledgments

William Arthur Ward once said, "Feeling gratitude and not express-ing it is like wrapping a present and not giving it." Please allow the time and space for the following to be signed, sealed, and delivered.

Let me first express my gratitude to my Creator, from whom all blessings flow. The first act of divine benevolence to me was the family I grew up in and the one I am privileged to lead. To my parents, James and Winell Thomas, I am nothing if not for you. You were my parent-ing models and my ever-present North Stars. Without you my family's story would have been very different, and there are no words or ways to thank you. To my sisters-in-law, Evelyn, Dawn, Tawana, Cookie, Connie; my brothers, Ralph and Howard, and the halves that make them whole, Donna and Pam: Thank you for always being there for me when my duet became a solo and I struggled with the notes. To my amazing son- and daughter-in-love, Jamaar and Dawn, thank you for completing the lives of the people I hold most dear to my heart, my children. And to them, Joy (Nikki), Wes, and Shani—thank you, thank you, thank you for tolerating my growing-up years and for teaching me how to become the kind of mother who is now humbled and blessed with the opportunity to write this book. The word *love* doesn't begin to describe my feelings for you, nor my excitement about the incredible adults you have become. You truly are my pride and joy.

My life has been anchored by unconditional presence and amaz-ing prides of people surrounding my family and me. To bring this book to life, presence and prides continued to have starring roles.

My pride of extraordinary editors and writers patiently and expertly helped me find my literary voice. To my book agent, Linda Loewenthal, who sensed there was a story to be told and a need to tell it: Thank you for guiding me through the long, winding, and rewarding process of discovery of direction and delivery of product. Along the way, I was blessed by the amazing vision, writing, and editing talents of Danelle Morton and Cheryl Woodruff. I was humbled by their selfless sharing of their time and talents, and by their encouragement that kept me moving forward. To the extraordinary writer and editor who brought me across the finish line, Michele Matrisciani: Thank you for being you. I loved talking copy and children with you, and I will be forever grateful to you for helping my thoughts and words take flight. Thank you as well to my researchers, advisers, thought partners, supporters, and, most important, dear friends throughout this book project: Kathryn Shagas, Grace Giermek, Kris Coffey, Jennifer Henderson, Lisa Nutter, Ralph Smith, and, of course, Mom, Nikki, Shani, Jamaar, Wes, and Dawn—you helped me make sure my memories were grounded in fact and my words connected to purpose. And rounding out my literary pride are the wonderful folks at Grand Central. Thank you for taking a chance on an unknown entity and giving me the freedom to craft a book that I hope people will enjoy, but that will also make a difference in their lives. Sarah Peltz, thank you for being my first champion before moving to the next leg of your professional journey, and Leah Miller, for assuming the reins as my editor and advocate in magnificent ways. To Katherine Stopa, Linda Duggins, Nick Small, Amanda Pritzker, Luria Rittenberg, Elisa Rivlin, Laura Jorstad, Melissa Mathlin, and the rest of the Grand Central team—from editing to design to production to marketing: I have so enjoyed being part of Grand Central during this entire process. Thank you for allowing me to join the family.

Embarking on this project, I was adamant that it had to contain more than the story of our family, because I knew and had heard about so many amazing families that were headed by single moms.

This book has its breadth of experiences, tips, and tools because of the generosity of spirit of the single mothers within who perfected their own brands of presence. I will be forever grateful to Mary Ann Boyd, Allessandra Bradley-Burns, Ona Caldwell, Maria del Rosario Castro, Rama Chakaki, Gina Davis, Loida Nicolas Lewis, Una McHugh, Calynn J. Taylor Moore, Hilary Pennington, Candace RedShirt, Susan L. Taylor, Pamela Warner, and Terrie Williams for the courage and the confidence in me it took to share the intimate details of their lives. Thanks, as well, to Ambassador Reverend Dr. Suzan Cook for her guidance in the faith chapter and Detective Tanya Carr, who along with Philip Banks III provided invaluable assistance in preparing the chapter on The Talk. Thanks go as well to all the other experts quoted throughout the book.

My parenting journey has had the benefit of sharing some inspiring experiences with a legion of dedicated single moms (and some incredible single dads and temporary surrogates too), who after a divorce, tragic death, deployment, or incarceration stepped up to raise amazing kids: Linette, Blossom, Carlton, Angela, Guy, Camille, Stephanie, Sharon, Evelyn, Dawn, Tawana, Connie, Cookie, Esther, Sandy, Tod, Desiree, Sherece, Maurice, Beverly, Rae Carole, Bethany, Yolanda, and Zelma. And while we have never met, I also want to acknowledge Mrs. Prothero, who lost her husband tragically and senselessly and who heroically raised their five children on her own.

And what can I say about my extraordinary girlfriends? Oprah, my guru on girlfriends, says, "Lots of people want to ride with you in the limo, but what you want is someone who will take the bus with you when the limo breaks down." Linda, Vicki, Gail, Pam, Mary, Thursa, Sujay, Alexis, Debbie, Edna, Kathryn, Kris, Linda, Ellen, Denise, and Cheryl: Thanks for always helping me get off at the right stop when the limo broke down.

And to all the courageous and hardworking single mothers I met at WMAL, WJLA, Riverdale, Valley Forge Military Academy and College, *Essence*, the Annie E. Casey Foundation, and the Campaign for Grade-Level Reading, as well as in the communities I have had the honor to get to know: Thank you for all you have done and continue to do to raise the children who became and will become the future leaders of this nation. Yours are the stories of sheroes, and my hope is this book will help to change the prevailing narrative around single mothers and instead start a movement to celebrate you and thank you for the enormous value you add to this nation and world.

Any presentation of gifts would not be complete without acknowledging those in the ancestral pride who have gone before us—Mama Gwen, Papa Moore, Ms. Elizabeth, the grandparents and those aunts and uncles in the Cannon family, the Moores, the Thomases, the Duncans, Vanzies, Moystons, Dwyers, Banks, Anglins, Stephens, Brandons, Flythes, Spences, Bailey-Hayes, Weatherbys, Boyds, Carolinas, and Meads. Thank you for the examples you provided, the love you shared, and the baton you passed to all those who followed. And to my father and my beloved Wes, my eternal gratitude. From you, Dad, I learned how a woman should be treated and that I could be strong and confident, whether I was an equal partner in a family or the head of it. And to Wes, even though our marriage was cut short, your influence on my thinking, your encouragement, and your support honors our vow of eternity. I raised our kids as we would have together, only your guidance was from your Heavenly perch. Thank you for your endless love.

There are so many others I am indebted to, who have stood by me, believed in me, and believed in and mentored my children. If I have not mentioned your name specifically, know that you are anchored in my heart and I will be forever grateful to you for helping me prepare my children, and all those whom they will influence, for brighter futures.

We are like lighthouses to our children . . . Beacons showing them the way. And when our light goes out, theirs will be at its brightest . . . ready to take over for us.
—Linda Poindexter

About the Author

Joy Thomas Moore is a Peabody Award–winning radio and television producer whose career has focused on connecting family issues to policy and practice. While she now runs her own media consulting business, she spent fifteen years at the Annie E. Casey Foundation in Baltimore, managing its media portfolio. Documentaries she championed earned numerous recognitions including Oscar nominations and Emmy Awards.

She is the mother of three grown children. Her daughter Joy (Nikki) is a successful event planner in the Washington, DC, Virginia, and Maryland area. Her son is Rhodes Scholar and *New York Times*–bestselling author Wes Moore. He now heads the Robin Hood Foundation, one of the country's largest anti-poverty organizations. Her youngest daughter, Shani, is a legal and business executive at NBCUniversal in Los Angeles and an independent television screenwriter. Moore's rewards for parenting are her two grandchildren, Mia and James.

Moore hopes to influence the prevailing narrative about successful parenting by throwing a spotlight on those voices not usually included in the conversation—single parents.

For more information, resources, and additional profiles, visit her website at **www.power-ofpresence.com.**